MEGARGEE'S GUIDE TO OBTAINING A PSYCHOLOGY INTERNSHIP

MEGARGEE'S GUIDE TO OBTAINING A PSYCHOLOGY INTERNSHIP

Third Edition
Revised and Expanded

Edwin I. Megargee, Ph.D., ABPP
The Florida State University

Foreword by Sanford L. Pederson, Ph.D.
Wright State University

ACCELERATED DEVELOPMENT
A member of the Taylor & Francis Group

USA	Publishing Office:	ACCELERATED DEVELOPMENT *A member of the Taylor & Francis Group* 1101 Vermont Avenue,N.W., Suite20 Washington, D.C. 2005-3531 Tel: (202) 289-2174 Fax: (202) 289-3665
	Distribution Center:	ACCELERATED DEVELOPMENT *A member of the Taylor & Francis Group* 1900 Frost Road, Suite 101 Briston, PA 19007-1598 Tel: (215) 785-5800 Fax: (215) 785-5515
UK		Taylor & Francis Ltd. 1 Gunpowder Square London EC4A 3DE Tel: 071 583 0490 Fax: 071 583 0581

MEGARGEE'S GUIDE TO OBTAINING A PSYCHOLOGY INTERNSHIP:
Third Edition, Revised and Expanded

1 2 3 4 5 6 7 8 9 0 B R B R 9 8 7

Editing by Cindy Long. Cover design by Michelle Fleitz.
A CIP catalog record for this book is available from the British Library.
∞ The paper in this publication meets the requirements of the ANSI Standard Z39.48-1984(Permanence of Paper)

Library of Congress Cataloging-in-Publication data available from the publisher.

ISBN: 1-56032-750-2 (paper)

ACKNOWLEDGMENTS AND DEDICATION

I am grateful to the many people who helped make this book and its two predecessors possible. First and foremost are the many Florida State University graduate students with whom I have shared the internship application process. Their comments, encounters, and reflections on their experiences form the essence of this survival guide. It is they who provided the questions in Appendices 5 and 6, and the "war stories" and examples that make this book real. I am also indebted to the many internship training directors and their staffs whom I have visited and interviewed from Los Angeles to Boston, and from Miami to Seattle, not only for their unfailing hospitality, but also for their thoughtful comments and insights on the internship selection process.

I also wish to thank the Association of Psychology Postdoctoral and Internship Centers for their contributions to all three editions and for allowing me to reprint the 1996 APPIC rules in Appendix 1. APPIC's First Annual Membership Meeting in Orlando organized by Carl Zimet and Sandy Pederson was an invaluable source of information on present and future changes in the Guidelines governing internship selection. I especially want to thank Sanford Pederson, the Chair of the APPIC Board of Directors, for answering my many questions over the years and for taking the time from his all-too-busy schedule to prepare the Foreword for this edition. In addition, I want to thank Bernhard Blom and Robert Klepac for their advice regarding computer matching and many other aspects of the selection process, and Connie Hercey, APPIC's Central Office Administrator, for providing back copies of the APPIC *Newsletter* and advance copies of the new Uniform Application Form that assisted in this revision.

Sue Cunningham did much of the library research and abstracted the data from the 1996-1997 APPIC *Directory* that I used in computing the statistics on the competitiveness of various types of internships in different parts of the country. James Stedman provided me with reprints and preprints of his many insightful papers on internship selection. Deborah Beidel furnished the latest APA accreditation information, and Peggy Cantrell updated me on the progress of the new Uniform Application Forms.

I also wish to thank Cindy Long of Accelerated Development for copy-editing the manuscript under the pressure of an imminent deadline and my publisher, Dr. Joe Hollis, for taking a chance and publishing an unconventional book for a specialized readership. If you find this book helpful, thank him for bringing it to you.

Most of all I wish to acknowledge the contribution of my wife, Sara Jill Mercer, for all her work on this and the previous editions. She is the production manager who takes the words and transforms them into an attractive camera-ready manuscript. This year she had the added chore of entering the *Directory* data into the computer and preparing the tables and graphs, as well as providing counsel and therapy while I grappled with a new word-processing system. She was my partner and collaborator on all phases of this enterprise, as she is on everything worthwhile in my life. It is to her that this edition, like the two previous ones, is dedicated.

CONTENTS

PREFACE

There have been dramatic changes in the internship marketplace and in the rules governing intern selection since the first edition of *A Guide to Obtaining a Psychology Internship* was published (1990). Whereas in 1990 only 95 applicants remained unplaced after Uniform Notification Day ("UND"), by 1996 the number had increased to 489. Previously the Clearinghouse managed by the Association of Psychology Postdoctoral and Internship Centers ("APPIC") had been able to find placements for virtually all of the qualified candidates who chose to participate, but in 1996, 98 applicants remained unplaced after all the slots listed in the Clearinghouse had been filled. This trend continued in 1997, with 469 remaining unplaced after UND. After the Clearinghouse had completed its matchings in the summer of 1997, there were still 150 applicants from 41 programs unplaced, with only eight positions from three unaccredited internships still available.

Since the first edition of this *Guide* was published, the rules governing intern selection have been changed and changed again. Computerized matching was given a trial run, was abandoned, and is now being reconsidered. The time applicants are allowed to consider offers on Uniform Notification Day has been decreased from 28 hours to four hours, and applicants can no longer hold more than one offer while they are considering which one to accept. Given the changes in the rules and the increase in the number of well- qualified applicants that are available, Internship Training Directors ("ITD"s) no longer need fear that they will be unable to fill all their slots. Nevertheless, cheating has grown to such epidemic proportions that the APPIC Board passed an emergency rule change in March, 1997, forbidding Internship Training Directors, applicants, and university faculty from soliciting, providing, accepting, or even using information about how applicants rank programs and vice versa prior to Uniform Notification Day. In short, the internship selection process is in a state of flux, and the only certainty is that the overall process has become even more difficult for the students.

If you are just beginning the process of seeking an internship, you will probably find this information and these terms... "APPIC," "UND," "Clearinghouse" and the like... troubling and bewildering. What or who is APPIC? What are these rules, and how are they being broken? Why is the internship selection process so difficult and stressful? You may feel as if you have entered the "Twilight Zone" and been transported to a seat at a high stakes poker game that everyone else has been playing for some time. You don't know who the other players are or what they want. No one has told you the rules. Nevertheless, you are supposed to ante up and play the next hand as if your life depended on it. Unfortunately, you are not in the Twilight Zone. Crazy as it may seem, this is reality.

The purpose of this book is to explain to you the nature of this game in which you have found yourself. It has been revised and expanded to incorporate the latest rules, to explain how and why they are often broken, and to anticipate the effects of planned changes, such as computerized matching. Most important, it has been designed to help you understand and cope with the process successfully.

Applying for a psychology internship has always been exceedingly stressful. It involves an inordinate amount of your time, effort, and money. Now that the number of applicants exceeds the supply of positions, normal applicant anxiety is escalating into panic. Because of these shortfalls, some students have markedly increased the number of applications they submit and the number of interviews they seek. In response, many internships have been limiting the number of applicants they interview, screening out those who don't seem well-prepared or well-suited to the setting. This has caused some students to prepare even more applications.

Frantic activity and multiple applications are not the answer. Instead of working harder, you need to work "smarter." In today's marketplace, there is no point applying before you are ready. You must learn to assess your qualifications and evaluate them as an Internship Selection Committee will. When you are ready to apply, you need to select the settings that are best for you and your particular goals. You must also learn to prepare applications that emphasize your particular talents and skills, and learn to interview Training Directors effectively. Finally, as the selection date draws near, you must negotiate in an ethical yet effective manner to optimize your chances of being selected at the internships that are best for you.

Accomplishing all of this while maintaining your obligations to your training program, your job, and your relationships requires a great deal of specialized knowledge, as well as effective time management and the ability to cope with stress. It is essential that you understand the implicit as well as the explicit rules of the game and learn the underlying concerns of the other players, especially the Internship Training Directors. Your Academic Director of Clinical Training ("ADCT") can assist you to an extent, but you must realize that the ADCT's primary concerns are to your training program and not to you as an individual, because there may be times when your needs differ from those of your program.

The first goal of this book is to educate you about the internship selection game and why it works the way it does. The second is to advise you on how to assess your priorities, select the sites that will best meet your needs, prepare your applications, interview effectively, and finally negotiate with ITDs. The more information you have, the better able you will be to cope with and survive the internship selection process with as little damage as possible to your self-esteem, health, relationships, and bank account.

Plan for this volume

The first step in coping with the internship process is to understand it. The training faculty and, especially, the ITDs at the sites where you apply will typically have a long history of coping with the internship recruitment and selection process. It is often as traumatic for them as it is for you. Many, perhaps most, feel they have been betrayed by applicants in the past and are predisposed to distrust you and your fellow applicants. At this stage of the game, this will probably strike you as bizarre, but until you understand their point of view, you will not be able to deal effectively with them. Therefore, I will start by providing you with the background information you need to understand their viewpoint.

In Chapter One, I will give you a brief history of how professional psychology internships originated and developed to their present point. Since the earliest days of American psychology, there has been a strain between the scientific and the applied aspects of the discipline. Today this is epitomized by the uneasy, and sometimes downright hostile, feelings your academic mentors may have toward the internship requirement in general and internship training personnel in particular. This feeling is often reciprocated by the internship training staffs. You will be caught in the middle. The purpose of this chapter is to provide you with some insight into this uneasy relationship so you can better understand and evaluate the advice you get from both sides.

Building on this foundation, Chapter Two describes the politics of intern selection. You will learn how and why the rules governing the selection and notification process have changed almost annually, and why they will continue to change in the years to come. Different procedures give different groups ...the ITDs, the ADCTs, and the applicants... different degrees of power. If you are to make sense of the internship selection process and cope with it successfully, it is essential that you understand the concerns and vested interests of the other parties and how their power struggles have influenced the selection process over the years.

After this introduction, Chapter Three will give you an overview of the internship selection process. You will be provided with a month-by-month timetable of what you must do to identify the internships that best meet your needs and prepare successful applications. The succeeding chapters will expand on these points.

Your first task is deciding when and where to apply. Chapter Four, "Establishing Your Priorities," will help you examine your strengths and weaknesses and determine the personal set of priorities that will guide you in selecting the internships that are best suited to your particular needs. I will begin by discussing some of the fears and concerns most applicants have when they begin this arduous and anxiety-provoking process. You will see which concerns are realistic and which are mythical. I will then help you formulate your personal list of priorities that will guide you in seeking the settings that best meet your needs.

Chapter Five, "Compiling Your Application List," advises you on how to obtain accurate information about the internships that interest you, provides you with information about the competitiveness and the priorities of internships in various areas, and advises you on how to prepare a list of possible internships.

The next two chapters deal with the actual application process. Chapter Six will teach you how to prepare a resume or Curriculum Vitae (CV) specifically for internship applications in the light of the new Uniform Applications that APPIC is developing. (Appendix 3 provides a sample CV.) Chapter Seven, "Preparing Your Applications," gives you advice on preparing and submitting personal statements, application forms, and work samples and obtaining letters of recommendation. It introduces you to the new Uniform Application Form that APPIC is introducing and discusses the certifications your ADCT now has to fill out if your candidacy is to be successful.

Once your applications are all in, you should obtain interviews and visit as many of the internship sites as you can. Chapter Eight gives you practical advice on traveling to internship sites and reducing transportation and hotel costs. Chapter Nine, "The Site Visit and Interview," discusses interviewing and how to deal with ITDs who violate the APPIC rules. Appendices 5 and 6 provide you with questions you may be asked by ITDs and questions you can ask them.

By January, most of the interviewing is over. This is when the "Endgame" begins as applicants and ITDs dance elaborate minuets and attempt to second guess each other. Chapter Ten tells you what to do during the Endgame. It also provides explicit instructions on what you should do on Uniform Notification Day and describes how the APPIC Clearinghouse works if you should not get an acceptable offer. Finally,

Chapter Eleven discusses the frequency of rule violations and describes how APPIC deals with complaints. It concludes with a description of the computer matching procedures that will soon be adopted.

As you can see, this book is designed to help you with all phases of obtaining your internship. To get started, I suggest that you read the first three chapters to get an understanding of the internship selection process and the vested interests of the various participants. Next, skim over the rest of the book to give yourself an overview of what you will need to do in the weeks and months to come. Don't forget to examine the Appendices; they are included to help you. Later, reread each chapter more closely when it is time for you to deal with each of the tasks described. You can use the timetable in Chapter Three to keep on schedule.

FOREWORD

Dr. Edwin Megargee offers potential intern applicants a wealth of useful information in this book. I have been familiar with it since the First Edition, when I was involved with the APPIC Pilot Study of a Computerized Internship Matching Program, and Dr. Megargee called to discuss the Program for inclusion in the First Edition. Dr. Megargee and I have continued our correspondence about the book, and I am pleased to be writing the Foreword for this Third Edition.

This book is the best available source of the most information in one place about this complex and often confusing process. One "side effect" that many readers do not initially notice is its anxiety reduction effects. And in a process as anxiety-provoking as the current professional psychology internship market, any healthy means to reduce anxiety is helpful. I am pleased to see that applicants have found this compendium of information, opinion, and advice to be useful enough to warrant a Second, and now a Third, Edition.

The process of applying to, interviewing for, and selecting an internship in professional psychology has become a far from simple process. It has become more lengthy, time-consuming, and complex as time has gone on, with more and more strategic thinking required on the part of applicants. In times like these you need all the help and guidance you can get. This book is one comprehensive source of that help and guidance. But, as Dr. Megargee himself states, it is not (and should not be) your only source of help and guidance. As in any endeavor where you are entering uncharted waters, it is always wise to ask the advice of those who have gone before you and of anyone who has been around the area you are about to enter. After all, psychologists are intellectual folks, and we feel better the more knowledge, information, data, and opinion we have. But never rely solely on anyone's advice. It's your career and your life, and you need to make your own decisions.

The internship is a critical part of the training of the professional psychologist in many different ways. Many people spend their careers in the geographic locale in which they interned. Internship is the "capstone" of professional training, where all that you have learned and all that you have become are brought together in the culmination of a process that began many years before. Many crucial career decisions are made during internship, many new areas of practice and research explored. I have been involved in the training of professional psychology interns since I completed my own internship in 1982. I am continually struck by the transformative nature of the internship experience. One begins the experience with much potential that has yet to be realized, and by the end of the successful experience one is transformed into the realization of that potential. Yet, of course, you remain the same person with many of the same strengths and weaknesses as before. But this year of focusing on who you are as a psychologist, and on who you want to become as a psychologist, continues to provide a crucible in which careers are formed and lives planned.

Because of the importance of this transformative year, all prospective interns should find as many resources as they can. The level of detail that you will find herein in unmatched elsewhere at the present time. This book is like having a long and pleasant conversation with its author, who shares his knowledge and opinion from many years as a Director of Clinical Training in a university and his many contacts with a wide variety of internship programs over those years. It is not a textbook; it is not a guarantee. But it is a wealth of useful information and advice that covers not just the professional and strategic aspects of applying for professional psychology internships, but also the practical down-to-earth aspects of how to manage this whole complex process. For those of you without extensive travel experience, the travel tips alone are worth reading this book.

While this book will not guarantee you get the internship of your dreams, it will go a long way toward helping you be more effective, more comfortable, and ultimately more successful in your quest for the best professional psychology internship for you.

Sanford L. Pederson, Ph.D.
Dayton, Ohio
June 11, 1997

CHAPTER ONE

THE NATURE AND AVAILABILITY OF PSYCHOLOGY INTERNSHIPS: PAST, PRESENT, AND FUTURE

Preparation and knowledge are your surest keys to success in internship selection. Later in this chapter, I will demonstrate that there are now over 2,800 applicants competing for less than 2,500 internship positions. This imbalance is likely to continue for the next several years. As a result, students are filing more applications than ever before; 37,107 applications were submitted in 1995-1996, 17% more than in the previous year. Nevertheless, 489 applicants remained unplaced after Uniform Notification Day in 1996. The shortfall was even greater in 1997.

Cranking out more applications is not the answer. To maximize your chances for success, you need to evaluate your education, experience, and skills and then submit thoughtfully prepared, individualized applications to carefully selected internships that are seeking students with your particular qualifications. This requires time, effort, and research. Although you may find it distasteful, you should view yourself as a product that you must package and sell to the internships of your choice. Like any other successful salesperson, you must evaluate the marketplace and understand what your customers, the Internship Training Directors, are looking for in a candidate.

The idea of kowtowing to ITDs is anathema to many Academic Directors of Clinical Training and their faculty colleagues. They may resist and resent offering a curriculum designed to prepare you for internship. Their notions of the purpose and goals of doctoral education often differ considerably from the ITDs' perspectives, chiefly on the relative importance of professional as opposed to research training. One well-known ADCT recently remarked that he would have grave reservations about any internship that would select students on the basis of the amount of assessment and therapy experience they had accumulated, opining that the number of publications and conference presentations was a much more relevant criterion. However, a survey of 90 internships revealed that ITDs ranked publications and presentations ninth out of nine possible criteria, and that supervised therapy and assessment experience ranked second and third respectively (Petzel & Berndt, 1980). However, these data do not mean you can ignore your ADCT's advice to publish; letters of recommendation, one of which should be from your ADCT, ranked first in the study.

In short, you will need to do a delicate balancing act, simultaneously pleasing your academic mentors and impressing your future internship faculty. That is why it is important you understand their views and why you should also be aware of how the various organizations involved, namely the American Psychological Association (APA) and the Association of Psychology Postdoctoral and Internship Centers (APPIC) regard the role of the internship year in your graduate education. Therefore, we will begin with a brief description of the changing nature of professional psychology internships.

A Short Course on Predoctoral Internships

APA and the scientist model

The American Psychological Association has accredited doctoral training programs in clinical psychology for almost 50 years. From the beginning, a year-long predoctoral internship, ideally in an APA-accredited program, has been an essential requirement for the doctoral degree in clinical psychology. Although graduating from an APA-accredited degree program is not essential for state licensure, for inclusion in the National Register of Health Service Providers in Psychology, or for obtaining a diploma issued by the American Board of Examiners in Professional Psychology (ABPP), APA accreditation criteria have become the "gold standard" by which training programs are judged. If your degree is not from an APA-accredited program, you will continually need to convince various credentialing bodies that your program equaled or exceeded APA standards.

Some university faculty members have little use for APA. They feel that APA has become a trade union representing professional psychology at the expense of psychology as a science. It was not always so. When APA was founded in 1892, it was a learned society comprised of philosophers, educators, physicians, and an occasional psychologist (Resnick, 1997). In the early years, membership requirements included a Ph.D., an academic teaching position, and a record of published scientific research (Brems, Thevenin, & Routh, 1991). Sporadic efforts to establish clinical or applied sections within APA were largely unsuccessful, and APA remained a scholarly society for academics until the end of World War II. Early practitioners formed independent organizations (Brems et al., 1991). Since there were no formal training programs in applied psychology, would-be practitioners earned university degrees in scientific psychology and obtained whatever professional training they could from mentors, reading, or trial and error (Peterson, 1991). Practice in those days consisted primarily of testing and assessment (Resnick, 1997).

World War II created an acute need for mental health personnel to assist the military in screening and classifying troops upon induction into the service and, later, in treating GIs suffering from war-induced traumas. Recruits who were deemed suitable on the basis of interests or education were trained to serve as psychologists in the service, not only to administer and interpret tests but also to perform psychotherapy. From this time forward, professional psychologists would no longer be content with being limited to testing and serving as assistants to psychiatrists. Their desire to continue independent practice after the war was supported by a tremendous demand for mental health professionals in schools, state hospitals, and correctional institutions as well as Veterans Administration (VA) facilities (Brems et al., 1991).

The federal government prepared for the return of 16 million veterans, many of whom had suffered psychological as well as physical wounds and traumas, by making funds available through the VA and the National Institute of Mental Health (NIMH) to train clinical psychologists to meet their mental health needs (Peterson, 1991). This vast educational program created an urgent need for agreed-upon training models and for standards to evaluate the adequacy of training programs and the competency of their graduates. Joint task forces of APA and the American Association for Applied Psychology (AAAP) met in 1941 and 1944 to consider schemes for training and accreditation (Laughlin & Worley, 1991). They proposed a model that combined academic training with a year-long, closely supervised, clinical internship. The internship would involve direct supervised clinical experience in inpatient settings, combined with indirect experience, such as case conferences, and with administrative experience in which the interns familiarized themselves with the facilities where they worked by participating in staff meetings, maintaining patient records, and preparing reports. Under this model, the internship occurred in the third year of graduate training, after which students would return to their academic settings for a fourth and final year in which they could integrate their academic and clinical experiences (Davies, 1987; Laughlin & Worley, 1991). This model assumed that relatively little clinical training would take place in the university setting.

To implement these recommendations, further meetings were held between APA and AAAP, which resulted in the merging of the two organizations. The new APA bylaws stipulated that the goals of the organization were to advance psychology as a profession as well as a science and to promote human welfare. Publications were no longer required for membership, making it easier for practitioners to join. AAAP disbanded, and the new APA was begun in May, 1945, shortly before the end of hostilities with Japan (Brems et al., 1991; Resnick, 1997). The hostilities within the new organization were just beginning.

Development of the scientist-professional model

The new APA's first order of business was to consider a request from the VA and NIMH to develop a model for graduate level training in clinical psychology and to identify university programs that met these criteria. APA responded by forming a Committee on Training in Clinical Psychology headed by David Shakow. The "Shakow Committee's Report" followed the guidelines outlined by the joint APA/AAAP task forces. It recommended a four-year, doctoral level training program, including practicum training at the university combined with a one-year clinical internship in the third year. It further recommended that APA establish an accreditation program with on-site visits occurring every five years. These recommendations were adopted at an NIMH-funded conference on graduate clinical training held at Boulder, Colorado in 1949 (Brems et al., 1991). Thus was born the "scientist-professional" or "Boulder model" of clinical training.

As the Boulder model was designed and implemented, the "scientist-professional" was first and foremost a scientist (Peterson, 1991) (i.e., a "***SCIENTIST*** - professional"). The clinical aspects of the graduate program were generally added on to the existing academic requirements for the Ph.D. in experimental psychology. For example, in my doctoral program at the University of California at Berkeley, after three semesters of study, all graduate students had to pass the same three qualifying examinations, one in history and systems, one in statistics, and one comprising six content areas (learning, sensation and perception, physiological, personality, developmental, and social). Grading was norm referenced with only the top third of the distribution on each exam passing at the doctoral level and with only one retake allowed. The next hurdle was passing written examinations in two of these three languages: French, German, or Russian. While preparing for these examinations, all students were expected to design and complete an empirical research project each semester. Next came individualized written and oral comprehensive examinations in each student's area of study. If and when these were passed, students formed a committee and embarked on a dissertation project.

In addition to these basic Ph.D. requirements, clinical students also had to complete a required curriculum, which included courses in the Stanford Binet and Wechsler intelligence tests, projective testing, structured personality testing, case history and psychopathology, personality theory, and individual and group psychotherapy, as well as specialized elective seminars. We also had to fulfill the practicum and internship requirements. It is not surprising that only three of the 25 students who began the program with me in 1959 eventually received Ph.D.s in clinical, or that it took us all more than four years. As you might suppose, those clinical students who were primarily interested in professional careers resented the time and effort required to complete the research, language, and other non-clinical requirements of the program.

It was only the widespread availability of clinical training grants financed by the National Institute of Mental Health, United States Public Health Service (USPHS) that made it possible to implement the Boulder model. Because students were supported by USHPS fellowships, universities could prescribe the type of experience students would receive in their practicum settings. When an agency received students' services free in exchange for access to clients and supervision, they usually did not mind assigning students good "teaching" cases, allowing them to administer extensive test batteries or permitting them to pick up long-term treatment cases with limited financial resources.

The original Boulder model, supported by clinical training grants and VA stipends, placed the control of clinical education in the hands of the ADCTs and university faculties. They emphasized the scientific end of the scientist-professional continuum. Boulder model Ph.D.s were expected to become research producers, not just research consumers. Those who went on to do clinical research in academic and medical school settings were considered successes, whereas those who never published and went into full-time practice were regarded as "hand holders" who had wasted their mentors' time (Peterson, 1991). Other players, however, were less enamored of the Boulder model. Eventually the view of this latter group prevailed, and alternative training models were developed.

Development of professional models

With the emergence of the Boulder model, APA was finally committed to fostering graduate training in professional psychology. The Boulder model allowed traditional academic departments to retain their scientific values while reaping important practical rewards; by enrolling large numbers of graduate students in clinical psychology, such as me and my 24 classmates, and by winning large clinical training grants, academic departments of psychology were able to generate increased numbers of faculty positions and obtain more space from their universities. (The only thing more important than faculty lines and space in the academic marketplace is preferential parking, something not even the training grants could secure.)

As is so often the case in the internship game, when one player prospers, others become dissatisfied. While the ADCTs were, as the late Red Barber would have said, "sitting in the catbird seat," the ITDs felt as if they were at the bottom of the bird cage. It appeared to them that the universities promoted research training at the expense of preparation for internship. As Peterson (1991, p. 423) noted, "Situated as they were in academic departments, controlled as they were by researchers, the Boulder-style programs all too often neglected training for practice." Summarizing the results of a survey of ITDs, Shemberg and Leventhal (1981, p. 639) reported, "Consistent with previous data, considerable dissatisfaction exists among directors relative to university preparation in clinical skills. Interns are seen by many as not well-prepared in assessment or psychotherapeutic activities." In one brief year, the internship center was expected to provide the bulk of the students' clinical training. One ITD and his colleagues warned the academic programs, "In your attempts to mold a scientist-practitioner, beware of over emphasizing the scientist at the expense of the practitioner" (Stedman, Costello, Gaines, Schoenfeld, Loucks, & Burstein, 1981, p. 419).

Undergraduate psychology majors seeking admission into clinical training programs were also dissatisfied. Although the universities welcomed large numbers of undergraduate psychology majors and adopted undergraduate curricula that would prepare these majors for graduate school, there were few places for their graduates in their doctoral training programs (Stricker, 1997). Scientist-professional training typically followed the scientific tradition in which a faculty mentor worked closely with a limited number of graduate students on a research team. There was insufficient room in their laboratories for large numbers of students, especially those whose primary interests were in practice rather than research. Graduate students who were admitted to doctoral programs in clinical psychology were expected to prepare for research careers; however, after paying their research dues in graduate school, most clinical Ph.D.s went into practice and never published (Peterson, 1991). It appeared to many that the Boulder model programs' insistence on training researchers was wasting the time of students and faculty alike.

The Korean war exacerbated the VA's need for practitioners, and the deinstitutionalization of the mentally ill and the proliferation of community based mental health centers in the 1960s increased the demand for clinical psychologists--personnel needs that were not being met by the traditional programs (Peterson, 1991). For example, even though the California State Psychological Association urged the universities to expand their clinical training programs, the entire University of California system turned out less than 20 Ph.D.s in clinical psychology annually (Peterson, 1991).

In response to these pressures, various alternatives to the Boulder model were considered in a series of APA-sponsored training conferences at Miami Beach (1958), Princeton (1962), Chicago (1965), Vail (1973), and Salt Lake City (1987). In the 1960s, Psy.D. programs and free-standing schools of professional psychology were initiated. By 1982, there were 44 such practitioner programs in the United States with almost 5,000 students enrolled (Brems et al., 1991; Peterson, 1985; 1991).

At this stage of the game, faculty members at the traditional programs felt no particular animosity toward the new Psy.D. or professional school programs. As long as they were able to train their students as "***SCIENTIST*** - professionals," they did not object if other institutions adopted a "scientist - ***PROFESSIONAL***" model, especially if it led to a different academic degree. What did aggravate them was APA's increasing tendency to dictate the content of the clinical curriculum for programs to be accredited. The development of national licensing examinations induced training programs to develop curricula that would prepare their students to pass these tests. For example, a traditional Boulder model professor teaching a course on psychopathology might emphasize experimental research on the etiology of various disorders, whereas the students might prefer to focus on using the latest *Diagnostic and Statistical Manual*. The overall effect was pressure to place more emphasis on practice and less on basic science. Many traditional faculty felt this diluted the scientific rigor of their programs; they argued that their job was to *educate* students, not prepare them for internship or licensing examinations.

Financial constraints, too, were forcing the academic training centers to become more practice oriented. As the large training grants that had furnished the stipends for predoctoral students were phased out during the Nixon and Ford administrations in the 1970s, programs began negotiating with practicum agencies to provide stipends for the students they trained. Of course, once the agencies began paying their stipends, it was inevitable that the agencies' needs would begin to dictate the nature of the practicum experience. This resulted in less extensive test batteries; briefer, more cost-effective, interventions; less freedom to select "interesting" cases; and more time spent in direct service activities.

The advent of APPIC and the two-year internship

As long as the internship training centers remained isolated from one another, competing with each other for the best clinical graduate students, the academic programs had the balance of power in the internship selection game. This changed in 1968, when a group of ITDs founded The Association of Psychology Internship Centers (APIC), since renamed the Association of Psychology and Postdoctoral Internship Centers (APPIC). (For the sake of simplicity, I shall simply use the acronym "APPIC" regardless of the year being discussed.) Although it got off to a shaky start, APPIC is now comprised of over 500 predoctoral and 75 postdoctoral training centers, about 75% of which are APA accredited. Members are expected to adhere to APPIC policies and pay their dues; in return they get access to the internship pool by virtue of being listed in the annual APPIC *Directory*.

Defining internships. APPIC, APA, the American Association of State Psychology Boards (which coordinates licensing), and the National Register have all agreed on a uniform operational definition of what constitutes a satisfactory predoctoral internship training program. These criteria are reprinted in the front of the APPIC *Directory*. Briefly, they stipulate that a psychology internship is an organized program of training that goes beyond supervised clinical experience or on the job training. Each internship must have a clearly-designated licensed doctoral-level director who is on site at least 20 hours weekly and who is responsible for the quality and integrity of the program, as well as at least two full-time licensed doctoral-level supervisors (one of whom may also be the director) who provide each intern with at least two hours of direct individual supervision each week. An internship must have at least two full-time interns who must put in at least 1,500 hours over a nine- to 24-month period, at least 25% of which must be in direct face-to-face service with clients. In addition, at least two hours weekly must be spent in didactic training such as case conferences, grand rounds, seminars, and the like. The nature and goals and the quantity and quality of the work expected of the interns, who may also be called residents or fellows, must be written and made available in a brochure.

Standardizing selection procedures. APPIC's first concern was regularizing the then-chaotic selection and notification process. It did so by formulating rules on how the internship selection process should work and persuading the internship training centers to adopt them (Stedman, 1989). Whereas previously internships could select interns whenever and however they chose, the APPIC rules stated that members had to adhere to a uniform notification time. Prior to the magic hour of 9:00 AM Central Standard Time on the second Monday in February, APPIC members are prohibited from making formal or informal offers to applicants. This ended the chaos that stemmed from some ITDs cutting deals with ADCTs and making offers before other settings had even begun interviewing. Key provisions are that internships may not make more offers than they have positions available, and that once an offer has been made and accepted, it cannot be rescinded. Once a slot has been offered to a candidate, the candidate can choose to accept, decline, or defer his or her decision. If the candidate opts to defer, the slot remains committed to that candidate and cannot be offered to anyone else until the candidate rejects it or until time runs out on the notification process. We will explore the political implications of these policies in the next chapter. Suffice it to say that this set the stage for a continuing power struggle between applicants and ITDs and created a situation in which there were strong incentives for both parties to break the rules.

Although APPIC had formulated the rules and, over the years, tried to improve them, the organization has little power to enforce them in a timely fashion. Sanctions, such as a reprimand or censure, can be imposed only after an aggrieved party files a formal written complaint that is then investigated by APPIC's Standards and Review Committee, a group that has no power to subpoena records or obtain sworn testimony from witnesses and instead must rely on the cooperation and compliance of the parties involved. Since each party is allowed a reasonable amount of time to study the other party's allegations and responses before replying, this can be a protracted process. By the time the matter is resolved, UND is ancient history and the matter appears moot. (See Chapter Eleven.)

Consequently, while students and ADCTs often gripe about some APPIC members' actions, few follow through and file formal complaints. Without a formal complaint, the Standards and Review Committee is powerless to act. Because of the difficulty it has policing its members, and because APPIC has the power to make and alter the rules unilaterally, the organization is resented by many ADCTs.

Impact of managed care. Like the other mental health agencies, most internships have been operating under financial constraints in recent years (Constantine & Gloria, 1996). Whereas universities and professional schools are in the business of providing education, training is only an ancillary activity at most internship sites. In an era of reduced budgets and "downsizing," some centers are tempted to lower their costs by cutting back or eliminating internship training. Many internships rely heavily on fees generated by the interns and their supervisors to underwrite the cost of training. One of my students accepted a neuropsychological slot at a major medical center. There she was trained to administer, score, and interpret a complex neuropsychological assessment battery. Throughout her internship year, she administered several such batteries each week. The fees she generated for the facility helped defray the cost of her stipend and supervision. Although this activity limited the breadth of her training, she could hardly complain because all of her supervisors, including the ITD, also had to spend many hours a week in direct service to generate the funds for their salaries.

In this era of managed health care ("MHC"), internships, like other mental health providers, have had increasing difficulty billing for the services performed by interns and postdoctoral fellows. As part of their quality assurance programs, many third-party providers will only pay for services performed by licensed health care providers. If an unlicensed technician carries out a procedure, the licensed provider often must be in the room directly supervising the activity for it to be reimbursable. Reviewing a videotape of a procedure is not sufficient.

This model does not work well for psychologists. Unlike X-ray technicians, nurses, and physicians' assistants, most psychology trainees do not have any sort of license, even though they typically have a master's degree or the equivalent, and it is obviously impractical for an intern's doctoral level supervisor to be physically present throughout the administration of a lengthy test battery or psychotherapy session. In settings where rules such as this apply, the range of clients that an intern may see can be severely limited if the facility wishes to be reimbursed for the intern's services.

Possible solutions to this dilemma are being discussed. Since MHC systems are accustomed to reimbursing for services performed by medical interns or residents, one proposal is that students should defend their dissertations and be awarded their degrees *before* going on internship. This would present a major change, since APA has always insisted that a *pre*doctoral internship is a prerequisite for the doctoral degree in clinical psychology. Still, as we have seen, when money talks, educational programs listen. Another suggestion is to create some sort of limited master's level license that would permit third-party reimbursements for selected procedures. This would have to be done on a state-by-state basis, and, indeed some states already have master's level licenses. These discussions are continuing, and their outcome may well alter psychology internships significantly.

Constantine and Gloria's (1996) recent survey of 311 APPIC ITDs indicates that MHC is having a negative impact on internship training; 96 of the 311 ITDs (31%) reported that MHC had affected the number of internship slots, 90 (29%) indicated that MHC had affected the criteria they use in selecting interns, 96 (31%) stated that MHC had affected their ability to fund current internship positions, 87 (28%) reported an adverse effect on the quality of their training, and 142 (46%) responded that MHC had limited the types of services their interns could provide. One implication of these findings is that applicants who have some sort of license or credential may be preferred by some internships, as will students with expertise in brief assessments and interventions and those with experience dealing with Health Maintenance Organizations ("HMOs").

The 1987 Gainesville Conference. In 1987, APPIC convened a national conference on internship training at Gainesville, Florida. The Gainesville Conference made a number of recommendations that, according to Laughlin and Worley (1991, p. 435), "...may well set the stage for internship training in psychology into the 21st century." Whereas the 1949 Boulder Conference had been dominated by university-based academicians, most of the Gainesville participants were from internship training centers (Belar, Bieliauskas, Larsen, Mensh, Poey, & Roehlke, 1987). The policy statement they adopted strongly advocated more extensive professional training in clinical psychology than the APA standards required. It specified that students must complete all their academic requirements before going on internship. These should include courses on "assessment/diagnosis," "intervention/treatment," and "ethical and professional standards." Whereas the APA guidelines required at least 400 hours of practicum training, the Gainesville conferees called for at least 900, 450 of which are to be spent in direct provision of services, as well as 300 hours to be spent in group and/or individual supervision. At the time of application, the ADCT must certify that the student has successfully completed all these requirements and has demonstrated the ethical conduct and interpersonal skills required for the practice of professional psychology. The policy statement also stipulated that all academic and internship training should take place in APA-accredited programs.

The most controversial aspect of the Gainesville policy statement was set forth in the first three sentences: "The internship is defined as a two year training experience. The first year is predoctoral. The second year is postdoctoral" (Belar et al., 1987, p. 4). It further stipulated that before going on internship students should have completed all their doctoral research requirements including the dissertation. Given the fact that internship selection takes place in February and most internships don't begin until the following September, the delegates stopped short of actually *requiring* that the dissertation be defended before reporting to the internship. However, they all agreed that students must complete their dissertation proposals before they apply for an internship.

These latter proposals, if adopted, would minimize the number of "ABDs," students who complete their internships but never finish their dissertations, a vexing problem for academic and internship programs alike. Moreover, by having their dissertation out of the way, students would be free to devote their full attention to their internship training. The increased practicum requirement and the two-year internship would mandate a higher minimum amount of predoctoral professional training and should make all students eligible for licensing upon completion of the second internship year.

Although the target date for implementing the Gainesville proposals was 1992 (Belar, Bieliauskas, Larsen, Mensh, Poey, & Roehlke, 1989), they have not yet been adopted by APA. However, some of these provisions are now in effect. A few centers are offering two-year internships, and most require considerably more than 400 hours of practicum experience. Moreover, all ADCTs must now certify that their students are ready for internship for their applications to be considered. More important, the Gainesville policy statement has had an anchoring effect. It defines a prototype of what APPIC's most influential leaders regard as the ideal applicant.

The closer you match that template -- more professional training you have had and the closer you are to the completion of your dissertation -- the more successful you will be in securing an internship.

As you might suppose, the two-year internship proposal was extremely controversial. Most ADCTs vehemently opposed the proposition since it added even more constraints to the academic curriculum. However, quite apart from its educational merits, it is likely that financial constraints will prevent the adoption of two-year internships for the foreseeable future because such a plan would immediately double the number of internship positions required. A facility that presently admits ten interns a year would have to come up with an additional ten postdoctoral positions to cover the second year of training. Given the current shortage of predoctoral positions, doubling the number of stipends would appear to be an impossible dream. Alternatively, such a facility would have to reduce their annual intake to five predoctoral positions. If this strategy was widely adopted, it would exacerbate the current shortage of predoctoral internship positions. This leads us to a consideration of the supply and demand issue.

A Shorter Course on Supply and Demand

The sudden surge in the number of applicants not obtaining internship positions on Uniform Notification Day caught most academic and internship training directors by surprise. How could this happen? Why wasn't it anticipated? Why doesn't somebody do something about it?

At first glance, any shortfall seems eminently predictable. After all, there are only a finite number of internship centers and students enrolled in graduate programs. It seems easy to tally them up, compare the totals, and determine whether or not there is an imbalance. Unfortunately things are not that simple. As with horse races and stock market fluctuations, we are excellent at looking back and charting what has already happened, but not very good at discerning current or future trends. The only way to obtain prospective information is through surveys; unfortunately not all internship or academic training programs are "in the system," and surveys of those that are may only have about a 50% return rate. As an ADCT, I received weekly surveys on a variety of training topics. I soon discovered that apparently simple questions such as, "How many students are enrolled in your program?" were surprisingly difficult to answer. Should I count the post-internship students who are supposedly working on their dissertations but who have not been heard from in over a year? What about those who have taken a leave of absence? When asked to predict how many will apply for internship a year or two hence, I often had to respond with a "WAG" (i.e., "Wild Assed Guess"). I suspect many of my fellow ADCTs also used WAGs, if they responded at all. Therefore, I am understandably skeptical about the reliability and validity of surveys on clinical training.

Thanks to the annual APPIC *Directories*, it is much easier to chart supply than demand. The now-current 1996-1997 *Directory* (Hall & Cantrell, 1996) lists 534 predoctoral internship programs, 411 (77%) of which are APA accredited. These agencies indicated they had a total of 2,431 funded full-time positions and 65 funded part- (usually half) time positions. There were also 76 full-time and 65 part-time unfunded slots listed. Of course, changes can take place over the course of a year; some programs may be added and others subtracted. I personally know of one major internship that lost seven of its 13 slots the week before UND in 1997.

APA-accredited academic training programs in clinical, counseling, and school psychology are listed each year in the December issue of the *American Psychologist*. However, no one knows precisely how many students are enrolled in these programs, much less how many will apply for internships in any given year. Moreover, there are a number of unaccredited programs whose students also seek internships. In an extraordinarily painstaking survey that yielded an exceptionally high response rate, Stedman, Costello, Gaines, Solway, Zimet, and Carrington (1990) polled the ADCTs of all the APA-accredited programs as well as the directors of a number of unaccredited ones. They asked them to estimate how many of their students would be likely to apply for internships in the 1988-1989, 1989-1990, and 1990-1991 selection years. After correcting for students' tendencies to be overly optimistic in forecasting their progress, Stedman et al. (1990) estimated that there would be approximately 2,000 students applying for the 2,045 positions the APPIC members had available in those years. It thus seemed that overall supply would slightly exceed demand. This was reassuring because APPIC members had been concerned that the number of positions would greatly exceed the number of applicants during the 1990s.

Stedman et al. (1990) identified one likely shortfall. They calculated that in 1988-1989 there would only be 1,372 applicants from APA-accredited traditional clinical or counseling programs for the 1,606 positions at APA-accredited training centers. "The APIC member, with or without APA accreditation, seeking to fill all its positions with traditional clinical psychology graduate students is likely to find itself with unfilled slots" (Stedman et al., 1990, p. 19). To fill these slots, they speculated that internships would have to accept students from the less preferred Psy.D. and professional school programs. Thus, from the traditional students' standpoint at least, there were ample positions available at the beginning of the 1990s.

The nature of the imbalance between supply and demand

The only hard data I can find on supply and demand are in the summary statistics on the operations of the Clearinghouse that APPIC maintains to match unselected applicants with unfilled positions. Records on recent Clearinghouse activities have been maintained and distributed by Dr. Gordon Williams of the Michigan State University Counseling Center who coordinates the Clearinghouse. Immediately after UND, ADCTs with unplaced applicants can access the Clearinghouse, as can internship programs that have unfilled positions. These parties are then able to communicate and try to match applicants to positions.

After three weeks, these data are purged. Some students no doubt decide to discontinue seeking a placement, preferring to work on their academic requirements and reapply the following year. Similarly, some internships may decide to convert a vacant slot to a postdoctoral position. After the purge, ADCTs who still have unplaced applicants seeking internships and internships with vacancies they still hope to fill can again access the Clearinghouse. Sometimes new positions become available in the months that follow. In June and July, some internships learn more about their budgets for the following year and may add new positions. Occasionally some applicants who were accepted on UND find they are unable to attend after all for health, personal, or academic reasons. Thus, additional matching usually takes place over the summer, and until recently, most qualified applicants were able to find a position.

The peak time for Clearinghouse listings is about three weeks after UND, just before the data are purged. Williams (personal communication, May, 1997) has kindly provided summary statistics regarding the numbers of applicants and positions available in the third week after UND for all the years from 1986 through 1997 (except for 1987 and 1990 for which the data are missing). These data are summarized in Figure 1-1.

It can be seen from the data in Figure 1-1 that supply exceeded demand through 1989. The data are missing for 1990. In 1991, there were 66 more applicants than vacancies. This shortfall increased to 198 in 1993, 212 in 1994, and 229 in 1995. However, in these years, additional positions became available and the Clearinghouse was generally successful in helping applicants and internships sort things out.

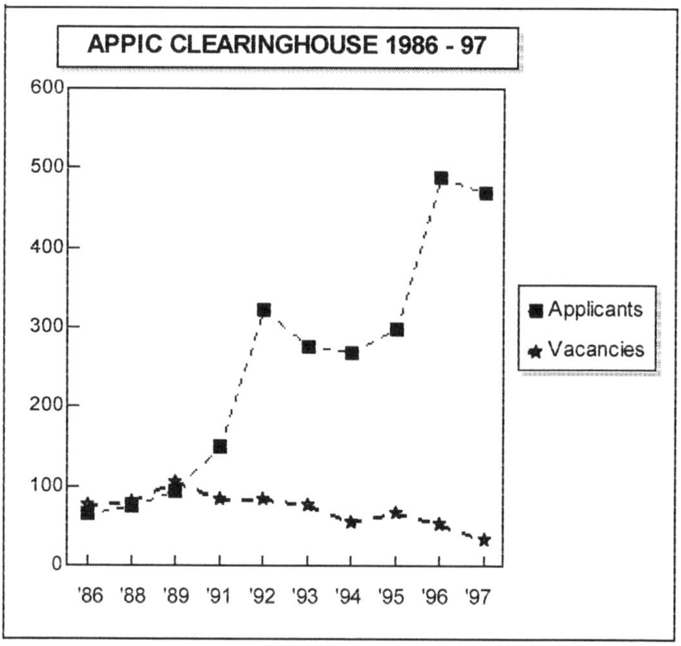

Figure 1-1. Comparison of number of applicants and vacancies after UND, 1986-1997.

This changed in 1996. The number of applicants accessing the Clearinghouse after UND soared to 489, and the number of vacancies dropped to an all time low of 53, producing a shortfall of 436. After the data were purged and throughout the summer, 99 applicants remained in the Clearinghouse, 88 of whom came from 34 APA-accredited programs, and there were only four vacancies for them to consider. In 1997, the picture was similar. The third week data showed 469 unplaced applicants and only 34 vacancies for a shortfall of 435. After the purge there were 150 applicants, 125 from APA-accredited programs and only eight unaccredited vacancies for them to consider.

Possible reasons for the shortfall

Insufficient positions? Earlier I mentioned how one major training center lost half its positions just before UND. Constantine and Gloria's (1996) survey indicated 14 centers had lost slots as a result of MHC. At the August, 1996, APPIC general meeting, it was announced that 40 APPIC members had lost a total of 64 slots but that four new centers with 34 positions had been added. All these rumors and anecdotes suggest that the total number of positions available is decreasing.

This impression is furthered by an analysis I recently carried out. In the second (1992) edition of this book, I included a list of the 41 internships that had reported receiving 100 or more applications in the 1990-1991 *Directory*. Collectively these centers had accounted for 25% of the total number of applications filed. What had happened to them? I looked them up in the 1996-1997 *Directory* (Hall & Cantrell, 1996) to see how they had fared. The good news was that seven programs had expanded, gaining a grand total of 15 positions; ten others had not changed. The bad news was that 22 other programs had lost a total of 67 positions, and three programs with 11 positions had folded. In all, 78 slots had been lost and only 15 gained for a net loss of 63 positions.

However, the results from these 41 large internships apparently distort the overall picture. Dr. Robert Klepac, Past President of APPIC and former editor of the *Directory,* recently provided me with a summary of the number of positions listed in the *Directory* each year from 1990 through 1997. These data are plotted in Figure 1-2. As you can see, there has been modest but steady growth throughout this period. In 1997 there were 2,431 full-time funded positions listed in the United States and Canada, an overall increase of 23% over the nine-year period. The proportion of the slots that are in APA-accredited centers has also remained constant, ranging from 85% to 88% of the total.

It thus appears that the phenomenon cognitive social psychologists' term the "availability heuristic" has mislead us. We all notice the loss of positions at old line internships that are familiar to us, and in our conversations we share this dismal news among ourselves. We pay less attention to new unfamiliar programs with additional slots that open to replace those that have been lost. Over the nine-year period, the number of APPIC members increased from 480 to 534 (11%). When all is said and done, the loss of internship positions is not the cause of the sudden shortfall.

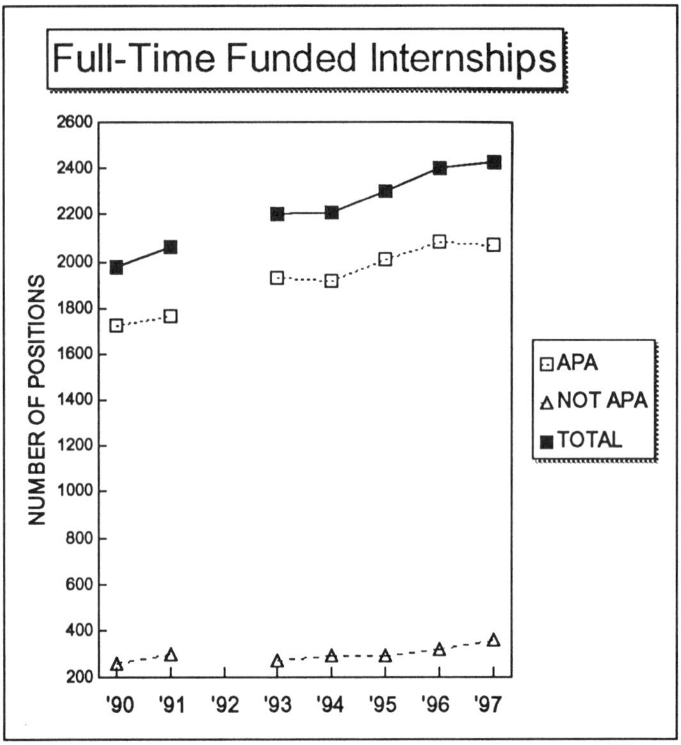

Figure 1-2. Number of full-time funded positions in APPIC internship facilities, 1990-1997.

<u>Too many applicants?</u> Given the overall increases in the number of internship training centers and the number of positions over the last nine years, the only explanation for the sudden surge in the number of unplaced applicants is an unanticipated overabundance of students applying for internships. In the last two years, the number of applications reportedly received by APPIC members has increased 23%, from 30,165 in 1993-1994 to 37,107 in 1995-1996. However, this could result from students increasing the average number of applications they prepare.

APA and APPIC conducted a survey to investigate how many students actually applied in 1995-1996. Under the supervision of Dr. Jessica Kohout of the APA Research Office, 307 graduate training programs were surveyed after UND in 1996; 55% of the programs responded. They reported that 1,498 students from their programs had applied, 79% of whom had gotten positions on UND. An additional 11% were placed after UND, presumably through the

Clearinghouse, for a total success rate of 90% (Clay, 1997; Pederson, 1994). If the programs that responded are representative of those that did not, these data would suggest that 2,724 students filed applications in 1995-1996.

I used a different approach to estimate the number of students applying in recent years. I added the number of available slots listed in the *Directory* for a given year to the number of unplaced applicants reported in the third week Clearinghouse summaries, and then subtracted the reported number of unfilled vacancies. (See Table 1-1.)

Table 1-1. Estimating the number of internship applicants in recent years

Source	Variable	1994-95	1995-96	1996-97
Directory	**Number of Positions**	**2,302**	**2,401**	**2,431**
Clearinghouse	**Number of Unplaced Applicants**	**297**	**489**	**470**
Clearinghouse	**Number of Vacancies**	**68**	**53**	**43**
Estimated number of applicants		**2,531**	**2,837**	**2,858**

This procedure suggests that there were about 2,530 applicants in 1994-1995. This number increased to an estimated 2,837 applicants in 1995-1996 and 2,858 in 1996-1997. No doubt the estimates for the last two years include reapplications by students who failed to secure internships the previous year.

Both the APA survey and my estimates indicate that there are several hundred more graduate students applying for internships now than there were at the beginning of the 1990s. In other words, the primary cause of the shortfall has been a real increase in the total number of applicants. It is not an artifact of applicants following unwise application strategies as some APA officials have suggested (Clay, 1997). Poor preparation and ineffective tactics no doubt influence which applicants will be unsuccessful, but they cannot account for the fact that so many students have been left without internships after all the positions have been filled.

Why the "sudden" increase in the number of students? The data summarized in Figure 1-2 suggest that the increase is not as sudden as it may appear. In most areas, heavy rains do not immediately produce a flood. But after a long period of heavy rains, when the ground can no longer absorb any more water, a flood results that suddenly gets everybody's attention. My guess is that the numbers of students and applicants have been quietly increasing for several years, but no one noticed until the system could not absorb the extra applicants and we had a flood of unplaced applicants in 1996.

I doubt if the increased number of students came from the university based programs, whether traditional or Psy.D. It is my impression that academic programs have been decreasing the number of students they admit. At my university, we admitted about 16 new students to our clinical program every year a decade ago. However, as the sources for funding students have decreased and the stipends we award have been increased, we have cut back on our admissions. This year we are only admitting five, and I don't believe we are atypical.

Free-standing professional schools, on the other hand rely on student fees to support their programs. When funds get tight, it is to their financial advantage to increase admissions. And, of course, every new professional school that opens for business eventually adds to the strain on the internships. If this is the case, we may have a real life example of Hardin's (1968) hypothetical "tragedy of the commons." APPIC and APA are continuing to study supply and demand, and soon there will be a national conference on the issue. Perhaps then, instead of speculating or pointing fingers at one another, we will have some hard data on which to base our conclusions.

Meanwhile, what do we do about the shortfall problem? APA is suggesting that clinical training programs regulate their admissions in the light of the availability of internships, and, of course, jobs for students who have graduated. Good advice, but it is too late to help you find an internship next year.

Fortunately, I don't have to solve the problem of the overall discrepancy between supply and demand. My only responsibility is to you, the readers of this book. Luckily, the odds are in our favor. We shouldn't let our concern over the shortfall blind us to the fact that 80 to 85% of the applicants *do* succeed in getting an internship. If my sales data are correct, more than half the applicants do not buy this book, so you already have an edge on most of your competitors. My job now is to reward your investment by helping you be one of the successful 85%. So, let's get on with it.

NOTES

CHAPTER TWO

THE POLITICS OF INTERN SELECTION

You will find that applying for an internship in professional psychology is unlike anything you have previously experienced. At first, the process will resemble applying to college or graduate school. The paperwork required is much the same, and your anxieties will be similar. But you will soon discover that applying for internship is different. When you call programs to inquire about the status of your application or innocently ask how things look, some may respond like CIA agents being interviewed by Mike Wallace, saying that they are not allowed to provide such information. When you ask for interviews, you may find that some places do not allow interviews and that others interview only those whom they invite. During the interviews themselves, you may be asked personal or probing questions unlike those you have experienced in previous employment interviews. Finally, unlike your prior experiences with college and graduate school, you may be pressed to make a decision and commit yourself to your first choice long before Uniform Notification Day and probably before you are ready to do so.

After it is over, many applicants liken the internship application process to dating and courtship. The comparison is apt. As in dating, there is a period of mild flirtation that gets more intense as certain relationships get more serious, and, as in courtship, there is the issue of which party should risk rejection by making the first commitment. You may feel that you have to decide whether you should try to win the spouse of your dreams and risk ending up with no one, or settle for someone who is more attainable but less attractive. Finally, once you have made your commitment, you will worry about being stranded at the altar. However, unless you have had the experience of managing several very serious relationships simultaneously while knowing that you will soon have to commit yourself to one and only one, you have not had an adequate foretaste of the internship applications experience.

Politics and poker

The reason you will find applying for internships unique is that, unlike college admissions or courtships, the internship selection process is basically political... political in the sense that it involves negotiations, compromises, and a delicate balance of power relationships. The locus of control has shifted over the years, and it will continue to change as the rules continue to be modified.

As we saw in Chapter One, the principal players in this poker game are 1) the Internship Training Directors, 2) the Academic Directors of Clinical Training, and 3) you, the graduate students who are applying for internship. Among the secondary players are the staffs at the internship sites, including the current interns, your major professor and other interested faculty members, your fellow graduate students, some of whom may have a vested interest in whether or not you are accepted at a certain site, and friends or family members whose lives will be affected by your choice of internship. At a tertiary level are the regulatory agencies, APPIC and APA. Correctly or not, all the principal players perceive this as a high stakes game in which their careers may be on the line; this perception generates considerable stress and tension for all involved.

This poker game has been going on every year since 1949, the date of the first Boulder Conference on professional training in psychology. Before you ante up and take a hand, you should get acquainted with the other players and learn what has been happening in the game so far. To play your hand effectively, you first need to understand the other players' goals, what it is they hope to accomplish if they succeed, and what it is they fear will happen if they fail. These hopes and fears are the keys to their game plans and the reason why people keep tinkering with the house rules in the hope of shifting the balance of power. The better your understanding of the game and its players, the more of an edge you will have.

In this chapter we will focus on two groups--the university and professional school faculties, who are represented by the ADCTs, and the internship centers, whose hand is played by the ITDs. These are the players who are involved in internship selection year after year and who have had the primary role in establishing and monitoring the selection procedures. (Don't worry, the rest of the book will focus on the applicants and their concerns.)

<u>The ADCTs and the academic training centers.</u> The first group consists of the Academic Directors of Clinical Training and the other faculty members at the degree-granting institutions. As you well know, this is hardly a monolithic group. Programs differ greatly in the emphasis they place on professional training, and, within each school, individual faculty members often have different attitudes and

opinions regarding what you should look for in an internship. Your clinical supervisor might recommend a program with a certain theoretical orientation. Your major professor may be more concerned with whether your internship will afford you time to complete your dissertation research. Your ADCT may urge you to apply to a program with which your university has strong historic ties.

In the first two decades following the Boulder Conference, the university faculties held the bulk of the power in deciding clinical training issues. Many graduate students were supported by USPHS Predoctoral Fellowships, which were controlled and distributed by the faculty. Others were supported by faculty members' research grants, that were also plentiful during the days of Lyndon Johnson's "Great Society." Driven by the need to educate the "baby boom" population which was engulfing the colleges and universities during the 1960s, academic departments were expanding and proliferating, providing a ready source of academic employment opportunities for research-oriented clinical psychologists.

In the earliest or *laissez faire* period when the academic departments held sway, the ADCTs and the major professors had a major role in placing students in internships. Successful ADCTs established networks of training centers, often staffed by former students, which could be relied upon to accept the current students they recommended. Some major professors had similar relationships with certain internships, albeit on a smaller scale. For example, a student working with "Prof. G. Whiteshark" could expect to intern at the "Halibut Hospital" where Whiteshark's prize graduate, "Dr. Almondine Dover-Sole," was Internship Training Director. By the same token, cooperative ITDs like Dover-Sole could count on regularly getting well-qualified students from these universities. The students had little or nothing to say about where they went, but they also did not have to go through all the hassle today's students must endure.

Most of the "Old Boys" are gone now, and the networks they created are moribund. However, sometimes they show unexpected signs of life. Several years ago I was advising "Fawn Doe," a student who had just interviewed at the "Moosehead Medical Center." She said she was very impressed with the program at Moosehead and planned to make it her first choice. Looking over the brochure she showed me, I noticed that the Moosehead training program was headed by "Dr. Carrie Boux," one of our alumnae who had taken her degree with one of our senior faculty, "Prof. Buck Muledeer." I remembered that Fawn had once taken a practicum with Prof.

Muledeer, so I suggested that she ask Buck to call Carrie Boux and put in a good word for her. Two days later I was astounded to receive a note from Prof. Muledeer saying that Ms. Doe had a position at Moosehead Medical; Uniform Notification Day was still a month away.

Nowadays, except for the ADCT, most university faculty members are much less involved in internship applications than they were when the Old Boy networks were more influential. Once university faculty members have written their letters of recommendation, they rarely get involved in the internship application process. As travel funds have become increasingly scarce, it has become difficult even for the ADCTs, whose job it is to monitor their students' professional training, to visit the internships where their students are training.

There are many reasons for the decline in faculty influence, interest, and participation. They include the decrease in the number of academic and research positions available for new Ph.D.s, the phasing out of federally-funded clinical training grants, the increasing competition for research grants, the increase in the proportion of professionally-trained psychologists seeking positions in applied rather than academic settings, and the entry of large numbers of young "baby boomers" into the profession, all of which have served to dilute the Old Boys' influence.

Although they are less overt now than they were in the past, informal networks still exist. Some ADCTs who take an active role in placing interns from their programs established good working relationships with the ITDs at the internships their students frequently attended. These relationships facilitated the exchange of information on students' progress during the internship year. They were also invaluable in sorting things out during internship selection. During the years when I was an ADCT, I could usually count on at least three training centers having one, and sometimes two, slots available for our students. Indeed, they depended on receiving applications from our students and counted on having at least one in each training class. Of course, the students we sent to these facilities had to do a good job for these relationships to continue. However, if your ADCT does not play an active role, do not despair. Most students nowadays work things out on their own. But an ADCT who is familiar with the various internships and their programs and who knows the training personnel at the agencies can assist you in selecting internships that are likely to meet your needs and be helpful in other ways during the application process.

The ITDs and the training facility staff. With the university faculty largely out of the picture, the principle players left in the intern selection process are the training center personnel and you, the applicants. Interestingly, each fears the other and feels the other has too much control over the final outcome of the selection process. The result has been continued tinkering with the rules for notification of candidates and shifts back and forth in the balance of power. As a graduate student about to apply for internship, it probably seems strange that Internship Training Directors may feel that you are too powerful and have too much control over the final outcome. Nevertheless, it is true, and until you understand their fears you will not be able to fathom their behavior. Let us see how this odd state of affairs came about.

As we have seen, the rules governing the internship selection and notification process were formulated and established by APPIC, which was created to regulate the unbridled competition among rival training programs that was making a shambles of the internship selection process, causing undue hardship for students and agencies alike (Fox, 1990). APPIC's first and greatest achievement was getting all the various internships to agree on a common day when offers would be made. This is variously referred to as "Uniform Notification Day," "Selection Day," and "Intern Calling Day," although at least one ITD refers to it as "Fear and Loathing Day" (Stedman, 1989).

Although many ADCTs viewed APPIC as a powerful, monolithic force, the older APPIC members remember the early day-to-day struggle to survive and the meetings held in a board member's hotel room with participants sitting on the bed and floor. In those days it was a poorly funded, loose confederation that literally lived out of a cardboard box, "... a traveling road show, moving from one location to another with each new election" (Stedman, 1989, p. 35). Just producing the *Directory* each year strained its resources, and only recently was APPIC able to establish a professionally staffed central office. The organization has little real power and must rely on the cooperation and voluntary compliance of its members. Aside from moral persuasion, APPIC has no real authority to investigate complaints. In view of these limitations, the organization has been remarkably successful in bringing some semblance of order to a chaotic process.

Although the Old Boy system had worked well for the Old Boys, in the late 1960s and early 1970s the increase in the number of academic clinical training programs had produced many "New Boys" as well as "New Girls" who also wanted a piece of the action.

Moreover, the lack of common ground rules in the intern selection process could put students in difficult, even intolerable, situations.

Imagine yourself as a student in the days before APPIC. If you had a well-connected ADCT or major professor, like Prof. Whiteshark or Prof. Muledeer, you attended the internship arranged for you. At some point you would be summoned to the Great Mentor's office, advised that next year you would be going on internship, and told which internship you would be attending. With that taken care of, you could go back to the laboratory. By the time this year is over you may think that was a pretty good system.

If you did not have a powerful mentor, you went through an application process similar to the current one. Of course, there was no APPIC *Directory* then, so you relied on the brochures sent by the various facilities. Let us suppose that after reading the brochures, interviewing at the several sites, and discussing them with faculty and friends, you decided that the best internship site for you was the "Codliver Consortium" and that your second choice was the "Septicemia School of Medicine."

In the days before APPIC and Uniform Notification, you might have received a call from the Internship Training Director at Septicemia in mid-January offering you an internship for the coming year and giving you 48 hours in which to decide, after which the offer would be withdrawn. You, or your ADCT, would then call the ITD at Codliver and discover that they were operating on a different schedule and were still actively interviewing applicants. While they had been very impressed with you and your credentials and considered you definitely in the running, no offers would be made to anyone until February.

Assuming your ADCT could not cut some deal with the Codliver ITD or get the people at Septicemia to back off, you would be left with two options: 1) you could accept the position at Septicemia and make a binding commitment to attend their program, or 2) you could decline and hope that you would get an offer from Codliver. (Don't even think about the possibility of accepting Septicemia and changing your mind if you subsequently got a Codliver offer. One thing that has remained constant in the internship game is that anyone who reneges on a formal internship commitment is doomed.)

In his recent history of the Association, Stedman (1989, p. 35) wrote, "APIC was organized primarily to deal with a lack of regularity in the intern selection process ... students of the late '60s complained about deals being made between internship sites and certain select students... [They]... complained that their clinical training directors didn't know what to do [and] there was often undue stress on students."

The idea behind APPIC was that internship training centers should agree on a common set of procedures and a uniform selection schedule to eliminate the unfair competition that all too often forced students to decide whether to accept offers from their second, third, or lower ranked internships before they had heard from their first choice. Under Uniform Notification, the APPIC members agreed among themselves that no Internship Training Director could make an offer before an agreed-upon time and that students were to be guaranteed a reasonable amount of time to consider these offers. Moreover, no ITD could make an offer to a student who had already accepted an offer from another institution.

In the interests of fairness to applicants and internship training centers alike, APPIC also stipulated that no training center could make more offers than they had slots available. Each internship has a limited number of funded positions that they feel it is vitally important to fill. Once an offer has been made to an applicant, that opening is committed and, until the applicant declines the offer, it is unavailable and cannot be offered to anyone else. In short, a student who is holding an offer owns that slot until the selection period ends. An agency with six positions cannot make eight offers figuring two people will probably decline. Once the sixth position has been offered, whether or not it has been accepted, the ITD is out of business. It is this rule that differentiates internship selection from college and graduate school admissions.

Every Internship Training Director knows of cases in which students for various reasons have held offers for lengthy periods of time. After UND in 1994, APPIC conducted a survey of 300 internship training centers. One question asked what had been the longest time an applicant held an offer. In 1994, UND lasted from 8:00 AM until 5:00 PM, CST. The longest holding times reported ranged from under an hour to over eight hours; 51% of the ITDs reported applicants held offers three or more hours, and 17% reported holds of six or more hours (APPIC, 1994).

Why the delay? Some may be unable to decide. One student who had been through the process noted "Some students will begin the day without knowing how they will respond if offered a particular internship" (Jacob, 1987, p. 154). In the early days, when students had days to respond, some would collect a number of offers and then choose among them. (Now applicants may not hold more than one offer at a time.) Deciding can be especially difficult when a couple is trying to make a joint decision. Of course the principle reason students hold offers is because they are waiting for an offer from another institution they would prefer to attend.

In order to protect itself, an internship with offers outstanding will urge the applicants on its alternate list not to accept another position until the agency has received definite responses of acceptance or rejection to all their outstanding bids. Indeed, it will probably try to maintain several viable alternates for every unresolved position. If it has offers out to a male and a female applicant, and it wants a class balanced for gender, then it will strive to keep both men and women on the alternate list. If the woman accepts and the man rejects the outstanding offer, then it will offer the freed-up slot to the first male alternate, and vice versa if the man accepts and the woman rejects. Race, ethnicity, interests in certain rotations, and theoretical preferences may all be factors encouraging the ITD to maintain as large a list of alternates as possible. If the alternates agree to wait, they will naturally hold on to any offers they have already received from their lower-ranked internships, which in turn will ask their alternates not to accept other offers and so the problem is compounded.

Sometimes "gridlocks" occur (May & Dana, 1990). In a classic gridlock, student A may have internship X for a first choice and Y as his second, while student B has Y as her first choice and X as the second. Let us suppose that at 9:00 AM, internship X offers a slot to B, while Y chooses student A. Both students decide to hold on to these offers hoping to get accepted at their first-choice institutions, and indeed program X calls applicant A, and facility Y calls candidate B, assuring them they are first alternates and will receive an offer as soon as an opening becomes available. Since the internships cannot withdraw offers once made, this deadlock can continue until either A or B decides to accept the second-choice offer or until the Notification Period ends. I was told of a three-way gridlock which was resolved only after one of the ITDs involved correctly diagnosed the stalemate, called the other two ITDs, and worked out a compromise whereby all three institutions agreed to settle for their second-choice candidates, thereby giving the applicants their first-choice placements. This initiative was no doubt a violation of some rule, but in this case it worked in the students' favor.

Gridlocks are miserable for everyone involved. ITDs are generally people who want to be in control, and as long as one or more students is holding an outstanding offer, they have lost control over their incoming class. All they can do is await the outcome and keep reassuring the students on their alternate list. Defining a gridlock as a period of two hours or more in which there are outstanding offers and no activity, the APPIC (1994) survey revealed that 157 of the 300 respondents (54%) experienced gridlocks on UND in 1994.

Gridlocks are even worse for the students. The internship year has much more impact on the life of a student than signing a particular intern does on the life of an ITD. Most students who hold offers do so because they would prefer to attend other internships that have them on their alternate lists. They know that before they can get the internships they want, the students who are holding those slots have to get the offers *they* are waiting for and release the desired positions. Then the ITDs at those institutions will decide which alternates should be offered the freed-up positions. Moreover, they also know that the longer they hold the offers they already have, the longer some other students will wait on those facility's alternate lists. Finally, there is always the agonizing possibility that they may be caught in a classic gridlock, such as that described previously, in which each student is waiting for the position the other one is holding. In the early days, such stalemates could go on for days!

The Internship Training Director's dilemma

Let us look at Uniform Notification Day from the viewpoint of Dr. "Jack Crevalle," the Internship Training Director at the "Coral Reef Internship Consortium." Coral Reef has six slots that Jack's boss, Chief Psychologist "Dr. Barri Cuda," wants filled with hardworking, brilliant, congenial interns from the nation's most prestigious universities, stratified to represent all the major ethnic groups and most of the typical genders. Dr. Cuda expects that these interns will all go on to achieve great success, which they will attribute to the magnificent training they received at Coral Reef. Dr. Crevalle shares these aspirations, but he will settle for filling all six slots with competent students who are reasonably free of psychopathology and will not precipitate any major lawsuits in the course of training.

If Dr. Crevalle's fondest hopes are realized, this is how Notification Day will proceed. Over the weekend, Dr. Crevalle and the admissions staff have ranked all the applicants, taking into account their qualifications and abilities as well as the likelihood that they will accept an offer. At 9:00 AM, Central Time, on UND, Dr. Crevalle calls the first-ranked applicant who promptly accepts. At

9:01, the second call goes out with the same results. By 9:06, all six slots have been filled with the six top-ranked applicants. At 9:07, Dr. Crevalle wonders briefly if they should have made an offer to the superstar that they put on the alternate list because it seemed likely she would go elsewhere. Deciding not to worry over what might have been, Jack notifies Dr. Cuda that they have signed up all their top applicants, tells a subordinate to notify the alternates that Coral Reef has filled all its slots, turns off his phone, and begins working on the quarterly evaluations of the current interns that have been neglected during selection season.

What would a bad day be like? Contrary to what you might suppose, a truly bad day is not one in which one or more of the top candidates reject their offers. When this happens, Dr. Crevalle can usually fill the six slots with applicants on the alternate list; indeed, Jack might be pleasantly surprised when the superstar accepts. No, a truly bad day occurs when one or more candidates inform Dr. Crevalle that they will neither "accept" nor "reject" but "**hold**" the offer. If this occurs, Dr. Crevalle will quickly start calling the lower-ranked applicants to inform them they are high on the alternate list, assure them that there is a good chance a slot will open up shortly, and ask them not to accept any offers until they have heard from Coral Reef. The rest of the notification period will be spent massaging the alternates and asking the students who are holding offers when they will be able to decide. Some may simply be having difficulty deciding where to go, but most will be on the alternate lists of other institutions that they would prefer to attend but that have offers out to other applicants who are waiting to hear from someone else and so on.

Meanwhile, Dr. Crevalle's list of alternate applicants may be melting away like a snow cone in a pizza oven. If a candidate takes a long time to reject an offer, most of the applicants on the alternate list may accept other positions. Coral Reef will be unlikely to get the exact mix of interns they wanted and may even be unable to fill all their slots. The 1994 APPIC survey indicated that 27 of the 300 internships (9%) had failed to fill when UND ended at 5:00 PM. When there were not enough intern applicants to go around, failure to fill positions could cause serious problems for an internship training center. Positions not filled could be lost in the next budget; commitments to faculty members or agencies to provide students for certain specific rotations might have to be revoked. Careful plans to ensure a balanced class were ruined. Now that the overall number of applicants exceeds the number of positions available, unfilled slots should not be as great a concern. Indeed, Dr. Jack Crevalle might find a better selection of candidates among the 450 or more students who are likely to access the Clearinghouse than he will on his list of alternates. However, in my conversations with ITDs, this does not seem to make any difference. It is a matter of pride. Not filling on UND, indeed not filling in the first hour, is a sign of failure.

As Notification Day proceeds, especially after 1:00 PM, some students have been amazed to receive calls asking if they are still available from internships that earlier refused to even grant them interviews or notified them they were no longer under consideration. ADCTs at major universities got calls from ITDs at internships that had failed to fill all their slots, asking if they had any students who were still uncommitted. If so, these ITDs sometimes indicated they were willing to accept them on the ADCTs' recommendation, sight unseen, so eager were they to achieve their quotas.

Given this background, you can see why many, perhaps most, Internship Training Directors feel the Uniform Notification system as it was originally designed placed too much power in the hands of students, especially when UND lasted for an extended period and there were not enough applicants to go around. Two coping strategies resulted. One, which we might call the "knowledge is power" strategy, was to make offers only to applicants who are certain to accept. The other was to change the house rules to make the game less risky for the internship centers or less stressful for the applicants. We will discuss each.

Knowledge is power

In a real poker game, all the players reveal their cards at the same time. However, on Notification Day, the ITDs have to show their hands before the students do. The rules state the ITDs are supposed to make their offers blindly, not knowing which students are planning to accept. No wonder many ITDs feel this is unfair. No wonder they would like to "peek at your hand" to find out how you will respond if they make you an offer. Training centers know they can mimimize their risks by making offers only to candidates they can rely on to accept their bids.

In the "Old Days," before APPIC, internships could make an offer whenever they chose and withdraw it if the applicant did not accept immediately. Or they would ask an applicant, "If we make you an offer, will you accept?"

When UND was first introduced, it was clear that no offers could be made before the appointed time. It was also understood, but not always clearly explicit as the rules changed, that ITDs were not supposed to solicit information on rankings or first-choice commitments. Clearly some did. Johnson (1986) reported that an informal poll of his friends and colleagues showed that every one had received an offer before the deadline, and many candidates in the East started getting calls at 8:00 AM *Eastern* Time instead of 8:00 AM *Central* Time. Using a more systematic but still flawed sampling procedure (Carifio & Grace, 1992), a survey of applicants after UND in 1985 indicated that 25% of them had received offers prior to UND and that 53% were asked for their rankings (Carifio, Buckner, & Grace, 1987).

In 1991 the rules were tightened to make it clearer what was and was not permitted. Rule 3 stated, "No internship offers in any form may be extended by agencies before the beginning of selection day," and section "c" further stated, "Internship programs may not solicit information regarding an applicant's ranking of programs or his/her intention to accept or decline an offer of admission until after that offer is officially tendered."

Rules or no rules, as UND approached, applicants discovered that many of the programs to which they applied tried to determine whether or not they would accept an offer if it were to be made. A few ITDs baldly stated during the interview, "If you want to get an offer from us, you have to tell us we are your first choice." Most were more subtle. Some waited for candidates to call them after interviewing and then asked them if they "needed any more information" in order to reach a decision. This ploy would lead to a subtle or not so subtle inquiry as to what that decision is likely to be. Others took the initiative and called the candidates directly to see "how things are going." Some would call the ADCT or major professor or use current interns as go betweens. To put this in perspective, however, 60% of the students surveyed anonymously by Constantine and Keilin (1996) after UND in 1995 reported that they had not been pressed to disclose their rankings.

These inquiries put students in a dilemma. Should they inform their first-choice that they will accept an offer? Would refusing to answer be interpreted as a lack of interest? Some simply assured all the ITDs who asked that they were their first-choice. (ITDs so frequently complain about students lying and reneging on their commitments, one wonders why they bother to ask.) If their second, third, or lower choice institution asked for a commitment, many students stalled and called their top-ranked internship to find out how they stood and ask whether making a first-choice commitment there would help their chances. Such calls put the ethical ITDs into a bind because APPIC Rule 2-b stated, "No other information (such as the agency's ranking of the applicant; status as alternate/first-choice, etc.) may be communicated to applicants prior to selection day." Some ITDs finessed the problem by discussing the student's status with the ADCT. Others refused to impart any information to anyone.

Changes in the selection procedures

A different approach to dealing with the UND power struggle has been to make fundamental changes in the basic selection/notification procedure.

Early Acceptance. If internship selection committees could be sure that their offers would be accepted, most of their risks would be eliminated. In 1986-1987, this led APPIC to adopt a procedure known as "Early Acceptance" ("EA"). Two weeks before Uniform Notification Day, students who chose to participate were allowed to notify one, and only one, internship that they would accept an offer if it was made. Unlike the present "first-choice" pledges, this commitment was binding on those applicants. If they were chosen by the internship, they were bound to attend, and all their other outstanding applications were withdrawn. The ITDs had one day to allocate as many of their slots as they liked to students in this pool of committed applicants. Those who were chosen were notified the next day. The following week the rest went through the regular UND procedure along with any students who had not participated in EA.

Early Acceptance provided the ITDs with a no-risk pool of committed applicants who would definitely accept an offer. Not surprisingly, many of the best internships filled on Early Acceptance Day, leaving the applicants who had not been chosen or who chose not to participate to scramble for the remaining slots on UND.

From the standpoint of many ITDs, especially those at the most popular programs, Early Acceptance was wonderful because it removed all the uncertainty from the selection process. However, from the standpoint of the applicants who had to decide whether to participate and then had only one chance to make a unilateral, binding commitment, EA was extremely anxiety provoking. The internships were still not supposed to disclose their rankings before UND, but some were more informative than others. Students frantically called ITDs trying to determine their chances for acceptance before they chose the best site to commit to. Krause and Lawlor (1990) later surveyed 191 students. They reported that 97% had participated in EA and 85% had been accepted at the sites they chose to call. However, 27% of them had played it safe; instead of committing to their top-ranked internship, they instead chose other lower-ranked sites where they had gotten positive feedback. A more extensive survey showed that 1,027 of the 1,399 applicants who participated in EA (73.4%) had been placed at their first-choice internships. However, they noted that this success had been accomplished, "...at the cost of significant increases in applicant stress, even as perceived by the sites - a clearly undesirable concomitant to any matching procedure, no matter how successful its outcomes" (Blom & Pederson, 1988, p. 47).

I was one of those who was vehemently opposed to the Early Acceptance procedure. However, in some ways it was better for students than the present situation in which about 80% of the applicants make unilateral pledges prior to UND without the safeguards that they had under EA (Constantine & Keilin, 1996; Thorne, 1997). In any event, the APPIC Board decided to drop Early Acceptance after the first year (Stedman, 1989). In its place, they decided to try computer matching.

Computer matching. The major drawback to both Early Acceptance and Uniform Notification is that both require sequential commitments. In Early Acceptance, based on the limited information they had available, the candidates had to make binding commitments to the programs. In Uniform Notification, it is the training centers that must make binding commitments to applicants. Under both systems, the party making the offer is relatively helpless and must wait while the other party decides whether or not to accept.

Under Uniform Notification, as in a poker game, it is to each player's advantage to know what is in the other player's hand. Internships would like to know which applicants will accept their offers, and candidates want to know how they stand with the internships. This is what drives all the phone calls and manipulations during the final phases of internship selection. In particular, training centers often attempt to get candidates to make commitments, or at least indicate their choices, prior to Notification Day (Zimet, 1991). When the training center is the candidate's first choice, there is no problem. But when a lower-ranked facility calls, any hesitation in saying, "You're my number one choice!" indicates that they are not the applicant's first choice (Johnson, 1986). Applicants fear that this may doom their candidacy.

Some empirical data may help at this juncture. Surveys conducted since the rules were tightened in 1991 show that about 80% of the applicants reported that they told their preferred internship that it was their first choice, but only 30% reported being pressured by the ITDs to disclose their rankings. In my experience, most ITDs play according to the rules and surveys by Constantine and Keilin (1996) and by Thorne (1997) are consistent with this impression. Unfortunately, those internships at which one or more staff members do violate the rules cause all the applicants a great deal of anxiety and stress. However, Constantine and Keilin's survey showed that despite "... their fears about whether or not they would still be considered as viable candidates by their second- and lesser ranked sites, ... applicants who did not disclose their rankings received more offers on selection day than those who did disclose" (1996, p. 313).

For many years it had been suggested that these disparities could be avoided if everyone made their decisions privately and then communicated them simultaneously, as they do in a real poker game. This would eliminate the problems of "stalling," "holding," and "stringing along" that have plagued the Uniform Notification process. Computerized matching is simply a *simultaneous* comparison of the choices made by the candidates and the training centers seeking the optimal fit. (It should be noted it is not essential to employ a computer in the process. However, without a computer it would involve weeks instead of hours and the likelihood of errors would be vastly greater.)

In the late 1980s, APPIC seriously considered adopting computerized matching. Proponents argued that computer matching had been used for years in medical internship selection, and that it would free applicants and programs alike to rank their choices on their merits without worrying about how their choices were ranking them. Not only would this remove most of the second guessing and skullduggery from the selection process, but it would also eliminate the time, stress, and expense associated with UND. Opponents feared losing control and argued that software programs could not deal with contingent choices such as, "If the first few applicants who accept are all female, we will make the subsequent offers to males."

Computerized matching was proposed as early as 1972, but it was 1988 before APPIC decided to give it a try. A special program had to be developed because requests to utilize the software developed for American medical schools had been denied and the company that did the matching for the Canadian medical schools wanted $105,000 a year for its services (Pederson, 1994; 1997). So a special APPIC committee developed their own matching program. Many APPIC members, however, had serious reservations about the very concept of using computers to match applicants and internships, so it was decided to test the program in a nationwide pilot study during the 1989-1990 selection season. The new program would be run in tandem with the actual UND selection process. The question was whether the hypothetical computer match would come up with assignments that were as satisfactory or better than those obtained using the regular UND procedure (Pederson, 1994).

This strategy proved to be a huge mistake. Although 2,000 students took part in the experiment, 15% of the internship sites, 5% of the universities, and an unknown number of applicants refused to participate. The software program, of course, was based on the assumption that all the sites and applicants would participate, as would be the case if it were adopted. It had no provision for missing data. As the committee noted, "We sadly realized that, inevitably, incomplete data produce incomplete and inconclusive results" (Blom, Pederson & Klepac, 1990, p. 20). Following this trial run, APPIC voted 183 to 141 in favor of staying with UND, and a five-year moratorium on changes in the selection process was imposed. That moratorium has ended, and it appears that computer matching will soon be a reality, perhaps as soon as the 1998-1999 selection year. This time the task will be contracted to a professional computer consulting firm. Any applicant or internship participating in APPIC-sponsored intern selection will be required to use the computer match procedure so that missing data cannot break down the system.

Computer matching should eliminate any advantage that now accrues to internships from knowing how they stand with the applicants. Applicants can make their rankings according to their actual preferences, without worrying whether placing highly competitive internships first on their lists might damage their chances of obtaining a less popular slot. Most ITDs and applicants probably will not believe this at first, so the poker games may continue for a while. But if computerized matching works as it is supposed to, this behavior will no longer be rewarded and these old habits should extinguish. We will discuss computer matching and how it works in more detail in Chapter Eleven.

Modifications in UND rules and procedures. After computer matching was defeated, APPIC considered other ways of improving the Uniform Notification procedures. A major cause of dissatisfaction on the part of internship personnel was what they regarded as the excessive amount of time students were allowed to hold offers. Applicants initially had five days to consider offers (Stedman, 1989, p. 36). In 1976, the time was reduced to three days, and by 1989 applicants had at most 28 hours to respond. In 1991, the time was reduced to nine hours, by 1994 it was seven hours, and since 1995 it has been only four hours. The current rules stipulate that no formal offers can be made until 9:00 AM, Central Standard Time, on the second Monday in February, and students have until 1:00 PM, CST *the same day* to accept or reject the offer. After 1:00 PM, CST, any outstanding offer that has not been accepted is void. This does not mean that all activity ceases and uncommitted applicants go into the Clearinghouse. Internships can, if they choose, allow candidates who were holding offers more time to decide. However, they may prefer to offer those positions to candidates who have been waiting on the alternate list. The new rule also gives the alternates a definite time by which they can expect to learn whether or not they will be offered a position.

The May, 1991, revision of the rules mandated several other changes aimed at making the selection process more equitable for applicants. It stated that programs *must* notify applicants who have been excluded from consideration as early as possible and no later than a week prior to Notification Day; previously the rules only stated that ITDs *should* notify such applicants. (Of course, there is no requirement that programs must exclude *any* applicants from consideration.) Similarly, another recent rule states that once a center has filled all its positions on UND, it *must* notify by phone as soon as possible all the remaining applicants who have not been selected and who have not notified the agency they have accepted positions elsewhere. Those who cannot be reached by phone must be sent a letter within 72 hours. (The previous rules only said that the internship *should* notify the remaining applicants and did not specify that it should be done promptly.)

The May, 1991, revision included a new rule stating that training centers should document the verbal agreement with each applicant in a letter specifying the terms and conditions of the appointment, such as the stipend, fringe benefits, and starting date. From a legal standpoint, this can be extremely important. Some internship programs have had their funding withdrawn or frozen after UND. Acceptance letters are important evidence that a binding commitment had been made to the trainees (Larsen, 1991).

The most recent change to the rules occurred in April, 1997. In the 1996-1997 internship selection period, rule violations and pressure on students to reveal their choices or commit themselves to their first-choice internships reached an all time high. After UND, the APPIC Board was subjected to such widespread criticism that they amended the APPIC rules without consulting their membership. They drafted a new policy statement that will take effect beginning with the 1997-1998 internship selection season. In order to be listed in the 1997-1998 *Directory*, internships will be required to adhere to this statement and include it in their brochures:

> We as representatives of the undersigned organizations, in the spirit of respect and fairness for all parties affected by the APPIC Policy on Internship Offers and Acceptances, endorse the following principles.
>
> I. No representative of an APPIC member internship program will solicit, accept or use any ranking-related information from any intern applicant prior to Uniform Notification Day.
>
> II. No prospective intern applicant will offer information or respond to questions about ranking-related information to any internship site prior to Uniform Notification Day.
>
> III. No representative of a doctoral training program will offer information or respond to questions about ranking-related information regarding an intern applicant to any internship site prior to Uniform Notification Day. Further, representatives of doctoral training programs will prohibit intern applicants from their doctoral programs from offering information or responding to questions regarding ranking-related information to any internship site.

The APPIC Board has presented this policy to the Boards of the following major groups involved in the internship-selection process and asked them to endorse this policy at their respective business meetings in August, 1997:

1. The American Psychological Association of Graduate Students (APAGS);

2. The Council of Counseling Psychology Training Programs (CCPTB);

3. The Council of Directors of School Psychology Programs (CDSPP);

4. The Council of University Directors of Clinical Psychology (CUDCP);

5. The National Council of Schools of Professional Psychology (NCSPP).

This is an extremely strong statement. For the first time, it places restraints on ADCTs and students as well as internships.

Surveys show that 78% of the students in 1994-1995 (Constantine & Keilin, 1996) and 81% in 1996-1997 (Thorne, 1997) communicated information about their rankings to one or more internships. This would now be against the rules. The ADCTs are supposed to prohibit students from offering such information to ITDs, and any ITDs receiving such information are pledged not to use it. This latter provision was especially upsetting to some of the ITDs at the First APPIC Membership Meeting and Conference in April, 1997, where this policy was announced. How can they not use such information, they asked. (The answer is that they should disregard such information just as a jury is instructed to ignore inappropriate testimony in a trial.) ADCTs, too, will be concerned because it prevents them from acting as brokers between the students and training centers.

Until it has been tried, no one knows what the effect of this new policy statement will be. It is, of course, even less enforceable than the previous rules because APPIC has no jurisdiction over ADCTs or students. No one I have discussed it with believes it will totally eliminate cheating or lying, but it may serve to curb the more egregious rules violations and make it easier for you, the students, to deal with overly inquisitive ITDs. Whether it will save you from yourselves and your compulsion to communicate your preference to your first-choice facility remains to be seen. I will discuss the implications of these rules on your negotiations with internships in Chapter Ten, "The Endgame."

The goals of the various players

As I noted earlier, it is essential that you understand the motives and objectives of the various players in this poker game. As an applicant, you have two basic goals. The first is obvious: obtaining an internship that meets the professional and personal needs you have defined for yourself. The second is less apparent, but no less important. That is to avoid making the kinds of mistakes that may later come back to haunt you, such as committing ethical lapses or offending people who may some day be in a position to influence your career.

Unless you are backed into a corner and not allowed to leave the premises unless you "first-choice," I feel that you should not lie about your intentions. Lying is unethical, and you should not begin your professional career by engaging in unethical behavior, even if you get the impression that others may be doing so. If you assure selection personnel at an internship that their program is your first choice and you later hold or reject an offer from them, they and everyone they talk to will regard you as being untrustworthy for the rest of your career. Later in this book we will discuss how to deal with internships that press you for a commitment. You can deal with them successfully without being dishonest, and you can emerge from the internship selection process with a network of positive professional contacts as well as with the internship of your choice.

The goals of the other principal players, the Internship Training Directors and Clinical Training Directors, are less clearly defined. An ITD's obvious objective is obtaining the "best" internship class possible, whatever that means. Basically it means pleasing the members of the training faculty at the internship by filling all the available slots with candidates who are ethical, reasonably competent, and free of flagrant psychopathology. The ADCTs hope to place all their applicants in settings that will a) enhance the prestige of their programs, b) please the applicants' major professors, and c) provide their students with good training experiences. The ITDs and ADCTs also have long-term concerns. They play this game every year, so they must establish and maintain good professional working relations with one another. The best ITDs and ADCTs realize that this means being honest with one another, and evaluating students and programs fairly and forthrightly.

CHAPTER THREE

APPLYING FOR INTERNSHIP: AN OVERVIEW

Applying for internship is like planning a political campaign or a military operation. It is impossible to begin too soon or prepare too thoroughly. Your first semester of graduate training is not too soon to start preparations. Internship application forms request an unbelievable amount of information, and if you start out keeping meticulous records of your academic work and, especially, your clinical activities, you will find it is much easier to fill out the various forms when the time comes to actually apply. One recent student summed up her advice in three words, "Compulse, compulse, compulse!"

There are two basic aspects to preparing for internship. The first is getting the academic training you need. You must make sure that you will complete all the eligibility requirements by the time you have to submit your applications. You must also develop the professional knowledge and skills you will need to profit from your internship training. The second basic aspect is making the preparations that are necessary to select a list of internships and to prepare your formal applications.

Preparing yourself for internship

The first step in the internship application process is to make sure you will be academically and professionally prepared to go on internship when the time comes. There are both formal and informal requirements that you will have to satisfy.

Formal requirements. Academic programs differ, but they all have criteria that you must meet before you can go on internship. One reason to plan ahead is to make sure that you have satisfied the necessary requirements by the time you submit your formal applications. If you are thinking about going on internship in the year 2002, you must complete all the eligibility requirements of your academic training program by the first week of November, 2001.

Perhaps your academic program requires you to pass your comprehensive examinations or have your dissertation proposal approved before you can go on internship. It is vital that these requirements be completed ***before*** you submit your applications. Suppose that you have not completed some requirement but plan to do so in the Spring of 2002, long before you would report to internship. Can't you and your ADCT simply assure the internship that although you have this last hurdle to leap you will certainly complete it before September, 2002? You can try, but if you do it is likely that you will be one of those applicants who is not selected in February. As long as there is a possibility that you will not be eligible and may have to stay at your university because you failed your examination or because some disaster prevented you from defending your prospectus, no worthwhile internship will risk wasting a position on you. ITDs assure me that if your ADCT's certification indicates there is even a remote chance that your university might not allow you to go on internship, your application will probably not be reviewed, much less selected. The bottom line is this: plan your program so that you will have completed all your formal requirements before you apply.

Internships have their own criteria, which typically exceed those imposed by the universities. For example, many academic programs require that students complete a minimum of 400 hours of practicum experience, at least 150 hours of which are in direct service and 75 hours in formal scheduled supervision, because these were the accreditation requirements stipulated in the American Psychological Association's (1986) *Accreditation Handbook*. However, most internships demand considerably more. Each individual internship's requirements are listed in its brochure and in its listing in the annual APPIC *Directory*. According to my calculations, the mean minimum number of practicum hours required by the 513 American predoctoral internships listed in the 1996-1997 *Directory* (Hall & Cantrell, 1996) was 744 hours with a standard deviation of 299 hours; the minimums ranged from 400 hours to 2,000 hours. In addition, 488 of the 513 internships (95%) stipulated that applicants must be doctoral candidates; if you have not attained candidacy by November, you should wait until next year.

Although the APPIC *Directory* does not list approval of the dissertation project or completion of the dissertation itself as a possible prerequisite, you will recall that the Gainesville Conference (Belar et al., 1987; 1989) concluded that all interns should have defended their doctoral proposals by the time they apply. Moreover, the conferees indicated a strong preference that the dissertation itself be completed before an intern reports for training. There are good practical reasons for these recommendations. Many internships feel they should help their interns find post-internship jobs, and those who still have a dissertation to complete are much harder to place or support. In my experience, students who leave on internship before defending their proposals or collecting their dissertation data are at a much higher risk of becoming ABDs. Even though they complete their internships a year earlier, it generally takes them longer to finish their degrees than students who defer going on internship for a year so they can complete their dissertations. For all these reasons, you stand a much better chance of obtaining the internship of your choice if you have defended your proposal and made substantial progress on your dissertation before you *apply* for internship.

Informal requirements. Preparing for internship involves more than accumulating practicum hours or satisfying a series of academic requirements. Your entire graduate school experience can be viewed as preparation for internship. From Day One, getting ready for internship should be an important consideration when you choose courses and practica. Although internships vary tremendously in their orientation and expectations, most will expect you to have a thorough grounding in traditional clinical skills and to be well-versed in professional ethics and behavior.

It is up to you and your advisors to determine when you are ready for internship. In the days when the university faculties played a greater role in the internship selection process and most students were supported by university-based research or training grants, students often went on internship in their third or fourth year of graduate study. By today's standards, the amount of clinical training some students received prior to internship was minimal. When I was at Palo Alto, a fellow trainee from a mid-western university had taken courses in test construction and theories of psychotherapy, but had never actually administered a test or counseled a client.

After the big clinical training grants were phased out during the Nixon and Ford administrations, more graduate students had to support themselves by working in clinical settings while at their universities. Practicum agencies insisted on a higher level of clinical competence when they paid their practicum students. As a result, by the time you go on internship, it is likely you will have had more clinical experience than your counterparts 20 years ago did. I have no idea how typical our program is, but the total number of hours of supervised clinical experience recorded by our students who applied for internship recently ranged from 1,848 to 10,257, with a mean of 5,121 hours.

One way to get ready for internship is to keep in touch with more advanced students from your academic program during their internship years and learn from them what skills they were expected to have when they arrived. Their advice may be more salient than that of some faculty members who have not recently been actively involved in clinical work. For example, your academic courses may have made you skeptical about the validity and utility of projective tests, or you may have been taught that formal diagnosis is a sterile enterprise. Remember to evaluate yourself as a product to be sold to the ITDs. If the internships to which you are applying want students who can make a formal diagnosis according to the latest *Diagnostic and Statistical Manual* and who are able to administer, score, and interpret projective techniques such as the Rorschach, you will find it is easier to market yourself if you have these skills.

Getting ready to apply

Since it is never too early to begin, I will first describe long-term preparations you can make. If you are reading this book at the last minute, do not despair. These long-term preparations are desirable and will make your job easier, but if, like most of us, you tend to put things off until the last minute, you can still prepare an effective application. You will simply have to scurry around even more frantically to get everything done. As Jacob (1987, p. 155) noted, "Gradual preparation would have eased the experience for me. Instead, ignorance and lack of preparation determined that 'internship hunting' was a full-time 2-month job."

Long-term preparations. Even if you are not planning to apply for internship for a year or so, there are many things you can do to get ready. One of the most important is what you are doing right now, namely, learning about what is involved.

As this is being written, there are two new developments in the works that will make both long-term preparation and the actual application process considerably easier. The first is a Uniform Application Form (UAF) that is being developed by APPIC. Not all internships will adopt it but enough should to make the application process considerably easier. The other development is APPIC's new World Wide Web site, which should be up and running by July, 1997. The address will be **www.appic.org**, and if all goes according to schedule, you will be able to use it to access and download the UAF and to keep abreast of other current internship information. The sooner you can obtain a copy of the UAF the better. Whether you are applying next month or next year, the UAF will show you the sort of information you will need to provide internships when you apply. If you still have a year or so to go before you start seeking an internship, this will enable you to set up a system for recording and retaining records of your academic and professional education and experience that will help you when you do apply.

Start keeping a detailed log in which you record all your practicum and supervision hours, the names and credentials of your supervisors, the number and the nature of the clients you have seen, the types of treatment in which you have participated, and a record of the various assessment devices you have administered, scored, and interpreted. Enter the basic information onto a spreadsheet program such as Excel or Lotus so you can sort your cases by type of client, presenting problem, diagnosis, setting, instruments or techniques used, and so forth. This will be very helpful when you prepare your Curriculum Vitae. (See Chapter Six.)

In anticipation of applying for internship, review the CVs of successful intern applicants from your program. How do your qualifications compare with theirs? Are there things you can do to improve your credentials in the year(s) to come that will make your application more competitive? This might be the time to take some specialized clinical courses in areas that might catch the eye of ITDs, such as minority mental health, neuropsychological assessment, or geropsychology. Consider taking professional workshops in assessment, psychopathology, or intervention techniques. They will not only enhance your credentials but also indicate your motivation to be well-prepared. If the advertised fees are more than you can afford, ask for a student discount or volunteer to help with registration and run errands in exchange for being allowed to sit in on the sessions. (These workshops are also a good place to make contacts and create networks that may prove useful when it is time to apply.) If you have some specialized skill such as a familiarity with a foreign language or American Sign Language, polish it up so you can present yourself as having competency in this area. If you have been meaning to write up your master's thesis for presentation or publication, this would be a good time to do so and submit it. In short, while there is time, consider ways you can make your CV stand out as being special when it is compared with those of other applicants.

Earlier, I described the difficulty some internships have getting HMOs to reimburse them for services performed by unlicensed practitioners such as interns. Your state may have licensing available for master's level psychologists, and it certainly licenses mental health counselors, marriage and family therapists, and other counselors. If you investigate these licensing laws, you may find that your master's degree in psychology goes a long way toward meeting your state's requirements. Perhaps with a course or two in mental counseling or an examination you can obtain such a license. If so, it might make you very attractive to some internships such as Community Mental Health Centers.

If you are in a clinical practicum, you can start preparing a work sample for submission along with your application to those internships that require them. Begin by discussing this with your supervisor. You will need to select a client who will afford you the opportunity to display your clinical skills. Before you start you will have to obtain informed consent and a release to allow you to use the materials, suitably disguised, in conjunction with your application. One of my students prepared two work samples, each dealing with a different problem in a different type of setting with a different supervisor so she could demonstrate her range and versatility. (She also hoped that if the internship staff did not care for one, they might like the other.)

You can also begin your preliminary reconnaissance for possible internships, identifying and investigating settings that interest you. If you start doing this a year in advance, you can benefit from the experiences of the people in the class ahead of you while they are applying for internships. They are going to be very busy and rather tense, so they may not want to spend a lot of time educating you. However, if you offer to help them by writing for brochures or assisting in preparing some of their numerous application forms, you will be more welcome. In particular, if you volunteer to help out by taking them to the airport and later meeting their planes when they return from interviews, you will not only be assisting them but also learning firsthand from seasoned veterans while the experiences are still fresh in their minds. This will be greatly appreciated since it seems to be an FAA regulation that the only flights intern applicants can take leave before dawn and return after midnight. (If they are scheduled to return at a civilized time, Murphy's Law stipulates that the flight will be delayed.)

Chapter Five recommends attending professional meetings as a cost-effective way to observe and meet personnel from internships that interest you. A number of regional meetings are held in the Spring, the American Psychological Association has its annual meeting in August, and the Association for the Advancement of Behavior Therapy ("AABT") meets in the Fall. AABT typically has an internship forum where students can meet the training directors and learn about a number of programs.

Advance financial planning can also help. Applying for internship can be expensive. Putting aside some funds, paying off the credit cards, taking advantage of tire, luggage, and clothing sales, and getting your car ready for long distance travel may make it less necessary to float a last minute loan.

Finally, long before you actually apply, you should discuss your plans with those people who are close to you who will be affected by your plans, such as your spouse or partner, children, parents, and others whose lives may be impacted. As you will see, your chances of success will be greatly enhanced if you are free to go wherever you find the best opportunity. This may mean moving hundreds or even thousands of miles. The sooner you start discussing this, the better. If someone is going to move with you, then the prospect of relocating in a year or two can make a difference in their educational, vocational, and personal plans. You should probably think twice about buying a new house, encouraging your widowed mother to move near you, or making plans to adopt a baby if it is likely you will be leaving the following year. If your family cannot relocate, will you go on your own for the year? How will your family cope during your absence? The sooner these issues can be explored the better. Once you have actually started applying you will have so much on your mind dealing with the application process that it will be difficult for you to explore major personal issues with your loved ones.

Short-term preparations. While it is never too early to start planning, the bulk of the effort involved in applying for internship will take place the year you apply. The internship application and selection season begins in the Fall semester and runs through the second Monday in February. Most students wait until the Fall semester begins to start thinking about internship applications. I have offered internship application workshops in March and April where not a single student signed up; six months later they are oversubscribed. This chapter will provide a general schedule of what must be done. We will be idealistic and start in the Spring of the year you plan to apply, even though I realize it is unlikely you will actually begin until that Fall.

As I noted earlier, you should plan your academic schedule so that you will have satisfied your internship eligibility requirements when the time comes to apply. The Spring semester before you plan to apply, make sure you know what all these requirements are and that it will be possible to satisfy them by Fall. When you have formulated a timetable for meeting these requirements and other goals you may have established, such as beginning your dissertation or completing needed courses, meet with your major professor. Discuss your plans and see if your major professor thinks they are realistic. When I was an ADCT, I had all the clinical students prepare "time lines" on which they projected what they would accomplish each semester. Writing, and especially rewriting, takes much longer than most students think, even without the time preparing internship applications consumes. Perhaps that required course you counted on taking in the Summer is not going to be offered. Perhaps your major professor plans to be on sabbatical next Fall. Now is the time to find out.

Once you have secured the general approval of your major professor, meet with your ADCT to discuss your plans and get advice. Under the new APPIC requirements, your Academic Director of Clinical Training must submit two signed statements for your application to be considered. The first is a "Verification of Internship Eligibility and Readiness." (This will be described more completely in Chapter Seven.) The first question asks your ADCT whether, A) you are ready to go on internship *now* (i.e., when your application is submitted), or B) you have outstanding requirements that will have to be satisfied before you will be allowed to attend. If your ADCT plans to check "B," your first order of business is to take care of those deficiencies before you apply. If you cannot do so by the application deadline, wait until next year. Going through the application process this year will be a waste of your time because, given the current oversupply of internship applicants, no legitimate training center will risk accepting any interns whose ADCTs may not allow them to attend in the Fall.

Next, your ADCT must sign a statement attesting to the fact that you have the emotional stability, maturity, academic preparation, clinical skills, ethical standards, integrity, and ability to benefit from supervision that will enable you to profit from the internship experience. This is a relatively recent requirement, and some ADCTs may balk at making such a blanket declaration, especially if you have had some difficulties in the program. If your ADCT is reluctant to sign, you need to have a discussion about what you need to do to reassure him or her. Perhaps you need to have your faculty mentor or clinical supervisor discuss your candidacy with the ADCT. If the bottom line is that your ADCT feels you need additional seasoning or experience before you are ready to go, it is probably best to wait another year before applying. In this climate, applying without your ADCT's certification is probably a waste of time, effort, and money.

Self-evaluation. Once you have your timetable approved and have made plans to satisfy all your academic goals and requirements, examine your credentials from an Internship Training Director's point of view. As we shall see, different internships have vastly different expectations and requirements. Nevertheless, they are all seeking applicants who can hit the ground running, people who can quickly assume a professional role and capably represent the Psychology Department, albeit as a trainee.

Next year, when you actually are an intern, you may be asked to help screen applications. Put yourself in this role now, and ask yourself how you would evaluate your own resume. Is this someone you would recommend? Why? If you can get some input from local practitioners or clinical supervisors, so much the better. Articles on the criteria used by internships to rate prospective applicants may also be helpful; several are contained in the chapter on "Selection" in Dana and May's (1987) book *Internship Training in Professional Psychology*. The purpose of this exercise is to identify possible weaknesses or areas that can be improved while there is still time to do something about it.

One student who went through this exercise one summer decided that he needed more experience in personality assessment with adult inpatients. As ADCT, I was able to arrange for him to obtain supervised experience in such a setting during the Fall Semester. I also made a point of noting in my letter of recommendation how this student had demonstrated professional maturity and eagerness to learn by taking an unpaid position two afternoons a week to enhance his skills in this area in preparation for internship. Concrete behavior such as this is much more impressive to a Training Director than the banal platitudes usually found in letters of recommendation.

Enhancing your academic credentials. Internships differ in the weight they attach to publications. Some say they are irrelevant, others state they are extremely important. One member of the Selection Committee at an internship housed in a major school of medicine remarked that he flips to the back of the CV and counts the publications before deciding whether to read the rest of the application. I hope he was jesting, but it is a fact that all of our students who have been accepted at that internship have had strong publication records.

Fortunately there are often steps you can take to enhance your CV to make it more competitive. This is a good task for the summer before you apply, but even the fall of your application year is not too late. If you have been putting off writing up your master's thesis or some other study, now is a good time to prepare it for publication and submit it. You can list it as "under review," and even if it is later rejected it will still enhance your CV while it is being evaluated. Similarly, take the time to prepare proposals for local or regional professional meetings. If you have collaborated on some research with some faculty members who have been dilatory about getting it written up, fuss at them or offer to write it up yourself.

Admissions committees are also favorably impressed by a commitment to the profession. A time-effective way to enhance your CV is to join professional societies and to enroll in some specialized workshops for continuing education credit. If you belong to a graduate student organization at your university or in your state, the next time the opportunity comes to volunteer to head a committee or to stand for office, go ahead and put yourself forward. This will enable your ADCT to comment on the high regard in which your peers hold you and how you have demonstrated leadership. These are little things, to be sure, but they will help differentiate your CV from those of other students who have not engaged in these activities.

Forming a support group. Programs differ greatly in the amount of assistance and support they provide for their internship applicants. As you can see from this book, our program does a great deal to prepare our applicants. If you are enrolled in a similar program, do what you are told, even if it conflicts with my advice. It is very important that everyone in a program works together; if you are marching to a different drummer you will have problems.

It is especially important that you meet whatever application deadlines your program establishes. Missing a deadline may not seem like a big deal, but it often creates a lot of extra work for the faculty and staff. It sometimes took me longer to process one late letter of recommendation than it did to do an entire batch of letters that were ready on schedule.

If you are in a program that does not provide a great deal of assistance, there is a lot you can do to facilitate the application process. I suggest that you form a support group of fellow applicants and work together to make things easier. For example, we provide our students with a copy of the latest APPIC *Directory of Internship and Postdoctoral Programs in Professional Psychology* which is published annually in July or August. The *Directory* is absolutely indispensable. It not only describes all the internships but is also the only source for the addresses and phone numbers of the various programs. If your school does not do so already, suggest that they subscribe to APPIC. The cost for graduate programs to subscribe is currently $125.00, which includes a copy of the *Directory*, the APPIC *Newsletter*, which contains important information about APPIC policies, access to the APPIC Clearinghouse, and a discount on additional copies of the *Directory* for graduate students in good standing. If your program has subscribed, you can purchase your own copy of the *Directory* for $15.00, which is half the regular price. Order your copy on your graduate program's letterhead with an endorsement from your ADCT or major professor certifying you are a student in a subscribing program.

If your program prefers not to subscribe, then I suggest that you chip in and order a *Directory* for your support group. APPIC's current address is:

APPIC Central Office
C/O Ms. Connie Hercey, MPA
733 15th St., NW, Suite 719
Washington, DC. 20005
Phone: (202) 347-0022
Fax: (202) 393-0079

Before ordering you might want to check the address and the prices at the APPIC Web site, which once again is **www.appic.org**.

Starting in September, the internships mail copies of their brochures to the various clinical training programs around the country. Ask your ADCT where your program files them. If there is no systematic procedure for making them available, I suggest that you volunteer to create and maintain a file for them in some convenient location. One word of advice: get a date stamp and date them as they come in. Otherwise you will soon find current brochures intermingled with those that are hopelessly out of date.

As internships get increasingly computerized, I expect more and more of them to develop pages on the World Wide Web. When that occurs, you should be able to download brochures and application forms. Give the person in your group who is the most cyber savvy the task of navigating the net in search of internship information.

A support group can also divide up the chores of writing for information, share impressions of internships, and see to it that you do not interfere with one another. Many internships will not take two people from the same program. By coordinating your applications, you can cut down on the competition within your group. We have found that mutual cooperation enhances everyone's chances.

Your responsibilities. No matter how supportive your program, the responsibility for selecting the internship that best meets *your* needs is *yours*. *You* must make sure that you have met all the requirements. *You* must convince the internships' Selection Committees that *you* are a person they want to have work and study with them for the coming year.

As a psychologist in training, you may have been told that you should not be judgmental. When it comes to selecting an internship, forget it. Making judgments is what the selection process is all about. As you prepare your applications and participate in your interviews, do so in the certain knowledge that you will definitely be judged. At the same time, you must judge yourself and the facilities to determine which is best for *you*. This requires doing your homework and learning everything you can about each internship. If at all possible, you should visit each site and meet the training staff and present interns in person. In every group of internship applicants I have worked with, some students return after interviewing having discovered that some of the celebrated luminaries they had admired from afar proved to be arrogant asses, while others who appeared less prestigious on paper were much more impressive in person. Invariably, after interviewing, some candidates eliminate their former top choices from consideration in favor of other programs they had formerly ranked considerably lower.

What to do month by month

In this section, I will provide you with a month-by-month time line of what should be done the year you actually apply for internship. In the chapters that follow, you will find detailed discussions of *how* to accomplish these various tasks. This is simply a list, without much explanation of what needs to be done.

September. If you began your preparations six months to a year ago, you should be in good shape. If you are like most people who are planning to apply this Fall, you are probably just beginning to think about what needs to be done. Get to work; you have a lot to do:

1. Read this entire book as soon as possible. Don't worry about the details; you will come back to them as you do each step.

Just get an overall picture of what has to be done between now and February.

2. If, after skimming the book, you are convinced there is no way you can possibly accomplish everything that must be done in the time you have left given all your other commitments, you may be right. If it looks like you will have serious problems meeting some important goal in the time remaining, it may be better to wait and apply next year.

One year, one of our students who was employed half-time and carrying an average course load told me that during the Fall semester she planned to a) complete her major area paper, which in our program is equivalent to the Comprehensive Examination, b) apply for internship, and c) arrange her wedding, get married, and go on her honeymoon. I advised her that this seemed to be an overly ambitious schedule and suggested that she cut it back somewhat. However, she was sure she could do it all; for example, she felt her Caribbean honeymoon would afford her ample opportunity to complete her major area paper and fill out her internship applications. By the time the semester had ended, she had actually managed to maintain her employment and her course load and accomplish two of her three goals. I thought this was a triumph, but she was very disappointed. (Sorry, but it is none of your business which two she completed.)

3. If you have not done all the things that I suggested you should do last Spring, take care of them now. That is, make sure you will meet all the requirements for going on internship this Fall, meet with your major professor, ADCT, and clinical supervisors, discuss your plans, get feedback, and work out a schedule to accomplish all the necessary tasks in the time allotted.

4. If you have already prepared a resume or CV, update it and do what you can to enhance it as noted above. If you have never prepared a CV, read Chapter Six and start to work on it. To help you assemble and record the information you will need, download APPIC's Uniform Application Form from their Web site and also get "Standard Form 171" from your local Post Office. Start assembling the information they require and begin filling them out.

5. Read Chapter Four and prepare your list of priorities. If you have dependents or are involved in relationships with people who will be affected by your decisions, it is time for some serious conversations. Are you going to go alone, or will one or more people

go with you? Either way, their needs will influence your choice of an internship site.

Whether or not other people are involved in your decision, some brainstorming with your support group and discussions with former interns and faculty will also help you in establishing priorities.

6. Start reviewing the APPIC *Directory*. As you identify places in which you are interested, write for brochures and application materials. Some especially well-organized students ask if they should write earlier. Since many internships wait until after the APPIC meeting in mid-August to update their brochures, I think it is generally best to wait until August or September to write for information.

7. Prepare for travel by joining automobile and airline frequent traveler and hotel discount clubs. Be alert for Fall luggage and clothing sales.

8. Get a flu shot. Airplanes are the world's most efficient virus-transmission devices, especially in the winter. In January, students returning to campus from Christmas break bring with them all the various germs they have collected flying around the country. On most campuses, the flu epidemics begin in mid-January, just when you will be doing most of your interviewing.

October. In October, I scheduled individual meetings with my intern applicants to discuss their priorities and the various sites that they included on their preliminary lists. They also brought their CVs to this meeting. We went over them in detail, and I made suggestions on how they could be improved. These interviews provided the students with feedback and they gave me information that I used in preparing my letters of recommendation. If your program does not have some comparable procedure, I suggest you seek out your ADCT and/or major professor for a similar session.

In any case, whether or not you are going to have such a meeting, by early October and preferably before you should have:

1. Completed your list of personal priorities to be used in evaluating internships.

2. Formulated a preliminary list of possible sites, obtained brochures, and started to evaluate them in the light of your priorities.

3. Completed your CV.

After meeting with your ADCT or advisor and revising your list of potential sites, you should:

4. Write each site for application forms if you have not already done so.

5. Go to the Registrar's Office and order transcripts to be sent to each place you are considering.

6. Get that flu shot you have been putting off.

November. Each internship will have its own individual date by which all materials must be received. However, the earliest due date drives the overall schedule since it is easiest and safest to send everything out at once. The earliest due dates used to be during the first week in December, but they have been moving steadily forward. In recent years the earliest date has been the Friday closest to the middle of November (i.e., on or about Nov. 14). This means you should plan for everything being placed in the mail *at the Post Office* by the previous Monday. This goal leaves you a couple of days leeway for the various disasters such as computer failure that might occur. To accomplish this:

1. Provide your major professor, ADCT, and clinical supervisor with copies of your CV and a list of addresses to which letters are to be sent. Make sure the addresses are complete as noted in Chapter Seven, and do exactly what you are told to do with regard to postage and so on.

2. Complete all your application forms, personal statements, cover letters, and CVs and mail them by the Monday before the Friday due date.

3. Make sure all your letters of recommendation and your transcripts have actually been *sent.* (I have known major professors who wrote the letters but forgot to mail them.)

4. If you hope to visit internship facilities during Christmas break, you may have to obtain advance purchase tickets during November. Unfortunately, those facilities that interview by invitation only will probably not be ready to decide whom they should invite, so don't be surprised if they put off your request for an appointment. Whether or not you actually need to purchase tickets, given all the holiday travel, the sooner you can book reservations the better, especially if there is no penalty for changes or cancellations.

December. By December 1, all the internships should have received and filed your applications and supporting materials. Call and find out if your application is complete. If not, send in any missing items as soon as possible.

Now is the time to arrange for interviews and make your travel plans. If you have not already done so, start scheduling appointments. Some popular places do not have the time to interview everyone, and latecomers may be out of luck. If you cannot visit in person, arrange for a telephone interview. Before your first internship visit, dress up and do some role-playing with faculty members or the other applicants in your support group, using the questions in Appendix 6.

If you have not gotten your flu shot by the end of December, forget it. It is too late to do any good. Budget time for being sick when you return, and stock up on tissues and chicken soup.

January. This is when you will do most of your interviewing. It is also the time when the weather is apt to be poorest for traveling. Follow the advice in Chapters Eight and Nine, and be sure to keep in touch with your home base so you can receive messages from other internships. A cellular phone may be a good investment; one can be rented if you don't want to purchase one.

After you have returned from interviewing, compare notes with the other internship applicants, seek the advice of faculty and friends, and rank the places to which you have applied. If you have some remaining questions, now is the time to call and ask. If you were unable to do so during your visit, talking with some of the present interns might help. Send thank you notes to all the places you visited.

If there are any places you are not willing to attend, consider withdrawing your candidacy. If your list has gotten too short, consider filing some more applications. There will be some internships with late due dates.

Even though Uniform Notification Day is not until the second Monday in February, some ITDs may start calling the last week in January, ostensibly to see if you have any questions but actually to try to ascertain whether you are a viable candidate. Review Chapter Ten and the APPIC rules in Appendix 1 so you will be prepared to respond.

__February.__ Unless the new APPIC statement is more effective than most authorities predict, you will probably receive some calls from Internship Training Directors or other internship personnel such as current interns trying to determine how you rank their programs. Other ITDs will not call you, but they will be paying close attention to whether or not you call or write them. If they do not hear from you, they may conclude that you are not interested. If you are seriously interested in an internship, you should definitely touch base with them during this period.

No matter who calls whom, it is absolutely essential that as soon as possible you formulate a ranked list of desirable placements and stick with it. Your response to a call from your first choice will differ from your reply to one that is ranked lower. As noted in Chapter Ten on the "Endgame," when talking to ITDs, be absolutely honest. Tell the truth and nothing but the truth, but do not feel that you have to tell the whole truth.

Your ADCT and, possibly, your major professor may be receiving similar calls from ITDs attempting to ascertain the likelihood that various applicants will attend their programs. Keep your ADCT informed as to your preferences. In the past, most students have notified their first choices that they will accept an offer if it is made. The new APPIC policy states that you should not do this. However, it will not hurt your chances to let your top choices know that you hold them in high regard.

The week before UND, some programs will notify you that you are no longer considered a viable candidate. Be grateful for their honesty, especially if it is your first choice. Knowing you are out of the running at some settings gives you a chance to improve your chances at the remaining internships on your list. Unfortunately too many internships "string along" too many applicants who have no realistic chance of acceptance.

__Notification Day.__ Your school will probably give you a set of instructions to follow on Notification Day. If so, comply with them exactly. Otherwise, follow the instructions in Chapter Ten.

Under UND, formal notification of candidates begins at 9:00 AM, CST, the second Monday in February. Once UND has begun, ITDs and applicants can and should talk frankly with one another about how they rate one another. (If you made the mistake of assuring more than one internship that it was your first choice, you may hear some very frank talk when you hold or decline their offers.)

When you receive an offer, you must indicate if you accept, reject, or will "hold" the offer. If you hold it, you have until 1:00 PM CST to decide whether or not to accept the offer. During that time, the internship cannot retract the offer, nor can they offer that position to anyone else. You can hold only one offer at a time, and if you have not accepted by 1:00 PM CST, the offer is automatically rescinded and the program can offer the slot to someone else.

Once you accept an offer on Notification Day, you have made a binding commitment that you cannot break. The internship marks that slot as being filled, and for you the internship selection season is over. If any other internships call you, you must tell them you are no longer available. You must immediately notify any program whose offer you were holding, and, as a courtesy, you should inform the other sites where you applied that you are no longer available. Then you can go celebrate.

If you have not accepted an offer by 1:00 PM, call any settings that you may not have heard from or lower-ranked programs you may have rejected and see if they have slots remaining. Notify your ADCT and discuss accessing the Clearinghouse.

Once computer matching is adopted, you will not have to go through the UND procedure described above. Instead, you will probably access the APPIC web site on line. Using the Personal Identification Number (PIN) you have been given, you will type in up to 17 sites in order of preference. You can change your list anytime you choose up to "one nanosecond" before midnight when the system is locked. Your choices and those of the internships are then automatically compared using procedures I will describe in Chapter Eleven. After the program has run, you will be informed with what internship you were matched. (Since you would be foolish to enter any program that you are not willing to attend, your acceptance of the match is, I presume, automatically assumed.) If there was no match, then you will go into the Clearinghouse automatically where you can find out what slots remain open.

After Notification Day. After Notification Day, when you have accepted an offer from the internship of your choice, send a formal letter of acceptance to the ITD with a copy to your ADCT. This should include your understanding of all the details of the agreement you have reached.

You should shortly be receiving a confirmation letter from the internship. If you do not receive one within a reasonable period of time, you or your ADCT should check with the program to make sure there is no problem. It is also appropriate to send nice notes to those places that made you offers which you did not choose to accept. Remember, soon after you complete your internship you will be out there again looking for a job.

NOTES

CHAPTER FOUR

ESTABLISHING YOUR PRIORITIES

You are embarking on one of the most challenging enterprises of your graduate education: seeking a predoctoral psychology internship. For some, applying for internship combines the worst aspects of getting married, applying for graduate school, and taking comprehensive oral exams. On the other hand, obtaining your first full-time professional position can also be challenging, exhilarating, and fulfilling. My goal is to help you minimize the strain and maximize the satisfactions.

Why do so many psychology graduate students find applying for internship so stressful? Some apprehension is justified. Obtaining a good internship is important for your career, and in recent years approximately one out of seven applicants has failed to secure a position. Any applicant who does not experience any anxiety probably does not understand the situation or is not especially serious about a career in professional psychology.

However, much of your trepidation is unwarranted. Some probably stems from fear of the unknown. You are applying for a professional psychology internship and you do not know what to expect or how to go about it. Relax. By the time you finish reading this book you will have all the information you need. Other worries may be caused by irrational beliefs. In the course of your professional training you have undoubtedly counseled clients to put aside their unrealistic expectations so they can cope more effectively with realistic concerns. It is time you did the same. Let us begin by exorcising some of the demons that haunt many intern applicants.

Some unrealistic worries

Obtaining the perfect internship. Many internship applicants operate under the illusion that somewhere there exists the one perfect program that is ideal for them and that their careers will be ruined if they do not procure a position there. Some are even convinced that there is a single special slot or rotation within that ideal internship that they must seek and obtain. This is utter nonsense.

In the course of seeking an internship you will become intimately acquainted with the annual APPIC *Directory* of internships. The 1996-1997 *Directory* listed 534 predoctoral training centers in the United States and Canada with 2,431 funded full-time slots, 85% of which were accredited by the American Psychological Association (APA). For the last eight years, the number of positions listed has increased, so there should be even more available when you apply. (See Figure 1-1.) Unless your needs are very unusual, many, probably most, of these sites would meet your basic training needs. At the same time, it is extremely unlikely that any one site would meet all your requirements perfectly. So, although your decision is an important one, try not to get too obsessive about it.

After reading the above, you probably nodded and proceeded to this paragraph secure in the knowledge that my admonition not to seek the perfect placement as if it were the Holy Grail does not apply to *you*. *You* are much too sophisticated and professional to subscribe to such a naive belief. Wonderful. Just remember your sophistication and professionalism the week before Notification Day when you are starting to panic over the possibility that you might not get into your first-choice program.

<u>Evaluation anxiety.</u> Internship selection involves evaluations, and evaluations make some people nervous. As a psychologist, you are going to be making appraisals every day of your professional career. Whenever you make a diagnostic assessment, perform a therapeutic intervention, or consult with another professional, you are constantly evaluating other people, and they in turn are examining you. The same thing happens when you are applying for internship. You will be sizing up the program and staff, and at the same time they will be appraising you. If you think of the internship interview as just another professional assessment, your anxiety should decrease.

<u>Competition anxiety.</u> Many students get scared by the numbers. According to the 1996-1997 APPIC *Directory*, there were 37,107 applications filed in 1995-1996. The average APA-accredited internship received 71 applications, or about 16 applications for every slot. Before you panic, you must remember that this is the number of *applications*, not *applicants*. In 1997, a survey of 480 students indicated that the average student applied to 11.45 places (Thorne, 1997). If my estimate of 2,837 applicants in 1995-1996 is correct, the overall mean would be about 13 applications per candidate. Even a "superstar" who got an offer from every place she

applied can take only one position; the other ten to 12 will go to other applicants.

As you will see later, there is great disparity in the numbers of students applying to various facilities. Data that I extracted from the *Directory* show that 20% of the internship centers received 41% of the total number of applications. The remaining 80% of the internships are considerably less competitive. And don't forget the non-accredited internships that only received eight applications per slot. Obviously an APA-accredited position is preferable, but you can still get good training at a non-accredited facility. Certain parts of the country consistently have a much higher ratio of applications to slots than others; if you are willing to travel, you can improve your chances. So while there is certainly cause for concern, there is no reason to panic.

Fear of rejection. A third irrational fear is that of experiencing rejection. You may as well accept the fact right now that you *will* be rejected. No matter how fabulous you are, it is unlikely that *every* setting you visit will decide that you are a good match for their program. I know of one internship that passed over an applicant because they felt he was *too* good; even though this program is highly competitive, they felt this student was so outstanding that he would probably go somewhere even more prestigious. Another candidate was a brilliant researcher, a gifted clinician, and fluent in two languages. Most training programs pursued her as if she were the graduate student equivalent of a Heisman Trophy winner. However, even this paragon did not get accepted everywhere. One program turned her down because they felt she was too physically attractive. "The head nurse would have killed me if I brought her in here," the Training Director later confessed.

If these two candidates could get rejected, so can you. But relax; you will soon discover that you do not like every program you apply to. Some will not meet your needs; others will simply not appeal to you. So why should you expect every program to fancy having you as a trainee? Such rejections, often mutual, are inevitable. Worrying about them is a waste of time.

Some realistic concerns

Once you stop stewing over the irrational worries that plague many students, you can deal more effectively with the realistic difficulties applying for internship poses. Virtually all of these problems can be anticipated. If you prepare for them, you will be able to cope with them more successfully.

Applying is a hassle. This is a legitimate concern. The Dean of a school of professional psychology described the present process as "disruptive to the lives of our students," (Fox, 1991, p. 34) and, indeed, applying for internship will come to dominate your life in the months to come. Identifying the training centers that will best meet your particular needs, filling out application forms, preparing a Curriculum Vitae ("CV"), traveling to the sites, interviewing and negotiating with training centers -- all this will require a lot of time and effort. I will tell you what to do and how to do it, but it will be up to you to get the job done correctly and on time.

Applying takes too much time. This is also true, so in planning your schedule for the year you apply, be sure to budget adequate time for the internship application process. Figure on it requiring at least as much time as the most rigorous graduate course you have ever taken, and modify your academic schedule accordingly.

Applying is expensive. Costs are another realistic consideration. Dean Fox (1991, p. 34) recently noted, "Going for interviews... creates real financial hardships for most students...It is not unusual for our students to have expenses of $2,000 in interview costs alone." A recent survey of 480 students undertaken for the Council of University Directors of Clinical Psychology (CUDCP) reported a mean expenditure of $1,084 with a wide range of variations (Thorne, 1997). Obviously the farther you travel, the more you will spend. If you follow the advice in this book, you will save hundreds of dollars. Nevertheless, you should be prepared for substantial extra expenditures for travel, telephone, and wardrobe additions.

Impact of your decision. Another realistic concern is that selecting an internship is an important professional decision that will significantly influence your career. The skills you develop and the techniques you learn will stay with you throughout your career, and the professional relationships you acquire and contacts you make will have a major influence on your subsequent opportunities. Choosing an internship is indeed an important task that deserves your serious attention.

Effects on family life. During the five months or so that your are applying for internship, you will be under considerable stress. Depending on how you cope with stress, you may be irritable, moody, or preoccupied. You may find it difficult to "be there" for your family or those who depend on you during this time. This can have an adverse effect on your relationships. That is why I recommend discussing these issues with your family and friends early in the game, so they will know what to expect and be more understanding during this period.

Lack of control. Feelings of uncertainty and lack of control over the eventual outcome are major sources of anxiety for everyone involved in the internship selection process, ITDs and ADCTs, as well as students. No one can predict exactly what will happen, and no one can control the outcome. For applicants, this lack of control is often compounded by not knowing exactly what is involved in the internship selection process. While your university or professional school training program may have provided you with excellent academic training, few prepare you for the process of finding and obtaining an appropriate internship. You can be forgiven if you feel like Alice playing croquet with the Queen of Hearts. Until you understand the process, it is indeed like playing a game on someone else's field with whimsical rules that often appear arbitrary, if indeed they are ever articulated. True, APPIC has published a formal set of explicit regulations, but at times these are incidental to what is actually happening. This book is designed to give you the information you need. You will also find it helpful to read accounts written by previous interns such as Burt (1985), Gollaher and Craig (1994), Jacob (1987), and Kingsley (1985) who have "been there" and successfully coped with the system.

Establishing Your Priorities

The first step in applying for an internship is probably the most important. This is establishing your priorities: deciding what it is *you* are looking for in your internship. If you do this honestly and insightfully at the outset, all the remaining steps will be infinitely easier. On the other hand, if you put this step off or fail to discern your real needs, the whole application process will be much more difficult, especially during the final stages in which you must come to some definite decisions.

I cannot overemphasize the importance of analyzing your priorities in the very beginning, *before* you start surveying the *Directory*, writing for brochures, composing your resume, and preparing your applications. Each person's needs and goals are different; there is no one internship that is best for everyone. Take the time to reflect on what it is *you* want from *your* internship.

You may find it helpful to formalize this process by listing all the features you do and do not want in an internship setting. Weigh the importance of each by indicating whether you regard it as "essential," "important," or "desirable." For examples, see Jacob (1987) and Stewart and Stewart (1996a). After you have refined this checklist and gathered more information, you can use it to help you decide which programs you will apply to, and, later, to help you rank your choices. It is because every person's list is unique that there is no internship that is ideal for everyone.

There are two sets of factors to consider in evaluating internships, professional and personal. The first set has to do with the training you will receive. These include whether a program has APA approval, the nature of the setting, the population(s) you will be exposed to, the rotations available, and the personnel with whom you would be working. The second set has to do with quality of life. It includes such aspects as geography, family ties, and finances (Stedman, in press). I will discuss a few of the most common considerations below.

Professional considerations

There are many factors to consider in evaluating an internship program. Important considerations are whether or not a program is approved by the American Psychological Association and whether the internship is for one year or two. With regard to the nature of the training offered, you need to consider whether you prefer diversity or wish to specialize, if the number or the nature of the rotations available is important to you, and how you value the opportunity to attend didactic presentations and seminars. The training faculty is extremely important. Their expertise, theoretical orientations, supervision styles, accessibility, and commitment to training are all factors you must weigh. The facilities and equipment that are provided and the opportunity to do research will be more critical for some applicants than others; you will have to decide for yourself how you weight these aspects. Less tangible, but still influential, is the atmosphere that prevails; this includes morale, collegiality, and the degree of respect or rivalry that may prevail among different services or disciplines. The prestige of an institution, and the degree to which it fits with your perception of your present training needs and your future plans also need to be considered.

In the pages that follow, I will comment on some of these factors. While I will offer my recommendations and opinions on these issues, this is done with the intent of helping you determine your own attitudes so you can decide which aspects are most important for you. For example, since I value internships for the clinical training they provide, I do not weight opportunities for research very high, but for you this might be a vital consideration. If my comments help you diagnose your feelings, they will accomplish their purpose; on the other hand, if you copy them down and say to yourself that certain things are important because Megargee says they are, you will be missing the point.

After you have formulated your personal list of priorities, when you start evaluating actual programs, you will soon discover that no place will have everything exactly as you would like it. If it fits your professional goals, it may conflict with your personal needs. Inevitably there will be tradeoffs and compromises. You will have to decide for yourself which aspects are most important for you. By establishing your professional priorities at the outset, before they are intertwined with any specific programs, you will be better able to analyze objectively how important these considerations are for you.

APA accreditation. Training programs in professional psychology are accredited by the American Psychological Association. Each year the accreditation status of predoctoral internship training programs is listed in the December issue of the *American Psychologist*. The APPIC *Directory* also notes the APA accreditation status as of June 15 when the *Directory* goes to press.

Of the 513 pre-doctoral internships in the United States listed in the 1996-1997 *Directory*, 398 (77.6%) were APA-accredited, and they had 1,923 of the 2,248 (85.5%) full-time funded positions. The 115 non-accredited internship centers had the remaining 325 funded positions (14.5%) as well as 97% of the unfunded positions.

If your application is "competitive," that is you are an advanced student in good standing at an APA-accredited clinical or counseling doctoral program, you should definitely set your sights on a funded APA-accredited internship program. The fact that a program is not APA-accredited does not mean that you cannot receive good training there. Indeed, every accredited program had to train several classes of interns before they could obtain accreditation. As long as you graduate with a doctoral degree from an APA-accredited doctoral program, it is usually possible to get licensed even if your internship was not APA-accredited. It is up to your graduate school to determine whether you have satisfied your degree program's predoctoral internship requirement.

Why then do I recommend that you concentrate on APA-accredited internships? First, even though it is now possible to obtain a license or other credentials, such as a listing in the *National Register of Health Service Providers in Psychology,* without having attended an APA-accredited internship, this could change. Future legislation might be more stringent. The primary reason, however, is the hassle involved. The typical license application asks if you completed a one-year APA-accredited predoctoral internship. If you did, you simply check "Yes" and skip to the next part of the application. If you check "No," however, you will probably need to describe *and document* all the details of your internship experience so the authorities can judge whether it was equivalent to a an APA-accredited program. This may include the number and the nature of the clients you saw, the various rotations on which you served, the number of clock hours of supervision you received, and, as if all this were not enough, you may have to establish all your supervisors' qualifications and credentials. The older you get, the more difficult this becomes. It is far better to apply only to programs with full accreditation.

One-year or two-year internship. To graduate with a degree in clinical psychology from an APA-approved doctoral program, you must have a one-year predoctoral internship. Most states, however, require an additional year of supervised postdoctoral experience before you can be licensed. The Gainesville Conference recommended that a two-year internship, one year predoctoral and one year postdoctoral, be required (Belar et al., 1987) and Blom (1990, p. 7) recently noted, "Should prescription privileges become a reality...the additional training required may add further weight to the arguments that two years of internship are not only desirable but necessary to ensure adequate preparation for the practice of professional psychology." There is also general agreement that specialty training in areas such as pediatric psychology, neuropsychological assessment, and forensic psychology will typically require one or more years of additional postdoctoral education. As a result of all these considerations, some internships now stipulate that they are for two years.

It is up to you to decide whether to apply for a one- or two-year internship. If you have had relatively little practicum experience, or if you are seeking specialty training, a two-year internship makes more sense than if you have already had considerable experience and have more general interests. I do not foresee APA *requiring* two years. Even if it did, it would not be retroactive.

Diversity vs. specialization. Some programs, such as those in pediatric psychology, provide very focused and specialized training.

Others require a variety of more general experiences. Which is best for you?

Other things being equal, I suggest you seek diversity. Your predoctoral internship may be the last chance for you to get such a varied experience. The broader the range of clinical cases, approaches, and settings, the better. In evaluating internships, examine not only the range of cases seen by the internship as a whole, but also the diversity that any given intern such as yourself is likely to encounter. For example, if case selection is driven by the availability of third-party payments, are you, as an unlicensed provider, going to be restricted to cases not covered by an HMO?

I also recommend that you choose a setting that will complement your previous practicum experience. If all your work has been with outpatients, now is the time to get some inpatient experience. If you have been working at a prison, consider a medical setting and so on. Look beyond the specific facility and determine what other opportunities exist in the area. Often there will be a number of hospitals or agencies that are geographically contiguous, and one can attend colloquia or Grand Rounds at neighboring facilities, or even have a rotation there. Visiting one VA hospital, I discovered it was across the street from a major children's hospital so that it was possible for the VA interns to do a pediatric rotation even though it was not mentioned in the brochure.

Number of rotations available. While I favor diversity, do not be seduced by the sheer number of rotations that are listed for some internships. An internship is not like a buffet or salad bar where you can have a little bit of everything. Instead it is like ordering a fixed-price family dinner in a Chinese restaurant: you get one choice from Column A, one from Column B, and so on. Moreover, just as everyone automatically gets rice and a fortune cookie, you will probably be required to take certain rotations. For example, it is common to require all interns to be involved in both assessment and treatment, to work with both children and adults, and to have both inpatient and outpatient rotations over the course of a year.

There is only a finite amount you can experience within a year. You will probably have two, possibly three, major rotations and two or three minor ones. However, you may simply be assigned to one setting for six months and another for the remaining six months, especially in a consortium in which the various participating institutions are miles apart from one another. In such internships, it is up to the interns and their supervisors to work out a varied array of experiences within each facility.

You may be expected to pick up three or four long-term therapy cases in your first rotation and carry them throughout the year. In addition, there will usually be a standard array of seminars for everyone plus some electives. Given all these obligations, your degrees of freedom are limited.

A vital consideration is who gets to participate in the various rotations. Some internships' brochures display an extraordinary number of rotations. Closer examination may reveal that several are funded from particular sources, such as a specialized hospital within a consortium or a foundation focused on a specific disorder. If so, the interns who receive those stipends may spend a major portion of their time in those settings and have relatively little opportunity to learn about the other settings except over coffee with fellow interns. Moreover, it may be that *only* the interns on those stipends get to work in those areas, especially if highly specialized skills such as administering a neuropsychological assessment battery are required.

Many settings have track-specific selection in which applicants are chosen for particular rotations. Such commitments should be part of the bargaining process prior to Notification Day. If it is especially important to you to have a specific rotation or to work with a particular faculty member, you need to find out how these assignments are made and determine whether you are likely to obtain this position. Do you have the qualifications they look for in applicants for this rotation? It does you no good to have an item on the menu if you can't order it.

In short, before you pass over an internship that has a relatively small selection of rotations in favor of one that appears to have more variety, determine how much of the variety you will actually be able to experience. It may be that you will discover that in both settings you would have pretty much the same program.

Didactic training and seminars. Some internships offer a wealth of didactic training and seminars with top-notch people in their fields. In contrast to the university courses you are familiar with, these are more apt to be mini-seminars with one to three sessions devoted to a given clinical topic or proseminars with a series of experts discussing their specialties. Grand Rounds and case conferences are another important aspect of internship training.

Since internships vary greatly in their resources and their geography, the opportunities to participate in these additional educational experiences will differ. You must decide for yourself how much weight you will place on this aspect of internship training.

Personnel. More important than the specific rotations, the populations available, and all the other aspects of the curriculum, are the actual people with whom you will be working. These include the Director of Training, your supervisors, and the other interns.

Good Internship Training Directors are sincerely interested in their students and the quality of their educational experience. If necessary, they are ready to do battle with the administration to preserve the quality of their interns' education and prevent them from being exploited. Poor ones are hassled, disinterested, and looking for ways out. If their morale is low, yours will probably suffer as well. How do you discriminate the good from the poor? Tenure in office is no reliable criterion; some who have been directors for many years continue because of their commitment to training, but there are other long-term directors who are obviously burned out and waiting for retirement. A new director may be excited and filled with ideas to improve training or resentful over the time that is required. I am always interested in whether the ITD sought out the post or was stuck with it because no one else wanted it. In any event, ask the present interns about the dedication, enthusiasm, and accessibility of the ITD.

Supervisors are also very important. Most of your actual training will take place in one-to-one interactions with individual supervisors. More than any other single factor, a good supervisor can make a rotation, while a poor one can be devastating. You may have to dig a bit to learn about the nature, quality, and quantity of supervision, but it will be one of the single most important aspects of your training.

In evaluating a facility, you may be dazzled by the eminent names listed on the brochure and the chance to work with such people. That is fine, but make sure you establish whether these individuals actually supervise trainees, whether they will be available the year you intern, and whether you have any say over who you get as a supervisor.

Supervisors are not always people on staff. When I was a trainee at the Palo Alto VA, I was assigned a chronic schizophrenic who had been hospitalized for 14 years as my long-term individual psychotherapy case. Not a likely prospect. However, I also had an outside consultant from Stanford named Albert Bandura as a supervisor who made it an excellent learning experience.

The other interns will be your primary support group during your training. They may become your best friends or your worst enemies. While each class is somewhat different, observing the present interns and their interactions can give you some clues about the types of people selected, and whether the institutional atmosphere is divisive or congenial. Are they all Type A's or more laid back? Are they doctrinaire and rigid, or tolerant of differing opinions? Are they trustworthy or treacherous?

Sometimes you can pick up important clues when you are given a tour of the interns' offices. I recently visited an internship in which three trainees shared an office they had decorated with numerous snapshots of the three of them and their families socializing together on Halloween, Thanksgiving, and other occasions. A series of charts on the wall, to which they had all contributed, recorded the amusing things their child clients had said, and done, to them during the course of the rotation. Clearly this was a congenial group.

Theoretical orientations. Settings differ greatly in theoretical orientation. Some places are very formal and authoritarian, expecting everyone to formulate and discuss cases according to the "official" orientation, whether it be behavioral or dynamic. Other places are more flexible and enjoy a wide range of viewpoints among the students and staff.

Your own theoretical orientation and your degree of commitment to it will be of interest to the internships, as theirs will be to you. While a setting will probably not require that you share their frame of reference, they will expect you to be open to exploring their point of view. Moreover, you should have a sufficient grasp of the basic principles and vocabulary of the prevailing orientation so as to be able to understand what is being said. Other things being equal, they may prefer students who share their frame of reference.

I feel that you will probably learn more from a setting with a variety of viewpoints than one with a single-party line. One intern I visited had six different supervisors with as many orientations. She learned to shift smoothly from a psychoanalytic to an ego psychology to a cognitive behavioral to a radical behavioral frame of reference in the course of an afternoon as she went from one supervisor to the next.

This intern's experience brings up another issue with regard to supervisors. Where are they located? In the case of this internship, they were consultants on soft money who were located in their practices around town and it was necessary for her to travel to them. In other settings, most supervision will occur on the premises, even if the supervisors are not on staff. Not only does this mean they will be more readily available for consults, but also that they are more likely to attend case conferences.

Service vs. training. Internships vary in their commitment to training. This is reflected in the numbers of hours allotted for supervision, in the number of seminars offered, and in the number of cases you are expected to process. Are you expected to give minimal batteries and turn out as many reports as possible, or are you encouraged to try various techniques and given an opportunity to read and reflect on a puzzling case? In some programs, the interns feel they are being exploited and used to provide low-cost service to the facility with minimal educational benefits. In some, interns are expected to "eat what they kill" by generating fees that will reimburse the agency for their stipends and supervision. Emphasis on service and generating fees seems to be becoming more common as state and federal support for training has diminished and centers have become more dependent on fees for their support.

This issue is best established by discussions with present interns during your site visit. You can also raise this issue with the training staff as long as you make it clear you are concerned about the quality of the training and not the quantity of work.

Facilities and equipment. The facilities that are available can also influence the quality of the supervision and training. Some internships have superb equipment; others do not. I recently toured one setting in which each intern had an office in which he or she could see clients. Each office was equipped with a complete video recording setup...camera, VCR and monitor... for taping sessions. Supervisors' offices were similarly equipped. Another internship had two cameras in every therapy room feeding to a central control console worthy of MGM Studios. There, technicians could alternate cameras to catch questions and responses in a dyadic therapy session in one room, while maneuvering the play room camera angles by remote control to track children as they scurried about. When I read the evaluations of the students interning at these settings, it was obvious that the supervisors closely monitored the actual therapy process and provided the trainees with detailed feedback.

Few places have such superb equipment. However, the availability of audio and video recording equipment, computers, electronic test scoring apparatus, and specialized equipment for neuropsychological assessment, biofeedback and the like obviously has an impact on what can be done there.

The nature and the amount of space for interns is another consideration. Some interns are provided with individual offices, some with individual desks in a shared office, and some with individual drawers in a shared desk.

Opportunities for research. Internships vary greatly in their emphasis on research, ranging from those where there is no research to those that view research as an important aspect of the training program. In the more research-oriented facilities, do not assume that the time allocated for research will necessarily be for your personal research. Some centers like to have all the interns collaborate with faculty members on a joint project that is relevant to the internship, such as a needs assessment of some service or an evaluation of some program being carried out by the facility. The results of such projects benefit the internship, enabling them to carry out studies they could not undertake without the assistance of the interns. Moreover, it provides a mechanism whereby students can work together, which should improve their *esprit de corps*.

Personal research is another matter. Except for a few places that are very academically oriented, do not count on having much time for personal research regardless of what is stated in the brochures. If you are the sort of person who took a big pile of "important" books home to read over Christmas or summer vacations *and actually read them*, maybe you will be able to accomplish a fair amount on internship, but most interns find there is so much clinical work to do that they quickly lose their academic mindset. After spending 60 to 70 hours seeing clients, attending staffings, writing reports, receiving supervision, and participating in seminars, you will probably have little inclination for crunching numbers or writing technical prose. I personally feel that spending a lot of time on your dissertation can detract from what should be a unique clinical experience. Most major professors will probably disagree.

A few academically-oriented internships do offer rich opportunities to collaborate with faculty in their ongoing research projects. This may enable you to get shared authorship on several publications. However, even in these settings, it is unlikely you will be able to formulate and carry out a personal research project. Given the amount of time it takes to settle in, observe the opportunities available, write a proposal, and get it approved, it is difficult to do much data collection in the span of a one-year internship, especially since you will be rotating through a variety of settings. If you plan to stay for two years, however, research can often occupy a larger portion of your available time in the second year.

If you feel you must do a great deal of dissertation work on internship, perhaps you ought to consider waiting another year and applying after you have completed your dissertation. Having a well-advanced or completed dissertation will not only give you an edge on other applicants, but will also make it easier to move smoothly from your internship into a full-time professional or academic position. More and more ITDs are maintaining that a completed dissertation, or at least a defended prospectus, should be *required* before students apply for internship.

Relations with other disciplines. The professional relations among disciplines should also be considered. They may be reflected in the formal table of organization that indicates who reports to whom (e.g., does the Chief of Psychology report to the Chief of Psychiatry?). However, it is the personal relationships and mutual respect among professionals from different disciplines that are most important.

The tensions between psychology and psychiatry on the national scene can be reflected in the relations between these disciplines in some medical settings. If the psychology interns wear white coats and are called "residents," I usually infer that psychology has a status problem *vis a vis* psychiatry.

As a psychology intern, you can get caught up in these factional disputes. One of my students was reprimanded by a psychiatric resident because he had the temerity to write a "diagnostic impression" ("patient appears depressed") in a chart, thus usurping the exclusive right of physicians to make medical diagnoses. The resident complained to the Chief of Psychiatry who complained to the Chief of Psychology. Eventually, a formal hearing was held before it all got worked out. Presumably all of this occurred because everyone wanted to make sure that the patient received the best possible care, but somehow I never learned how the client benefited from all this wrangling. You may enjoy such confrontations, but from my standpoint, with everything else you have to worry about on internship, who needs this sort of bovine residue?

Politics and purges. Apart from interdisciplinary harmony, as you travel around the circuit you may hear rumors about high level political struggles in which administrators resign or are fired.

Sometimes these struggles are real, sometimes simply gossip. They are usually conveyed in hushed tones by some interns who are presently at the facility and are eager to display their inside knowledge of programmatic politics. The implication is that you should avoid that setting until the conflicts have been resolved or new people appointed.

An unstable political climate, if in fact it exists, is certainly a factor to consider, but its effects should not be overemphasized. To put the matter in perspective, suppose that as a graduate student you teach introductory psychology to undergraduates at your university. If the Chancellor of the University System fired the President of your school, would it really make any difference in the quality of instruction for the freshmen enrolled in your class? At the intern level, these political battles, unlike the territorial disputes described above, probably have relatively little impact.

Prestige. Some internships are more prestigious than others. Graduating from an eminent internship enhances your CV and may open some doors. It also makes your ADCT look good. However, prestige does not necessarily guarantee that the training afforded interns is better, or even as good, as it may be at other, less renowned facilities. The famous people whose names add luster to a program's reputation may spend most of their time off doing the things that make them famous instead of working with the trainees. It is up to you to discern how important an institution's prestige is to you and weigh it accordingly.

Fit with your training needs. In reviewing your readiness for internship, you will no doubt conclude that you are well-prepared in certain areas and adequate in several others, but that there are some professional skills that need to be enhanced. Unless you plan to be a Renaissance psychologist, it is unlikely that you want to achieve the highest levels of proficiency in all areas. I am pretty good at using traditional assessment techniques, but I doubt if I ever will have occasion to measure evoked potentials.

In formulating your priorities for internship, you need to establish your personal training goals. What is it you want to accomplish during your internship year? Consult with your faculty advisors and clinical supervisors. What are the areas you most need to work on? With what patient populations and treatment settings should you gain more experience? By asking yourself and your mentors these questions, you should be able to formulate a list of the types of training experiences and rotations you are going to seek on internship, as well as an idea of how much you want to emphasize various areas.

<u>**Fit with future plans.**</u> Every applicant has different career goals. Consider what you want to be doing five and ten years from now. When evaluating possible programs, keep these objectives in mind and ask yourself how each setting will influence your chances of achieving your ambitions. If, for example, you plan on postdoctoral training in a particular area, will this internship prepare you for the postdoctoral program and enhance your chances of getting accepted? If you are planning to relocate, you may want to inquire about the licensing laws in the different states you are considering.

Look beyond the professed goals of the training program and examine the actual achievements of its graduates. What kinds of jobs do they get? What are they doing five years later? Some places that profess to prepare you for academic positions, for example, may have virtually all of their former interns enter professional practice.

Some Training Directors and their staffs work very hard at helping their interns find full-time positions at the conclusion of their internship. Obviously this is easiest when the intern has completed the dissertation and the facility is located in the area where the student hopes to locate. Other internships do not regard intern placement as part of their responsibility and do not get involved with this aspect. Such assistance will be more important to some students than to others.

<u>**Balancing professional priorities.**</u> As we have reviewed some of these professional considerations, it may have seemed that some choices were obvious or trivial. Everyone wants high quality training, dedicated supervisors, congenial colleagues, and a free choice of desirable rotations. What you must do is decide on their *relative* importance to you, because you will find that tradeoffs are inevitable. In order to get that neuropsychological rotation you covet, you may have to go to a place where there is considerable interdisciplinary strife. An institution with considerable prestige may emphasize service at the expense of training. If you can decide on the relative importance of these professional issues before they get linked to particular places, you will find it easier to evaluate actual internships.

<u>**Truth in advertising.**</u> Don't believe everything you read in the internship brochures (Grace, 1985). Some rotations may have long since been discontinued; other training experiences may exist only

in the vivid imagination of whoever wrote the brochure. One recent applicant found that the statements regarding the theoretical orientations of the settings she visited bore little relation to the types of treatment actually being done. Some places that called themselves dynamic were actually more eclectic. One ITD confessed that the paragraph on theoretical orientation was included for historical reasons to please members of the Board of Trustees of the foundation that helped support the internship.

In short, even though APPIC has guidelines for internship brochures, and APA site visitors will examine them every five years, it is safest to regard an internship brochure as you would any other piece of advertising, like a circular you might pick up in an auto dealership or real estate office. Maintain a healthy skepticism and check out the claims they make for yourself.

Personal and practical considerations

In addition to these professional factors, there are personal preferences and practical concerns to consider. Since you are going to spend at least a year of your life in your internship, it is important that you consider these aspects as well as your professional priorities.

Family and personal relationships. Family ties and relationships often play a vital role in selecting a site. Aged or infirm parents may want you to locate near them. If you have a spouse, partner, or children, the first big decision that must be made is whether they are going to travel with you to the internship.

Sometimes it is undesirable, impractical, or just plain impossible for your loved one(s) to relocate. If this is the case, you may decide to intern close to home. This is obviously much easier in some parts of the country than in others. If your region is rich in training resources, interning near your home base may not present much of a problem. If good local training facilities are scarce, however, the decision to stay near home may mean sacrificing some professional goals such as attending a fully-accredited training program.

If you decide to leave your family or friends behind while you go away on internship for a year, accessibility will probably be an important consideration. An internship within driving distance will allow you to come home some weekends. If you must go farther afield, choosing an internship located in a "hub" city will make air travel easier and less expensive.

If family members or partners are going to move with you to the internship site, then their needs for employment, education, and so forth will have to be considered along with your training requirements. Having a partner who is unable to find work in a new city can be devastating to a relationship that may already be strained by the stresses induced by the training program.

If you are traveling in tandem with another intern applicant, compromises will be necessary. Some internships make an effort to keep couples together, even when it involves different disciplines such as psychology and social work. Others prefer not to take two people from the same university. This is the sort of issue that can be investigated during the reconnaissance phase.

The best strategy for couples who wish to remain in proximity is for them to limit their applications to a single geographic area. Other things being equal, metropolitan areas with a variety of settings such as Boston, the New York Metropolitan area, the District of Columbia and its environs, Atlanta, Chicago, St. Louis, Houston, Los Angeles, and the San Francisco Bay Area afford couples the best chance to stay together (Stewart & Stewart, 1996b). It is easier to travel from one major city to another in the Northeast than in the Northwest.

Caring for children is difficult while on internship, especially in those settings that expect 60- to 70-hour work weeks. Some interns rely on their non-interning spouse or other family members to care for their children during the internship year, especially when circumstances dictate it is best to leave the children behind. Others may have to rely on relatives to provide day care; if so, they need to select a program located where they have family members who are willing and able to assist them.

Parents lacking family or other child care resources may seek other alternatives. Commercial day care for preschool is one possibility, but internship stipends are limited and most communities do not provide adequate public care, especially for new arrivals. Nor do many training programs provide on-site centers. The solution that is most often discussed is the half-time two-year internship that enables parents to complete the APA requirement within 24 months (Blom, 1990, 1991; Ochroch, 1990). Unfortunately, of the 2,313 APPIC positions available in the United States in 1997, only 65 (2.8%) were part-time. This is half the number (123) that were available in 1991 (Zimet, 1991), so it appears such positions are becoming scarcer.

By and large, ITDs do not seem to care for half-time positions. At a recent meeting one complained that they are not cost-effective because APPIC and APA regulations state that a half-time intern requires the same number of hours of weekly supervision and didactic training as a full-time intern, leaving fewer hours to be spent in direct clinical work. Blom (1991, p. 3) also noted, "Political issues also enter the process; for instance, should half-time internships be available to all applicants regardless of parenting status or gender, or should they be exclusively or preferentially provided only for parents of young children or females with young children? Will this open the door for litigation for discriminatory practices?"

Location. In addition to proximity to family members, geography is an important consideration for other reasons. You will make many contacts on internship and no doubt generate some job offers. For this reason, it is sensible to consider a site in the area where you eventually plan to locate. Going to Boston will not help you find a job in Southern California.

If you still have your dissertation work to complete, proximity to your university or professional school may be another geographic consideration. If there is a lot of work remaining on your dissertation, you may have to select a site nearby, choose a topic that can be investigated at your new location, or decide to postpone applying for internship.

Geography also interacts with financial concerns. Living expenses are much higher in some places than others. During the application process, you can reduce travel expenses by developing a list of several places in a particular region instead of applying to internships that are scattered all over the continent.

Of course, geographic considerations need not always be practical. If you would like to spend a year in Hawaii or there is some other place you have always wanted to visit, put that down and give it an appropriate weight. Quality of life, rural vs. urban environment, climate, proximity to a beach and similar factors are also worth considering.

Financial considerations. Finances are another factor. Among the funded positions, stipends vary greatly. My calculations of the data reported in the 1996-1997 *Directory* (Hall & Cantrell, 1996) showed a range from $3,600 to $40,000 per year for a full-time position. The mean was $15,300, and the standard deviation was $4,447. Thus, 68% of the stipends would be in the range from about $10,600 to $20,000.

Given the shortfall in the number of positions, some students whose financial resources permit it opt for an unfunded position in preference to waiting a year or accepting a funded position at a less preferred site. I have never favored this strategy. Funded or unfunded, an internship will expect the same workload. I feel that unpaid interns who are working the same hours as the other trainees sooner or later will begin feeling exploited, although some disagree (Carlin, 1982). In certain situations, this may be the only way to get the experience you wish. For example, various regulations limit the types of stipends available for students who are not US. citizens. Certainly an unfunded position is preferable to those now being offered by some professional schools where *you* pay *them* for the internship experience.

Fringe benefits also vary greatly. They range from none at all to some that have very generous benefits including health care for the trainee and his or her family, housing and subsistence allowances, commissary privileges, and paid attendance at workshops and professional meetings. Ironically, the latter are also those with the highest stipends, namely the internships offered by the military.

Pay particular attention to whether medical benefits are provided, especially if you have a family and/or health problems. While you are at it, check and see if your university provides health benefits to students who are not in residence and if so, what fees you must pay to keep your health plan active. You may discover that the cost of health insurance makes an enormous difference in the actual value of a stipend.

To people accustomed to the usual graduate school deprivation schedule, a stipend of $15,000 or so may seem quite adequate. However, you may find that your expenses are significantly higher on internship. Additions to and maintenance of your wardrobe, transportation expenses, and rent will often be higher. If you re-register your car, you may have to pay an impact fee. You may have to budget travel back to your university, and, if you are separated from a loved one, you can count on the phone bill being higher.

If your graduate school is in a relatively rural region and your internship is in a metropolitan area, you can expect the cost of living, especially rents, to be substantially higher. If your stipend is modest, you may have to live at some distance from the site where housing is more nearly affordable; this increases the time and money spent commuting and decreases the time spent at the facility. Consortiums may require you to travel back and forth from one facility to another, which has the same effect. No one is going to get rich on internship, but if the stipend is so low and/or the living expenses so high that you must take a second job to survive, you will get less out of the experience.

Evaluate the local cost of living by asking other interns and by checking the rents in the classified ads when you visit. If possible, inspect the areas with the rents you will be able to afford on your stipend. Is the neighborhood so bad that you will have to budget $100 a month for ammunition and emergency room expenses? You can ask your insurance agent for the auto liability and theft rates and provisions at possible sites. In addition to their impact on your budget, the rates might be a good unobtrusive index of the relative safety of various locales.

I recently visited one of our interns in the Northeast. He was unable to meet me at the train station because his car had been stolen from his driveway. What astonished him was that none of the staff members at the training center were surprised because all of them at some time had had their cars stolen or boosted. Needless to say, no one had informed him of this probability when he had interviewed at the internship.

You might also want to check your insurance coverage; my intern's car was recovered in another city, but by the time the police notified him, the daily storage charges had accumulated to the point where they exceeded the value of his automobile. Partly because he had relocated in another state without informing them, his insurance company refused to reimburse him, and he was forced to abandon his car.

Quality of life. One aspect of an internship that is not readily apparent from the brochures is the pace and the amount of stress placed on interns. Some are frenetic...the interns all carry beepers and rarely complete a meal or a trip to the bathroom without being summoned to a phone. Others are more leisurely and laid back. Some places require interns to work 60 hours or more and a six- or seven-day week to keep abreast of their duties; others expect no more than the standard 40-hour, five-day work week. What you choose is up to you, but a Type B personality can be miserable in a Type A setting and vice versa.

How rotations are assigned is another important factor influencing intern morale. If the trainees feel that assignments are distributed honestly and fairly, morale is generally good, but any perceived favoritism is corrosive. The worst morale I ever observed was at a program where the trainees had been assembled on the first Saturday, placed in a room together, given a list of the rotations that had to be covered each quarter, and told to decide among themselves how they were to be distributed. Hours later, the most powerful individuals emerged with all their preferred placements; the rest got what was left as well as a bitter attitude that poisoned the rest of the year for all concerned.

Another potential stressor is the type of clients you will be treating. Psychopaths and sex offenders pose special problems, and a pediatric AIDs or oncology ward requires extraordinary emotional stamina. You need to evaluate yourself on these dimensions and select accordingly, especially if you are applying for specialized programs such as the VA's gerontology slots.

Amenities will vary greatly from one site to the next. I have visited interns ensconced in brand new, beautifully furnished private offices that I would kill for and others that had to share a battered desk in a room crowded with other trainees. Some sites, usually VA facilities, have magnificent, well-maintained grounds with ocean views, tennis courts, and golf courses; others are in inner-city ghettos where staff venture outside only in groups. Availability of secretarial help, the adequacy of the library, the accessibility of parking, and even the quality of the cafeteria can all influence morale.

Negative items

In addition to all the things you are seeking from your internship, there are undoubtedly some other things you do not want. Jacob (1987), for example, did not want an inpatient psychiatry rotation and negatively weighed those internships that had such a requirement. The more inpatient psychiatric time that was required, the more it detracted from the overall score on her "decision grid." Other trainees may want to avoid any settings where they may encounter snow or ice.

You may feel so strongly about some things that they constitute "veto items." These would cause you not to go to a program under any circumstances, no matter how desirable it was in other respects. These items may be professional or personal, rational or irrational. Most students will not consider an unfunded position, and many will not attend an internship that is not APA-accredited. Others will not apply to an internship that does not offer a particular rotation or experience they consider essential. Some may rule out settings with a strong theoretical orientation that is alien to their own. On the personal side, a setting that does not offer health benefits or does not have adequate job opportunities for a spouse or partner may be considered out of the question.

Whatever these veto items are, you should note them down and make them explicit. By eliminating any settings that have this negative characteristic, you will save yourself a good deal of time. Of course, if you have so many veto items on your list that you are left with only a handful of potential internships, that do not fit well with your qualifications or needs, perhaps you should reconsider your veto items and be more flexible.

All of these considerations, professional and personal, positive and negative, are unique to each individual. This is why there is no one internship that is best for everyone. Once you have formulated your list and weighted the various aspects in the abstract, you should use it to evaluate possible programs and identify those you wish to investigate further. These lists will also guide you to the information you need to gather about each setting.

CHAPTER FIVE

WHERE TO APPLY? COMPILING YOUR APPLICATION LIST

Once you have established your personal priorities, you need to compile a list of possible internships that you are interested in investigating in greater depth. Although students spend hours poring over internship materials, this is probably the easiest part of the process. You already know how to do library research, and, since you have already established your priorities, you know what it is you are looking for.

Preliminary Reconnaissance

Some preliminary explorations can take place early in your academic career. You probably already have some internships that you are interested in. Perhaps you have heard about them from faculty or students who interned there. Maybe they are in a part of the country that has always appealed to you. If it is convenient, you might find it helpful to make a preliminary informal visit to the internship site just to get a feel for the place and see what it looks like. If it is a real "turn off," you will save yourself the trouble of applying. However, keep a low profile; most Internship Training Directors have more than enough to do without feeling obliged to entertain casual visitors who may someday apply for internship.

If someone on your faculty interned at one of these sites, or if fellow graduate students are presently enrolled there, solicit their opinions. Often current interns return during the course of the year for committee meetings and other academic chores. Ask their major professors when they are likely to be in town, and see if you can schedule some time with them. If they are located at an internship that is not too far away, you might be able to arrange for an informal visit. Failing this, you may send them an e-mail, write a letter, or phone them at home.

Another cost-effective way of reconnoitering is to identify personnel connected with the training sites in which you are interested and observe or make contact with them at regional or national professional meetings such as APA or AABT. If you are really interested, you might write or call in advance to see if they are free for coffee or a chat. Otherwise, attend one of their presentations and introduce yourself afterwards. This will not only give you a chance to study the person during the presentation, but may also be advantageous later if you apply. When you interview, you won't be just another nameless applicant but someone the interviewer has previously met at a professional meeting.

However, unless you are one of those super-organized people who always mail all their Christmas cards the day after Thanksgiving, you are probably reading this in the fall of the year you plan to apply and you have not taken any of the above steps. Given the fact you will soon have to begin filling out applications, how do you develop a list of places and check them out?

Using the APPIC Directory

Begin by surveying the literature on a number of internship facilities. Although your ADCT probably has a file of brochures distributed by various clinical training programs, your best source of comprehensive, recent information is the *Directory of Internship Programs in Professional Psychology* published annually by APPIC. Consult this source first. (If your program does not provide a copy, see Chapter Three for instructions on how to obtain one.)

You will find the APPIC *Directory* includes a wealth of valuable information on each facility. It lists the names, degrees and Diplomate status of the Chief Psychologist and Training Director, and the number of full- and part-time doctoral level psychologists employed. It provides the training program's complete mailing address and phone number, as well the date applications are due. It indicates the number of full- and part-time funded and unfunded internship slots expected. It stipulates what requirements applicants must meet with regard to citizenship, number of practicum hours completed, progress toward degree, and nature of the training programs from which they welcome applications. It states what major and minor rotations are available, the stipend level and fringe benefits afforded, and, finally, how many completed applications they received the previous year. This last item, in conjunction with the number of stipends available, is very helpful in determining how competitive a program is. Much of this information is not available in any other source, including the internships' brochures.

While the APPIC *Directory* also includes each program's APA accreditation status, this information could be somewhat dated. The *Directory* goes to press in June and, of course, the programs provided their data earlier in the year. Moreover, some programs do not update their entries annually, so their accreditation status could have changed in the interim. Fortunately, the December issue of the *American Psychologist* always provides the most recent list of APA-accredited programs; use this source to check the program's current status.

Organization and contents of the *Directory*

Although the APPIC *Directory* is your best source of information regarding psychology internships, it has no index to help you locate programs with certain specific characteristics. Instead it is organized geographically, first by states and then by cities within states. So, if you do not already have some places in mind, you need to wade through it state by state and city by city. A support group can make the task of searching through the *Directory* easier. If you are interested in identifying those programs that have certain attributes, such as a major child rotation, you can each take a region and flag the settings with the desired characteristics.

Since the cities are listed in alphabetical order, tracking down a particular program can sometimes be difficult, especially when it is a consortium involving facilities in several different towns. Although it may be located in a metropolitan area and have several urban sites, the actual headquarters may be in suburb or a smaller town whose name is unfamiliar.

If geography is not your strong suit, it helps to keep an atlas handy. I have had students who wanted to intern in the Los Angeles area who skipped right over listings for programs in Culver City, Downey, Irvine, Long Beach, Orange, and Santa Monica, CA. Remember that training programs situated in different states can be geographically contiguous even though their listings may be at opposite ends of the alphabetically-ordered *Directory*; Baltimore, MD is next door to Washington, DC, and Newark, NJ, is just across the Hudson River from New York, NY. Although it is not 100% effective, it often helps to check out programs in communities with the same telephone area code as the city you are focusing on.

Statistical summaries. The first Appendix in the APPIC *Directory* provides aggregate data listing the total number of agencies, funded and unfunded vacancies, and numbers of applications received by all APPIC members. It also furnishes you with information regarding the average stipend levels and the average number of applications received for each funded slot overall. In addition, it breaks out these data separately for APA-accredited and non-accredited internships, and provides subtotals for 11 different types of internship settings.

Thus, Appendix A of the 1996-1997 *Directory* shows that there were 534 internships in the United States and Canada, 411 of which (77%) were APA-accredited. Collectively these internships had a total of 2,431 funded positions, 2,070 of which (85%) were at APA-accredited facilities. Overall, the internships reported receiving 37,107 applications, which averaged out to 71 per internship and 14 per slot. The accredited internships received 33,451 of the applications (90%), for an average of 90 applications each or 16 per slot, while the non-accredited facilities received 3,553 applications, which came to 30 per training center or eight per slot. By comparing subsequent summaries with these data, you can determine whether the numbers of positions, applications, and so on are increasing or decreasing.

Aside from these overall statistics, which include internships in Canada as well as the U.S., all the data in the *Directory* are raw, consisting of the information listed on each individual site's entry. To assist you in your survey of settings, I entered all the data for the 513 American internships into a computer so that I could compute some additional averages. These findings will be cited throughout this chapter.

Preferences. For each program listed in the APPIC *Directory*, there is a section with the heading, "Applicants welcome from what programs?" There are six academic program categories: 1. Clinical, APA-accredited; 2. Clinical, Non-accredited; 3. Counseling, APA-accredited; 4. Counseling, Non-accredited; 5. School, APA-accredited; and 6. School, Non-accredited. ITDs from various settings have indicated whether they welcome applications from each type of program by rating them as "Only," "Preferred," "Acceptable," or "Not Welcome."

In Table 5-1, I have summarized these rankings for the 513 American internships, combining the "Only" and "Preferred" categories. As you can see, applicants from APA-accredited Clinical, and, to a lesser extent, Counseling, programs are the most desired applicants. Within this category, Stedman et al. (1990, p. 36) suggested that internships prefer candidates from traditional Clinical and, to a somewhat lesser extent, Counseling programs. The few settings that do not welcome such candidates tend to be school-based internships, which, naturally, prefer candidates from APA-accredited School Psychology programs. Although applicants from non-accredited Clinical programs are deemed Acceptable by half the internships, those from School Psychology programs and non-accredited Counseling programs are not generally welcomed. As

Table 5-1. Programs from which applicants are welcomed by APPIC internships

	APA Accredited			Not APA Accredited		
	Clinical	Counseling	School	Clinical	Counseling	School
Only	160 31%	131 26%	12 2%	2 0%	0 0%	0 0%
Preferred	316 62%	186 36%	41 8%	14 3%	7 1%	2 0%
Acceptable	32 6%	137 27%	72 14%	249 49%	195 38%	56 11%
Not Welcomed	5 1%	59 12%	388 76%	348 48%	311 61%	455 89%

you might suppose, it is generally the non-accredited internships that welcome applicants from non-accredited academic programs.

Pay close attention to this section when you are reviewing the *Directory*. Unless your individual credentials are outstanding, you are probably wasting your time applying to an internship that indicates in its listing that it does not welcome applicants from programs such as yours. If you are not enrolled in an APA-accredited Clinical or Counseling program, you have a smaller pool of potential places to which you can apply. This means you should do everything you can to build up your individual qualifications and credentials. Even if you are not in a Clinical program, you may be able to take clinical courses and practica that show you are capable of doing clinical work. Perhaps a year at an unaccredited clinical internship will prepare you for a second year at an accredited facility. In short, you will probably have to work harder and do more to demonstrate to the selection committees that you are as good or better than the applicants from the preferred programs. You will also probably have to submit more applications and include a greater proportion of less competitive internships on your list.

If you are fortunate enough to be enrolled in a preferred program, don't think you can rest on your laurels. Remember that most of the applicants who were not placed on UND were from APA-accredited Clinical programs.

The *Directory* may not appear very user-friendly, especially when you encounter it for the first time. It is hard to assimilate all the different types of settings, rotations, and other information included. If you are just starting out, you may not have given much thought to the type of setting in which you want to do your internship. To get you started, I have compiled some basic information about the characteristics of the various kinds of internship agencies listed.

There are about a dozen different types of settings listed in the *Directory*, and they differ in a number of ways. Figure 5-1, illustrates their relative frequency, and Table 5-1 indicates the types of applicants each setting prefers. The best sources of information about these different types of internships is, of course, their individual listings in the *Directory* and the brochures they prepare. However, I will provide some descriptive comments to help you decide which settings interest you.

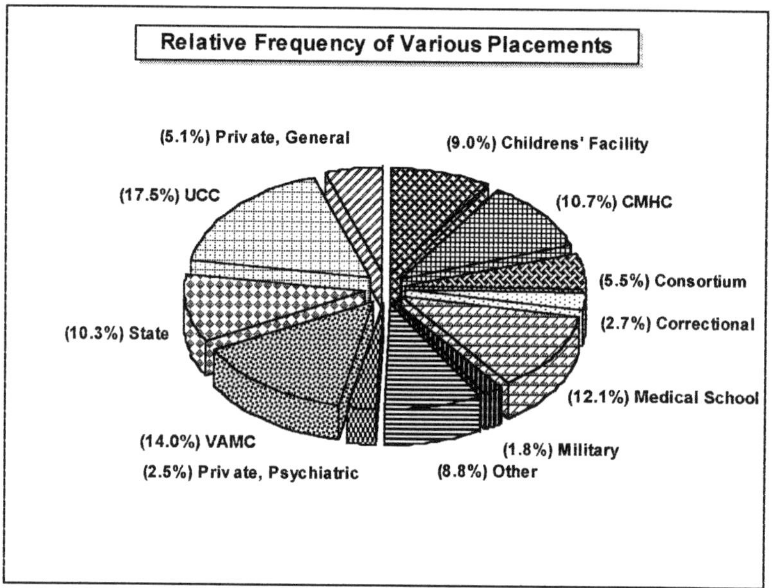

Figure 5-1. Relative frequency of different internship settings.

Children's facilities. Children's hospitals and other child-oriented internships are, naturally, most attractive to students in child-clinical training programs. Clients, naturally, tend to be children, adolescents, and their families. They include children with medical as well as mental health problems, and young people with acting out and conduct disorders, substance abuse problems, and neurological disorders. Most include both inpatient and outpatient psychiatric services. Compared with other settings, there is less opportunity to work with adults.

There were 46 children's' facilities listed in the 1996-1997 *Directory*, 37 (80%) of which were APA-accredited. They reported having 176 funded full-time positions, seven funded part-time positions, and 11 unfunded slots. The number of hours of practicum experience they required ranged from 300 hours to 1,500 hours with a mean of 699. Their stipends ranged from $7,400 to $20,300 with a mean of $13,900. As can be seen from Table 5-2, children's facilities were the most eclectic with regard to the applicants welcomed. Students from APA-accredited School and Counseling Psychology programs as well as Clinical programs were acceptable, and some settings indicated they also accepted applicants from non-accredited training programs. On the average, children's facilities reported receiving 58 applications each, and the mean number of applications per funded slot was 14.6.

Community mental health centers. Comprehensive community mental health centers ("CMHCs") deal with clients of all ages. Naturally there is an emphasis on outpatient treatment, although some CMHCs also treat inpatients at short-term, county-run, acute mental health units and in alcohol and drug abuse rehabilitation programs. Short-term interventions, both individual and group, may be emphasized. Behavioral medicine and neuropsychological rotations are rare.

There were 55 CMHCs, 41 (75%) of which were accredited, listed in the 1996-1997 *Directory*. They had 224 funded full-time and 16 part-time positions, as well as three unfunded slots. They required anywhere from 200 hours to 1,500 hours of practicum experience with a mean of 750 hours. Stipends ranged from $8,000 to $26,300 with a mean of $15,000. Virtually all welcomed applicants from APA-accredited Clinical and Counseling programs, and applicants from non-accredited Clinical, and, to a lesser extent, Counseling programs were generally acceptable; 26% welcomed candidates from accredited School Psychology programs, but only

Table 5-2. Agencies' expressed preferences for applicants from six types of academic programs

Internship Setting	Preference	CLINICAL APA-Accredited Yes	CLINICAL APA-Accredited No	COUNSELING APA-Accredited Yes	COUNSELING APA-Accredited No	SCHOOL APA-Accredited Yes	SCHOOL APA-Accredited No
Children's Facility	"Only" or "Prefer"	98%	2%	37%	0%	41%	0%
	"Acceptable"	0%	54%	48%	33%	37%	26%
	"Not Acceptable"	2%	43%	15%	67%	22%	74%
Community Mental Health Centers	"Only" or "Prefer"	96%	2%	59%	0%	11%	0%
	"Acceptable"	4%	61%	31%	48%	15%	13%
	"Not Acceptable"	0%	37%	7%	52%	74%	87%
Consortium	"Only" or "Prefer"	82%	0%	61%	0%	11%	0%
	"Acceptable"	14%	46%	29%	36%	18%	18%
	"Not Acceptable"	4%	54%	11%	64%	71%	82%
Correctional	"Only" or "Prefer"	100%	14%	93%	7%	7%	7%
	"Acceptable"	0%	57%	0%	50%	0%	0%
	"Not Acceptable"	0%	29%	7%	43%	93%	93%
Medical School	"Only" or "Prefer"	100%	0%	29%	0%	5%	0%
	"Acceptable"	0%	27%	32%	11%	19%	5%
	"Not Acceptable"	0%	73%	39%	89%	76%	95%
Military	"Only" or "Prefer"	100%	0%	100%	0%	0%	0%
	"Acceptable"	0%	33%	0%	33%	0%	0%
	"Not Acceptable"	0%	67%	0%	67%	100%	100%
Private, General	"Only" or "Prefer"	96%	12%	27%	4%	15%	0%
	"Acceptable"	4%	65%	58%	42%	23%	27%
	"Not Acceptable"	0%	23%	15%	54%	62%	73%
Private Psychiatric	"Only" or "Prefer"	92%	0%	46%	0%	8%	0%
	"Acceptable"	8%	62%	46%	38%	8%	0%
	"Not Acceptable"	0%	38%	8%	62%	85%	100%
State	"Only" or "Prefer"	98%	6%	57%	0%	9%	0%
	"Acceptable"	0%	57%	32%	38%	15%	8%
	"Not Acceptable"	2%	38%	11%	62%	75%	92%
University Counseling	"Only" or "Prefer"	88%	3%	97%	4%	0%	0%
	"Acceptable"	12%	71%	2%	72%	2%	2%
	"Not Acceptable"	0%	26%	1%	23%	98%	98%
VAMC	"Only" or "Prefer"	100%	0%	97%	0%	0%	0%
	"Acceptable"	0%	0%	1%	0%	0%	0%
	"Not Acceptable"	0%	100%	1%	100%	100%	100%

13% found non-accredited School applicants acceptable. The number of applications averaged 64 per agency, with a mean of 14.6 per slot.

Consortiums. Consortiums are groups of mental health facilities that band together to create a joint internship training program. The exact nature of the rotations available depends on the nature of the facilities in the consortium, but typically both inpatient and outpatient mental health settings are included. One advantage of a consortium is that it may be able to provide a broader range of clients and settings than any single mental health facility can. In some, "rotations" consist of spending a day or two each week in two or three different settings; in others, interns may spend four to six consecutive months in a single setting and then rotate to a different facility. If the facilities are in different locales, as often is the case, interns may not have much opportunity to interact with one another. Typically one afternoon a week interns gather at a central location for training meetings, case conferences, and didactic training experiences.

The 1996-1997 *Directory* listed 28 consortiums, 21 (75%) of which were accredited. They had 209 full-time and three part-time funded positions, as well as 11 that were unfunded. Practicum experience required ranged from 400 hours to 1,500 hours with a mean of 816 hours. Stipends ranged from $7,500 to $22,100 with a mean of $14,600. There was a clear preference for applicants from accredited Clinical and Counseling programs, and 29% also welcomed candidates from accredited School programs. Candidates from non-accredited programs were generally not welcomed. The mean number of applications was 92 per internship, and there was an average of 12.2 applications per vacancy.

Correctional. There were 14 internships at correctional agencies, many of which were at institutions run by the federal Bureau of Prisons; nine (64%) were accredited. Altogether they had 47 funded full-time positions as well as two that were unfunded. As a general rule, the range of clients seen in a prison setting is more limited than at most internships; the clientele is generally limited to adults, and typically only one gender is represented at any given institution. However, within these limits, prison populations can be surprisingly heterogeneous. A correctional facility is a good setting for someone interested in forensic psychology, and, in recent years, substance abuse programs have been increasingly prominent. Unlike many other settings, correctional institutions are not fee-driven, so interns may be able to administer a broader array of assessment techniques or consider longer-term as well as short-term interventions.

The number of practicum hours expected by the correctional agencies listed in the *Directory* ranged from 400 hours to 1,000 hours with a mean of 705 hours. Stipends were higher than in most settings, ranging from $13,500 to $24,900 with a mean of $20,300, and good fringe benefits are common. Applicants must undergo a background and security check. As can be seen from Table 5-2, applicants from APA-accredited Clinical and Counseling programs were definitely preferred, although half the facilities accepted applicants from non-accredited Clinical or Counseling programs. School psychology applicants are almost never sought. The mean number of applications received was 37, and there was a mean of 11.0 applications per vacancy.

Medical schools. Medical schools are one of the most popular internships. They typically afford trainees a wide variety of experiences and clients, and there is often more emphasis on research than is found in most settings. Obviously such "medical" specialties as behavioral medicine and neuropsychological assessment are more likely to be found in these internships. The work load and the pace in medical schools are apt to be higher than at most settings, and there may be turf wars with psychiatry and other medical specialties.

The *Directory* listed 62 internships based in medical schools, 60 (97%) of which were APA-accredited. They reported having 392 full-time and three part-time funded positions, and one unfunded slot. Practicum experience expected ranged from 400 hours to 1,500 hours with a mean of 892 hours. Stipends ranged from $11,000 to $18,000 with a mean of $14,700. There was a clear preference for candidates from APA-accredited Clinical training programs, some tolerance for those from APA-accredited Counseling programs, and little or no interest in School Psychology candidates or students from non-accredited training programs. There was a mean of 100 applications received per internship and 17.3 applications per slot.

Military internships. The nine military internships, all of which were accredited, are unique in many respects. Applicants who are accepted are commissioned as officers and are expected to serve on active duty for three years after completion of the internship. To be considered, they must be U.S. citizens, 18 to 33 years old, and able to pass a rigorous pre-induction physical examination. Since interns go directly from the internship to active duty, their dissertations should be completed by the time they finish their internships. As military officers, they receive much higher pay and allowances than any other group of interns. However, like any other service personnel on active duty, they go where they are sent and do what they are ordered to do. If they choose to continue in the military after their payback period, there are good opportunities for travel and for early retirement. The clients served by military interns are service men and women and their families, typically at military hospitals, so there is opportunity to work with a wide variety of cases in the younger age ranges in both inpatient and outpatient settings.

The nine military internships had 49 funded full-time slots. The practicum hours required ranged from 400 hours to 500 hours with a mean of 480 hours. The stipends are by far the highest of any type of internship, ranging from $35,500 to $40,000 with a mean of $38,400; 20% to 25% of the salary is considered a housing allotment and is therefore tax exempt, and there are generous fringe benefits. All nine settings indicated they were only interested in candidates from APA-accredited Clinical or Counseling programs, although three stated they would also consider applicants from non-accredited Clinical or Counseling programs. None were interested in School Psychology applicants. The mean number of applications received by the military internships was 52, and there was an average of 9.5 applications per slot.

Private general hospitals. Private general hospitals treat a full range of medical problems, in contrast to private psychiatric hospitals, which are strictly mental health facilities. Interns can be involved in medical psychology and behavioral medicine as well as traditional mental health services with both inpatients and outpatients and their families. Most have inpatient psychiatric units geared toward short-term hospitalizations.

There were 26 private general hospitals listed, 13 (50%) of which were APA-accredited, an accreditation rate considerably lower than other settings. They reported 87 full-time and 12 part-time funded positions as well as six full-time and one part-time unfunded slot. The practicum hours expected ranged from 500 hours to 2,000 hours with a mean of 929 hours. Stipends ranged from $3,600 to $17,200 with a mean of $12,700, the lowest of any setting category. Perhaps because of the relatively high rate of unaccredited facilities, these internships are less restrictive with regard to the applicants they will consider. As usual, APA-accredited Clinical and Counseling students were preferred; and 77% accepted students from non-accredited Clinical programs, and 46% would take students from non-accredited Counseling programs. About a third also considered students from School programs, whether or not they were accredited. The mean number of applications these facilities reported receiving was 63, and the mean number of applications per slot was 16.6.

Private psychiatric hospitals. Private psychiatric hospitals are primarily mental health facilities treating both inpatients and outpatients for various mental disorders and substance abuse problems. Interns are more likely to see seriously mentally ill patients in these hospitals than in general hospitals or community settings. Patient fees and third-party payments are typically significant sources of revenue.

The 1996-1997 *Directory* listed 13 private psychiatric hospitals, ten (77%) of which were accredited. They reported having 49 funded full-time positions and 11 unfunded full-time positions. They required applicants to have completed 500 hours to 1,000 hours of practicum with a mean of 667 hours. Stipends ranged from $12,000 to $18,800, with a mean of $13,500. They had a clear preference for students from APA-accredited Clinical and Counseling Psychology programs; 62% would also accept students from non-accredited Clinical programs, but there was little interest in students from non-accredited Counseling programs or any sort of School program. The mean number of applications received was 66 per setting, and the mean number of applications per slot was 17.6.

State hospitals. In contrast to private psychiatric hospitals, state facilities get more patients from the lower end of the socio-economic spectrum, including long-term, chronically mentally ill patients, a number of whom are involuntarily committed because they are considered a threat to themselves or others, and individuals with problems relating to substance abuse. Many state hospitals also treat cases in which the state has an interest, such as clients referred by the courts for competency and legal sanity evaluations, people remanded for treatment under mentally disordered sex offender acts, and, in some states, mentally ill state prisoners. Although some children and adolescents are evaluated or treated, most of the clients are adult men and women, including geriatric cases with various forms of dementia.

There were 53 state facilities listed, 37 (70%) of which were accredited. They had 206 full-time and five part-time funded slots, as well as 11 unfunded full-time and one unfunded part-time position. The number of practicum hours expected ranged from 400 hours to 2,000 hours with a mean of 732 hours, and stipends ranged from $10,000 to $27,600 with a mean of $16,500. Like most of the internships, the state facilities preferred APA-accredited Clinical and

Counseling program students and would also accept non-accredited Clinical students. Non-accredited Counseling and all School candidates were generally not accepted. On the average, the state hospitals reported receiving 70 applications each with a mean of 17.7 applications for each funded slot.

University counseling centers. University counseling centers ("UCCs") are the single most numerous type of internship. (See Figure 5-1). Given the recent shortfall in the number of internship positions, some academic training programs are considering ways in which they can create internships for their students. It would be natural for them to look at their own Psychology Department Clinics, if they have them, and to their University Counseling Centers as starting points for such endeavors. If you are planning to apply to a UCC, you should investigate where the current interns are from to determine how open they are to "outside" applicants.

The main disadvantage of a UCC is the relatively limited range of clients seen compared with other settings. Most treat with outpatient adults and students who are not seriously disturbed. Seriously mentally ill cases are often sent home or referred to other agencies. Vocational and career-development counseling is a strong suit, but students interested in such areas as neuropsychology, forensic psychology, or behavioral medicine should probably look elsewhere, as should those who are interested in children or geriatric cases.

The *Directory* listed 90 UCCs, 74 (82%) of which were accredited. They had 320 full-time and 16 half-time funded positions, as well as six unfunded slots. They expected applicants to have from 400 hours to 1,200 hours of practicum with a mean of 601 hours. Stipends ranged from $5,700 to $19,800 with a mean of $14,700. As one would expect, applicants from APA-accredited Counseling Psychology programs were most preferred, followed by those from Clinical programs; students from non-accredited Counseling and Clinical programs were also deemed acceptable by approximately 75% of the UCCs, but they were not interested in School students regardless of whether or not their programs were accredited. The mean number of applications received by the UCCs was 64 with a mean of 18.1 applications per site, making the UCCs the most competitive of these settings.

Veterans Administration medical centers. As we saw in Chapter One, the Veterans Administration took the lead in training clinical psychologists after World War II, and despite some shrinkage in recent years, the VA programs are still vigorous. Before women were admitted into the services in significant numbers, the VA clientele used to be almost exclusively male, but many more former female veterans are now being seen in VA facilities. As the World War II and Korean veterans have aged, the VA has begun setting aside some trainee positions for students interested in geropsychology in order to develop a cadre of clinical psychologists who are prepared to deal with elderly veterans. One can also work with children and their parents in the VA, but the "children" may be in their 50s and the parents in their 70s; young children are scarcer. As in the medical schools, the comprehensive VAMCs afford opportunities to practice medical psychology and behavioral medicine and deal with neuropsychological disorders. The VA operates outpatient as well as inpatient treatment facilities. Although historically the VA tried to treat veterans regardless of cost considerations, it is now undergoing a massive reorganization that will shift much patient care from an inpatient to an outpatient system and that will introduce MHC cost-containment measures such as capping the annual costs for certain types of cases (LaGana, 1997).

There were 72 Veterans Administration internship centers listed in the 1996-1997 APPIC *Directory*, 67 (93%) of which were APA accredited. They had 342 funded full-time positions and expected applicants to have completed from 500 hours to 1,200 hours with a mean of 925 hours. The stipends ranged from $17,000 to $18,300 with a mean of $17,025. Only students who are U.S. citizens and who are enrolled in APA-accredited Clinical or Counseling Psychology programs are eligible. The average VAMC received 76 applications, and the mean number of applications per position was 15.9

Regional differences

A glib explanation for the recent shortfalls has been that students are applying to the "wrong places," concentrating on the large metropolitan areas on the two coasts and neglecting facilities in the middle of the country (Clay, 1997). To investigate this hypothesis, I aggregated the *Directory* listings for each state, calculating the total number of internship training centers, both accredited and non-accredited, the number of funded full- and part-time positions, the mean stipends, and the mean number of applications per position available. Based on these data, I have divided the country up into six regions, based partly on geographical contiguity and partly on the mean number of applications per position. The data for the states in each region are reported in Appendix 2. The overall findings will be summarized here.

Region 1: East Coast, Northern Section. Proceeding from North to South, this region consists of the states of Maine, New Hampshire, Vermont, Massachusetts, Rhode Island, Connecticut, New York, New Jersey, Pennsylvania, and Delaware. With the exception of Vermont, all are on the Atlantic, and with the exception of Vermont and New Hampshire, all are highly competitive. This region has 137 internship centers, 83% of which are accredited, with 676 funded positions, making it the largest of my six regions. The mean stipends of the states in Region 1 range from $13,775 to $16,919, with an overall mean of $15,349. Except for Vermont and New Hampshire, which average 3.5 and 13.6 applications per position, the states in Region 1 have from 15.6 to 19.8 applications per slot with an overall mean of 15.8. Put another way, this region has 29.2% of the slots in the United States, but it receives 32.9% of the applications.

Region 2: East Coast, Southern Section. The Southern Section of the East Coast is the most competitive in the country based on its average application-to-slot ratios. The region includes Maryland, the District of Columbia, Virginia, North Carolina, South Carolina, and Georgia, but not Florida. This region has 54 internship settings, 51 (94%) of which are APA-accredited, with 247 funded positions. Region 2 has the nation's highest proportion of accredited internships and also the nation's highest mean stipends, ranging from $15,333 to $21,002 with a regional mean of $18,306. (This can be attributed in part to the large number of highly paid military internships in this region.) The mean number of applications per position in these six states ranged from 15.5 to 20.3, with an overall mean of 17.9 applications per position.

Region 3: Eastern Central. From North to South, this region includes Michigan, Ohio, West Virginia, Tennessee, Alabama, Mississippi, and Florida. These seven states are all less competitive than those on the East Coast and those in the North Central region. They have 85 internships, 57 (67%) of which are APA-accredited, with 379 positions. Stipends in this region range from $12,837 to $17,000 with a mean of $15,312. The average number of applications per slot for the states in this region are almost all lower than those in Regions 1 and 2, ranging from 7.8 to 13.6 applications per slot with an overall regional mean of 11.4. Although Region 3 had 16% of the positions available in the US, it received only 12% of the applications.

Region 4, Northern Central. This region consists of five states: Minnesota, Wisconsin, Illinois, Indiana, and Kentucky. These states share a higher application-to-position ratio than those that surround them. They have 75 internships, 54 (72%) of which are APA-accredited, and 290 positions. Stipends range from $14,711 to $18,696 with a mean of $15,653. The mean number of applications per position for the states in Region 4 range from 16.1 to 19.0 with an overall mean of 17.3 applications per position.

Region 5, Western Central. From North to South, this region includes nine states lying between the Mississippi River and the Rocky Mountains: South Dakota, Nebraska, Iowa, Kansas, Missouri, Oklahoma, Arkansas, Texas, and Louisiana. (North Dakota has no APPIC members.) Like the Eastern Central states, these are among the less competitive sites for internships. Region 5 has 61 internship centers, 52 85%) of which (are APA-accredited, and 294 positions. Stipends range from $14,075 to $21,300 with a mean of $16,813. The mean number of applications per position in Region 5 range from 5.0 to 13.5 with an overall mean of 11.4. Although they have 12.7% of the nation's internship positions, they receive only 9.4% of the applications.

Region 6: West Coast and Mountain. This region, which is the largest in area, includes the states of Washington, Montana, Oregon, Wyoming, California, Nevada, Utah, Colorado, Arizona, and New Mexico plus Hawaii. (Idaho and Alaska have no APPIC members.) Altogether these 11 states have 101 internship centers, 70 (70%) of which are APA-accredited, with a total of 427 positions. Stipends range from $13,799 to $17,000 with a mean of $15,247. Except for Hawaii (11.5) and Utah (12.0), the states in this region have relatively high application to slot ratios ranging from 15.7 to 22.9, with an overall mean of 17.0.

Other Sources of Information

The APPIC *Directory* is not the only source of internship information. The Society for a Science of Clinical Psychology, which is Section 3 of the APA's Division 12, issues a *Directory of Research Opportunities for Clinical Psychology Interns* (Blanchard, 1994) that is distributed to all ADCTs. In addition to informing you about research opportunities, it discusses the degree to which internships use various empirically validated treatments, the typical post-internship positions taken by previous interns, and other salient information. Other directories compiled by professional organizations provide listings of internships that provide training in behavioral techniques, health psychology, behavioral medicine, and clinical neuropsychology. An up-to-date list of the latest editions of these guides, along with information on how they can be obtained, including postal and e-mail addresses, can be found in Appendix B in the back of the annual APPIC *Directory*. In addition, the "Position Openings" section of the monthly APA *Monitor* lists some predoctoral internships.

Your faculty is another good source of information about internships, although some of their knowledge may be dated. Discuss programs with faculty members who interned at places that interest you or who share your particular clinical interests. In the course of these discussions, you may discover that certain faculty members are personally acquainted with members of the training staff at one or more of the institutions that interest you. If you decide to apply there, it may help to ask these faculty members to send reference letters or call their friends on your behalf. Recommendations from friends and people with whom we are personally acquainted always carry greater weight than those from strangers.

Most graduate programs have a staff member who keeps track of students and former students. This individual can probably provide you with addresses of students from your school who have recently gone on predoctoral internships. This information helps you in two ways. First, you can analyze the acceptance and attendance patterns at your school and find out which internships prefer your school's applicants. If your colleagues have consistently gone to certain training centers and done well, their achievements should enhance your chances of being accepted at those placements. As a general rule, applicants from my program have always had a much higher rate of success applying to internships that have had previous students from our university than they have applying to settings where we are relatively unknown. Second, you can use this list to contact previous students directly and get their opinions about the internships they attended.

Assembling Your Initial List

As you know, Maslow's motivational hierarchy distinguishes survival needs from those that are centered on fulfillment or self-actualization. You need to consider both in compiling a list of places to which you might apply. In setting forth your personal priorities in Chapter Four, you were probably thinking in terms of self-actualization. You probably tried to describe internships that would enable you to develop to your fullest in a congenial setting. That is good, but you also have to consider the survival aspects, because you won't get fulfilled if you don't get admitted.

Experienced photographers calculate the optimal camera settings to ensure a perfect photograph; they take most of their pictures using that combination, but to be on the safe side, they customarily make some additional exposures above and below that setting. In applying for internships, you need to do likewise. Most of the programs you apply to should be ones that appear to be "just right" for a person with your needs, skills, and abilities. But you should also add some that are more competitive in case you have underestimated your marketability, and others that appear easier to get into in the event that the competition is tougher than you expected. You should investigate enough so that, by the time you have finished interviewing and have discarded those that you did not like or where you got little encouragement, you have a list of about 12 places with two that you think may be out of reach, seven that are just right, and three in your safety net.

Making these sorts of estimates involves two sets of calculations. The first is assessing how difficult it is to get accepted into a given program. The second is estimating how strong a candidate you are.

Assessing the programs. How do you determine competitiveness? Unlike college admissions, there are no published guides to internships rating the difficulty of securing admission. However, there are data available that permit you to make some educated estimates. The information provided in the APPIC *Directory* and in this chapter should help you assess competitiveness in terms of the number of applications received for each slot.

Other things being equal, programs where students from your school have done well in the past, and where you or your faculty mentors have strong ties, are more likely to be favorably disposed toward your application. The reverse is also true. If you decide to apply to places where no one from your program has preceded you, you may find it more difficult to get accepted. To compensate, you might need to submit more applications and apply to more places that appear less competitive. If it is also impossible for you to visit these places personally, so that you will have to rely on telephone interviews, your task will be even more difficult. All of the things that enhance and detract from the strength of your application at various places must be considered when you are formulating your list.

Some programs attract more applications than others. Typically more applicants are interested in working with children than with geriatric patients. If you are interested in geropsychology, consider the VA and other settings that have specific gerospychology slots. If you have special skills, such as fluency in Spanish, consider internships located in cities or states with a large Hispanic population where your language skills will be an asset. In other words, do your homework and locate the internships where your particular combination of skills, training, and contacts give you an edge.

Assessing your chances. One of the frustrating aspects of evaluating the competitiveness of the internship selection process has been that, although the number of positions and the number of applications is reported each year, there is no way of ascertaining how many actual *applicants* there are until after UND. However, you can use the information provided thus far to help you evaluate your chances.

For each program you are interested in, pay close attention to the preferences listed in the *Directory.* You have an edge at internships that rate programs such as yours "O" (Only) or "P" (Preferred). Internships that are academically oriented and that pride themselves on their research will usually favor Ph.D. candidates from traditional university departments. Psy.D. candidates, especially those from free-standing professional schools, should do better at internships that are more practitioner oriented. You should also assess the match between your theoretical orientation and that of the internships you are considering. The two need not be perfectly congruent, but the greater the disparity, the more open you should be to points of view that differ from your own.

If you plan to apply for a specialized program or position, such as neuro-psychological assessment or pediatric psychology, you need to evaluate your chances of being selected for such positions. If you have little or no background in that particular field, you will be at a disadvantage in competing for such positions. Submit some applications for generalized training programs for which you are better qualified as well.

A number of surveys have analyzed the characteristics of successful and unsuccessful internship applicants. The one factor that has consistently emerged is that the more successful applicants were those who did what was necessary to obtain an internship. They were the ones who were willing to consider internships in a variety of locales, who spent the extra time and trouble to individualize their applications, and who studied the characteristics of the internships to which they applied so they could discuss them intelligently with the selection staff. They were also, of course, those who were best prepared for internship.

Consider the Gainesville Conference and its prototype of the ideal intern: a student who has had considerably more clinical experience than the APA minimum and who is on the verge of completing or has already completed his or her dissertation. The closer you match this template, the better your chances. Conversely, the farther you are from finishing your degree and the less supervised clinical experience you have, the more difficult it will be to find a placement.

Investigating Possible Programs

After you complete your reconnaissance, you should have an initial list of about 20 to 30 internships that interest you, ranging from some that are quite competitive to others where you feel reasonably sure you can gain admittance. These internships should all be ones that you think you might like to attend, but at this stage you know too little about them to be sure. Your next task is to investigate them more closely so you can select about a dozen to which you will submit actual applications.

Each Fall, your ADCT or professional training office receives numerous brochures from facilities around the country. These are generally mailed after the August APPIC meeting at APA. If a file of these brochures is available, consult it. If not, you and your fellow applicants should volunteer to create such a file. Meanwhile, write to the programs for information and application forms. It is best to wait until late August or September to write to make sure you get the most recent brochure; any earlier and you may get a packet left over from the previous year.

When you write to an internship program, whether you are asking for information or actually applying, it is essential you include *all* the information on the address you obtained from the APPIC *Directory*. Many students send their inquiries or applications to the training center without indicating the person or the program for whom it is intended. With thousands of patients and hundreds of staff members from dozens of disciplines passing through a major training center in the course of a year, hospital mail rooms have little time or inclination to deduce whom you wanted to contact. A common mistake is for applicants to write to the "Internship Program." As Belar and Orgel (1980, p. 672) pointed out, a major consortium may have a number of internship programs in a dozen different disciplines scattered over several hospitals.

As with other aspects of the application process, writing for brochures is easier if you have a support group to divide up the work. When you get the brochures and materials, stamp the date on them. Then try to ascertain when they were published. Be wary of brochures that do not have the current year printed on them. Some programs leave their materials undated so they can use the same brochure year after year. If so, some of the information, such as staff rosters, may be out of date.

Remember that the purpose of the brochure, like any other piece of advertising, is to sell you on the internship so you will apply there. Without a pool of applicants, an internship will go out of business. Every year I was surprised when a large number of students expressed enthusiasm for some program that previous classes had disregarded. When I checked the files I often found that the program in question had just issued a slick new brochure. Be wary about judging a program on the basis of its circulars. As Grace (1985, p. 475) gloomily noted, "The prospective intern should not accept on faith that the internship will meet his or her needs or even that it is primarily designed to do so. Nor should one assume that all information in written and verbal descriptions is accurate. Programs change and misrepresentation is not unheard of." Grace's warning takes on added weight by virtue of the fact that he himself was an Internship Training Director when he wrote his article.

Once you have received your materials, it is time to narrow your list and investigate the most appealing programs in greater depth. Discuss them with faculty and supervisors, especially those who may have interned or visited the site in which you are interested. When possible, talk with fellow students or recent alumni who may have interned there recently.

After doing all your homework, you may have some specific questions that will be critical to your application decision. Perhaps you really want a neuropsychological rotation, but it is not clear from the brochure whether one will be available this year. Or you may be attracted by the opportunity to work with the famous "Dr. Tibia Femur," but you have heard a rumor that Tibia is leaving the "Brachial Center" and moving to "Humerus Hospital." By all means call the ITD, or ask your ADCT to do so, to check out this information before going to the trouble of applying. Current interns can be an invaluable source of information. Ask for their names and give some a call. When you complete this information-gathering you should have narrowed your list down to about 12 to 15 possible programs.

Some universities require that you get clearance from your ADCT or from the clinical faculty before you may submit any applications. Others may have rules about where you may apply; for example, one university-based program reduces inter-student competition by having each student select one first choice and forbidding other students from applying there. Whatever the ground rules, make sure you get your list approved and verify that you have your program's permission to apply to the internships you have selected.

Once you have been cleared to apply and your list has been approved, you are ready to begin the application process. Take your list of sites, *with complete addresses*, to the Registrar's office and arrange for transcripts to be sent. This is a very low priority item with most Registrars, and it can take them forever to mail out your transcripts; therefore, get them ordered as soon as possible. Some applicants worry that the transcript may get lost if it arrives before the formal application; others fret that they may change their minds and not apply. Relax; this is the least of your worries. Internship selection committees are well aware that some materials arrive before a formal application is received, and they have drawers labeled "Incomplete Folders" set aside for that purpose. If you later decide not to apply so the rest of your materials never arrive, they are also skilled at emptying the "Incomplete Folders" drawer into the recycling bin after Notification Day.

After you have ordered your transcripts and paid whatever fee is required, it is time to prepare your resume or Curriculum Vitae. This process is described in detail in Chapter Six. And, of course, you will need to prepare your applications. This is discussed in Chapter Seven.

CHAPTER SIX

PREPARING A RESUME OR CURRICULUM VITAE

The purpose of this chapter is to help you write a successful resume for applying for internship. I use the term "resume" deliberately, because even though you will probably call your resume a "Curriculum Vitae" ("CV" or "Vitae" for short), the document you will prepare for applying to internship will differ in certain respects from an academic CV.

Your academic CV will focus almost exclusively on scholarship (i.e., your educational history, editorial appointments, professional memberships, and publications), whereas the resume you prepare for internship applications should also include a detailed account of your clinical and professional training, experience, and skills. In addition to listing your various jobs, it should contain a brief description of your duties, the types of patients you saw, the nature and extent of the supervision you received, and your competence with various psychometric instruments, items that would be inappropriate in an academic CV. With the understanding that I am not referring to an academic CV, I will use the terms "CV" and "resume" interchangeably in this chapter.

The purpose of your CV or resume is to present a complete and accurate account of all your qualifications in an attractive format that will help you compete successfully with other applicants. This is not the time to be modest. Include *all* your credentials and relevant experiences. When I was an ADCT, I interviewed all our internship applicants and went over their CVs with them. Every one had omitted some salient bit of information that would impress some ITDs. Among the most common omissions were professional workshops they may have attended (or even presented), undergraduate accomplishments such as graduating with honors, and special skills such as fluency in a foreign language.

While you should not be overly modest, you should not "pad" your CV by listing the same item several times, by including trivia, or by overstating your accomplishments or qualifications. For example, do not list your master's thesis under "education" and again under "publications," or claim expert status on the Rorschach based on five administrations.

Now that APPIC is developing a Uniform Application Form ("UAF"), most internships will probably require that you complete a formal printed application form as well as a CV. Since much of the information that is requested will overlap your CV, I suggest that you begin by assembling all the data you will need for both the resume and the application forms. Next, prepare the resume. Once that is completed, it may be possible for you to answer some of the questions you encounter on the application forms by referring the reader to your CV.

In preparing a CV, especially their first CV, many students get so overwhelmed by stylistic questions they tend to forget the more substantive ones. What font(s) should I use? Should I put my name in the middle or at the side, in regular type or boldface? Should I have it professionally printed? What color paper should I use?

I suggest that you divide the process into four steps and deal with them one at a time:

1. Gather together all the information you will need to complete the CV and the various application forms.

2. From the collected data, select the information you wish to include in your resume.

3. Decide the best way to organize the information you choose to include (i.e., the sequence of topics and what will be listed under each).

4. Present the information in a clear and attractive format. (This is when you decide the stylistic questions.)

Step One: Assembling the Information

Writing an initial resume is like filing your income tax...the biggest problem is amassing all the data you may need. In this section, I will provide you with a comprehensive list of all the information you should ever need for writing your CV and filling out application forms. First, obtain two forms. The first is the current UAF, which you can download from the APPIC Web site or obtain by writing the APPIC central office. (See Chapter Three for these addresses.) The second is "Standard Form 171," which you can obtain from any Post Office. This form is used in all applications for federal employment including VA internships. It will show you what details regarding education and previous employment you will need to have at hand when you fill out this and other application forms. Whether or not you apply to the VA, fill out your 171 and keep updating it every time you change jobs for the rest of your life. Even if you never apply for a federal position, it will serve as a useful repository of information for other applications. Eventually it will be of great assistance to your biographer.

Although I will concentrate on the information you need to assemble for internship applications, as long as you are going to all the trouble of gathering these data, it makes sense to collect and preserve other records you might need when applying for employment, licensing, or obtaining a National Register listing or Diplomate status at some future date. Information that seems unimportant now may be essential at some future date, but as the years go by and you move from place to place these data will become increasingly hard to obtain.

As you build up this data bank, don't worry about how to present or display material. That will come later. Just obtain and record the information in whatever manner you find most convenient. I suggest you use a system that will make it easy to add and subtract items such as a multi-pocket file folder or loose-leaf notebook. Most multi-purpose computer software packages include an information storage and retrieval system that will allow you to transfer the information to your word processing program. If you elect to store your data on a computer, make sure you back it up on a floppy disk and with hard copy. Make sure you preserve these data, whether computerized or not, in a place that is not only safe but also secure.

The list of information that I will propose is designed to be as comprehensive as possible; there will be many items included that you will not choose to put in your CV. Nevertheless it will be helpful for you to have these data available. Since I am trying to think of everything that anyone might have, there will undoubtedly be many items that do not apply to most readers; do not let this give you a feeling of inferiority.

Personal information and identifying data

This information is designed to tell the person who reads your resume who you are and where you can be found. Although you have considerable discretion about how much personal information you wish to disclose, and equal employment opportunity laws place severe restrictions on the information employers can require, for the purpose of assembling a data base I have listed everything you may want or need to include.

Name(s). List your complete legal name, including any suffixes such as "Jr." or "III"; any other or former names, especially if you have used them professionally; and any name changes you anticipate between now and Notification Day.

Addresses. Record your home and work addresses as well as the address of your academic training program and the address of someone who will always know how to locate you. Note any anticipated address changes. (Although it is not necessary for internship applications, for some purposes, such as high level security clearances, you may some day need to provide a complete list of the exact street addresses of all the places you have ever lived.)

Communication numbers. List all your phone and fax numbers and e-mail addresses, the days and times when you can be reached at each, as well as any special information that would be helpful in reaching you, such as "ring 12 times to activate the answering machine."

Social and demographic information. Include your date and place of birth, Social Security number, marital status, names and birth dates of children and other dependents, your ethnic, racial, or minority status, and your gender if it is not obvious to American readers from your name. If you are not a U.S. citizen, record your citizenship, passport number, current visa status, and other relevant data, such as whether you are married to a U.S. citizen.

Military status. If you have served in the armed forces, record the branch of the service, your dates of service, medals and honors, discharge status, military serial number, service connected disabilities and/or Purple Heart, and if you are eligible for a Veteran's preference. This information may be especially important if you apply for a VA placement.

Legal status. List any arrests, convictions, probation, parole, or imprisonments and explanations of each, as well as any ethical charges or complaints that might have been filed with any licensing boards or professional associations. (See Federal Form 171 and the APPIC Professional Conduct Form).

Health. Include any conditions that might have an impact on your ability to perform the duties of your position (e.g., need for a wheelchair accessible workplace).

Education

By and large, for your CV you will only need to list your undergraduate and graduate education, noting the degrees and majors, but some applications call for lists of courses and dates, so you should get copies of your transcripts and have them available. The more general the application form, such as Form 171, the more likely it is to ask for things such as the number of semester hours or credits you had in your major or minor.

Would-be employers do not usually ask for GRE scores, but you should keep a record of them in case you apply for admission for further graduate education. In addition to the regular graduate program, you should keep a record of all the relevant continuing education courses or workshops you attend.

High school of GED. Make a record of schools you attended with addresses, dates attended, and so forth. You will not use this in your CV, but some applications may call for it.

Undergraduate education. List every institution attended, noting for each the name of the institution, its address, the dates you attended, your major and minor, any degree you received and the date, and any honors or awards (cum laude, Phi Beta Kappa, etc.). Note any scholarships, awards, achievements, memberships in organizations, extracurricular activities, service on university committees, student government, and volunteer activities. Instead of using initials, use the full name of organizations or clubs. If you received an award that is specific to that school (e.g., the "Phineas P. Phollansby Senior Trophy"), record what it is for; other readers won't know and after a couple of decades you will forget. If you completed an honors project, record the name of your major professor or advisor and the title of your honor's thesis.

Graduate education. For each program attended, list the same basic data as above. Have available a transcript for those applications that inquire about specific courses or numbers of hours. Also include the specific degree program (e.g., APA-approved Ph.D. program in Clinical Psychology); the title of your master's thesis, major area paper, and dissertation; the name of your major professor(s); your current status (e.g., completed major area paper, candidate for Ph.D.); the date your dissertation prospectus was or will be defended; and the date you anticipate completing your dissertation.

Note any major gaps in your chronology (i.e., periods when you were not enrolled in school or were unemployed) and be prepared to explain them (e.g., raising small children, in a coma, beach combing, in prison, and so on).

Other educational experiences

1. List professional workshops you have attended, including the person who presented, the date, place, and number of hours for each.

2. Technical or professional courses such as computer seminars.

3. Personal therapy or training analysis.

Special skills

Include knowledge or skills that might be useful in some internship settings.

1. List any foreign languages you know and your proficiency level in reading, writing, speaking, and understanding.

2. Special computer skills.

3. Ability to operate relevant equipment such as biofeedback apparatus.

4. First aid or CPR training.

5. American Sign Language for the hearing impaired.

Professional credentials

Include any relevant professional licenses or certificates. Include the state, the license number, and the date awarded.

Memberships in professional organizations

List the various professional organizations to which you now belong, or have belonged, with the dates of membership and the level of membership (i.e., student, associate, member, fellow). Include any committees on which you served and any offices you may have held, such as program chair or nominating committee. Again, do not use initials to identify organizations.

Honors and awards

List any honors and awards you may have received in college and elsewhere. Later you can decide what details to include. Also record exceptional high school awards such as Girl's State Governor or a Presidential Scholar award, as well as awards from civic or professional organizations (e.g., Lou Brock Leadership Award or APA outstanding first paper award). Don't forget any athletic trophies or honors you may have earned. If the nature of the honor or award is not obvious, note the name of the organization that presented it and why you received it. If there was a citation, record it verbatim.

Record election to honorary societies such as Sigma Xi, any degrees with honors, and any fellowships or grants. Note offices you have held, both elective and appointed, such as Graduate Student Member on Clinical Training Committee, President of Psi Chi. (When it comes to organizing your actual CV, you can decide whether to list the college awards such as Phi Beta Kappa separately or under "Education"; at this stage redundancy is acceptable.)

Previous employment

In a resume you give a complete employment history, whereas in a CV you typically list only professionally relevant experience. For your internship applications, you will probably strike a balance, including all the positions of a strictly psychological nature and also others that may be seen as tangentially related--such as a weight-loss counselor, sleep lab technician, or computer consultant--but omitting other jobs--like being a bartender--that you may have taken to get through school.

On an application form such as Form 171, however, you may have to list all the jobs you have ever had in chronological order, beginning with your current position and working backward. This usually includes part-time as well as full-time positions. Don't forget to include military service, especially if your military experience was psychological in nature. At this stage it is a good idea to gather together all the data you will need for both your CV and an application such as Form 171.

Preparing a complete employment history is always difficult, especially the first time you do it. Unfortunately, you generally need to submit one for a federal or state position. If you keep a copy and simply update it as you move from position to position, it is less difficult.

These forms are all similar to one another. Starting with your present position and working backward toward the dawn of time for *each and every* job you have ever held, list:

1. the name and address of your employer;
2. the dates you began and ended your employment;
3. the average number of hours worked per week;
4. your starting and ending salary;
5. the name and phone number of your immediate supervisor;
6. the nature of the business;
7. the exact title of your job, (e.g., "Clinical Psychologist III, Step 4");
8. a description of the work you performed;
9. your specific duties and the percent of time doing each; and
10. your reason for leaving.

The specific application forms you have to fill out may ask for other information, but, with one exception, all of it should be included in the material you have been gathering. The exception is a question asking whether you have ever been fired from any job or quit because you were about to be fired, in which case you then have to go on and supply all the gory details. It is always best to 'fess up and answer these items truthfully, as well as any questions about professional misconduct or criminal convictions. Then explain the circumstances. A positive answer does not necessarily bar you from employment, but signing a false application is a criminal offense and subjects you not only to dismissal but prosecution for fraud and misrepresentation.

Professional experience

On a CV, in contrast to an employment application, you only include those jobs that are relevant to the position for which you are applying, namely a psychology internship. When you get to organizing your CV, you may want to subdivide your experience into two or three categories such as research, clinical experience, and teaching. For each, you should provide enough detail to give the reader a clear understanding of the nature of your duties and the extent of your experience. For each position, you should indicate:

1. the title of the position;

2. the employer;

3. the dates you were employed;

4. the number of hours you worked per week;

5. your specific duties and responsibilities and the percent of time doing each;

6. the name of your supervisor and his or her title and credentials (e.g., "Barri Cuda, Ph.D., ABPP, Supervising Clinical Psychologist [Licensed West Idabama]"); and

7. the amount of supervision received weekly and whether it was individual or group.

In addition, for future reference, it would not hurt to note where each supervisor obtained his or her degree and the year. The nature of the information you include under "responsibilities" will differ according to whether you are discussing teaching, research, or clinical positions.

Teaching. In the case of teaching experience, you should indicate the name and number of the course, its subject matter (e.g., abnormal psychology), the type of course taught (e.g., large lecture), the number and the level of students (e.g., 150 to 200 undergraduates, mostly freshmen and sophomores), and what your role was. Did you have sole responsibility for the course or did you handle the sections and proctor the exams? Do this individually for each course.

Research. Indicate the nature of the research and your specific responsibilities (e.g., running subjects, analyzing data etc.). Be specific regarding how long you worked, who your supervisor was, the nature of the project, and your specific responsibilities. Cover the specific skills you needed and the techniques you used (e.g., administered SADs interviews to 100 college sophomores). List unpaid as well as paid research experience, and include undergraduate as well as graduate experience. Remember, you are preparing a *comprehensive* summary.

Clinical experience. APPIC's Uniform Application Form will probably become the "gold standard" for applications; you should obtain a copy as soon as possible, ideally, your first week in graduate school, so you can set up a procedure for systematically recording the information that will be required when you eventually have to complete it for internship. If you have not been keeping a detailed clinical log, you will have to reconstruct the information from transcripts, supervisory records, and other sources. Allow plenty of time, because this can get very complex.

Familiarize yourself with the definitions used in the UAF. Assuming the preliminary draft of the UAF that is available to me as I prepare this chapter is not changed substantially, you will see that you are expected to report how many "clock hours" (which may be only 50 minutes) you spend in various activities. Although estimating overall hours such as "20 hours/week X 50 weeks = 1,000 hours," is all right on a CV, this is not true on the UAF. You will also note that you are expected to indicate how many hours you spend in "direct" services, which are hours spent with a client; "indirect services," which are hours spent reviewing charts, reviewing tapes, and the like; and hours spent in "supervision." Moreover, my current understanding is that "practicum" hours will be defined as hours spent in supervised clinical activities for which you received course credit.

By the time you apply for internship, the UAF will no doubt have evolved beyond its present, draft form. However, it will be important for you to keep very detailed records so you can report your activities in the form required. You should record the number of hours spent in various activities and the nature of those activities so you can later aggregate them according to the type of client(s) seen (age, gender, diagnosis) and the nature of the intervention (e.g., one clock hour of videotaped cognitive behavioral therapy). You should also keep track of the time spent supporting the intervention (e.g., 90 minutes writing summary and reviewing tape) and the nature and amount of the supervision you received on the case (e.g., 30 minutes individual supervision with Mary Marjoram, Ph.D.). Later you can aggregate the data for your CV or application.

I suggest that you summarize these data on Lotus or Excel computer spreadsheets. This enables you to respond easily to questions asking how many clients of various sorts you have seen or how many tests of different types you have administered by sorting the data and computing summary statistics. With regard to assessment, the present draft of the UAF lists no less than 47 different psychological tests and asks you how many of each you have administered and scored and written reports on. Other application forms may ask about the clients to whom such tests were administered. For interventions, you may be asked to break down the number of clients by setting (e.g., your university's Psychology Clinic), age (children, adolescent, or adults), inpatient or outpatient status, and presenting problem or diagnosis (substance abuse, marital problems, ADHD, noncompliance with a treatment regimen, etc.). Then you indicate the nature and extent of your contact with the individuals in each category (e.g., intake, assessment battery, group therapy, individual therapy etc.). (Remember that an hour spent with a couple or a group is still only one clock hour.) One successful applicant prepared a summary table that reported her experience with three types of treatment--individual, group, and family. For each case she reported the client's age (age range for the group), presenting problems, treatment approach (e.g., behavior modification, cognitive behavioral, etc.), the number of sessions, and the frequency of supervision. I would suggest adding outcome.

In addition to these statistical summaries, you may simply be asked to indicate your level of expertise with various tests or techniques. In responding you have to walk a fine line between overstating and understating your abilities. People will look askance if you claim "expert" status on the Rorschach after scoring only five, or even 25. On the other hand, don't sell yourself short. There may be some instruments with which you have only a nodding acquaintance, perhaps based on a lecture or a couple of case presentations. It is all right to list "exposure to" these techniques, indicating some familiarity but not implying proficiency.

In addition to your formal practicum placements for which you received course credit, you should also record in similar detail other clinical experience for which you may not have received actual course credit. If you work 20 hours a week at some agency to help support yourself, you need to be able to document and report on the nature and extent of these activities as well. And don't forget any additional relevant experience you have accumulated in the course of volunteer work, participating in a telephone counseling service, or serving on a crisis management team. List these activities along with dates and salient details such as the types of clients seen, the numbers of hours you spent, and the nature of your duties.

Publications and presentations

This is the section that is the core of an academic CV. Most internships will be duly appreciative of your scholarly credentials, as long as they are convinced you can pull your weight clinically. As in previous sections, put everything you can think of into this inventory, then later pick and choose what you will include on your CV. List all items according to the style in the current APA *Publication Manual.* In this section include:

1. Articles in refereed journals, including articles already published, those "in press," those being revised for resubmission, and those under review.

2. Papers presented at scholarly meetings, posters, symposium contributions, etc. in which there is a review for quality. Include those presentations already made and those that are under review.

3. Chapters or contributions to books or monographs that have been published or accepted for publication.

4. Reviews, notes, and comments such as published book reviews and published letters to the APA *Monitor* or the newsletters of learned societies, etc.

5. Unpublished writings, such as your thesis, dissertation, or major area paper, technical reports prepared for granting agencies, as well as training manuals or other internal documents published by your department or employer.

6. Unrefereed presentations, such as colloquia presented to groups of scholars (other than classroom presentations), workshops, staff training presentations at your workplace, creative writing, and film, TV, or other media presentations.

Other evidence of scholarly activity

In addition to publications and presentations, you should also keep a record of any other scholarly activities in which you have engaged. (These are in addition to the research positions you have held that are included above.) You should record:

1. Editorial activities, such as reviewing submissions for a journal or a scholarly meeting, or editing or being on the editorial board of a publication such as a journal, a newsletter, etc.

2. Grants applied for or received. Include intramural and local grants such as dissertation awards as well as extramural funding.

3. Consulting activities of a scholarly nature.

4. A summary of current research and plans for future research.

5. Anything else of a scholarly nature you can think of, such as writing software programs.

Miscellaneous

Note any accomplishments or activities not included above that might enhance your resume or help the reader get to know you. Include recreational activities, sports or hobbies, civic service, and non-professional honors, awards, or recognitions such as getting a ribbon in an art show, being elected to office in a civic organization, or winning a footrace.

Basic boilerplate

In addition to the data that will form the raw material for your CV and for your applications, there are certain standard questions you are likely to be asked or statements you may wish to include in your cover letter. It may be helpful to prepare them in advance, or at least list the points you will wish to make when these items come up. We will discuss this further in the next chapter.

Step Two: Selecting What to Include

Having assembled all the material you can possibly use, plus a lot more, you can select what information you wish to present in your resume. Since your CV is your creation, there are no formal or explicit rules about what you may and may not include. However, there is a large body of custom, and people will generally look askance at those who deviate from the generally agreed upon format.

One way to steer between the Scylla of appearing to overstate your qualifications or pad your CV with trivial items and the Charybdis of omitting potentially helpful information is to label items clearly. For example, whereas it is not appropriate to include unrefereed items like grant reports or training manuals under "Publications," you can include them as "Technical reports (unrefereed)" or "Training manuals." That way they get on the record, but no one can accuse you of misrepresenting these items as refereed publications.

As you scan the material you have assembled, deciding what to put in your CV, you may also note other items that are not appropriate for inclusion in your resume that you will wish to include in a personal statement or cover letter.

Personal information. Personal information is just that, personal, and it is entirely up to you what to include under "personal" material. You obviously need to list your name, address, and communication numbers.

Information as to marital status and dependents is optional. Female applicants note a lot of curiosity about their marital status; if it was not indicated on their resume, some interviewers craned their necks to check out their ring fingers. ITDs I have asked indicate that the two basic concerns internships have about marital status and dependents is, first, whether marital obligations will have an impact on the likelihood a candidate will accept an offer, and second, whether parental responsibilities will interfere with internship duties. Be prepared to deal with this issue whether or not you put it in your CV, mention it in your letter, or are asked about it in an interview.

If you are married and applying to an internship that involves a major relocation, expect some curiosity about whether your spouse plans to move with you or not. If attending this internship means living apart from your spouse and/or your children for a year, they may infer that you will be more likely to accept an offer that is closer to home. If this is not the case, you may have to disabuse them of this notion. If you have small children, expect curiosity about who will take care of them and, if you are bringing them with you, whether they will make it difficult for you to put in the necessary hours. When one of my students who had a small child interviewed at an internship in a distant city, she made a point of telling the interviewer that one of the attractions of that locale was that her aunt who lived there would be able to help her with child care. She got the position.

Realistically or not, there seems to be more concern over the relationships of female than male applicants, and for couples who are married rather than otherwise involved. My advice, which some of my female colleagues say is naive, is to be honest and forthright if you are asked about your plans for your spouse or children. I maintain that if this is going to be a big problem, it is better to find out about it now than after you have started an internship. My female colleagues say, "Get real." You will have to decide for yourself how to handle these issues.

One item I would definitely *not* include or reveal is the fact that you may be financially secure, especially if you a married woman whose husband is capable of supporting you during your internship. Some settings have unfunded positions, and it is my impression that internships are more likely to offer an unfunded slot to "Mrs. Lottery Winner," even if she is the best qualified candidate, than they are to other applicants with more limited resources. I have discussed this with women faculty at training centers, and many agree that this can occur.

If you are traveling in tandem with someone and you are both applying to the same place, I would communicate the fact that you are a couple. If you are applying to different programs in the same center (e.g., one to psychology and one to social work), some cooperation between the departments will enhance the chances of your both being accepted. Different institutions in the same locale may also cooperate if they are aware of your situation.

If you qualify as a minority, I would include this information since there are some stipends that are reserved for minority applicants. If you are not a U.S. citizen, you may be ineligible for some positions, so it is best to make this known in advance rather than after you have invested a lot of time and effort in interviewing.

I would not include health or legal status in the CV, but, if there are problems, be prepared to deal with them in interview or on an application form. Concealing relevant information or lying on an application form can not only cost you a job, but could subject you to prosecution. So if you are asked if you have a felony conviction, for instance, answer truthfully.

Education and special skills. Turning to education, do not include high school data on your CV, and do not list the courses you have taken. Save that for the application form or your transcript. Do list all the basic information for every college and graduate school attended and your current status in your program. Also include the workshops and continuing education seminars you may have attended, but under a separate heading.

Aside from language proficiency, special skills do not generally go in a CV. I would put them in an application or mention them in your cover letter. Do, however, list all your current professional organizations and credentials.

When it comes to honors and awards, some discretion is in order. You definitively want to include the important ones, especially those of a clearly professional nature, but do not include others such as being "Hilton employee of the month" or the fact that you won the local pub's wet T-shirt contest. High school awards can be included if they are truly exceptional; the more they relate to professional activities the better, such as winning a major science fair competition.

Previous experience. Under previous experience and employment, include all your relevant professional experience in your CV, but do not put in all the various other jobs you have held. Under "Step Three: Organizing your CV," I suggest that you subdivide your experience into homogeneous categories such as "research," "clinical," and so on. You do not need to limit this to paid positions; for example, you might wish to include a research apprenticeship, even though it was unpaid, under "research experience." With regard to other activities such as volunteer work, you should decide for yourself how significant this activity is and whether it enhances or detracts from your CV. It may be better to allude to it in your personal statement or in your discussion of goals.

In describing your experience, write clearly and directly, stating what it was that you accomplished. Be forceful; avoid weak, passive, or "wimpy" constructions. One university's guide to preparing resumes advises, "Concentrate on the positive and use active verbs in the past tense when stating what you did. To say that you planned, organized, supervised, coordinated, implemented, or designed is far better than saying you were 'involved in' or 'participated in,'" (Stanford University Career Planning and Placement Center, 1988, p. 2). While this advice is aimed at bachelor's level business applicants, you get the idea.

Opinion is divided on whether you should include tables summarizing your therapy experience and instrument competence on your CV if this information is also available in an application form. I advise my students to include them, but some ITDs feel that if these data are in an application form it is redundant to list them again in a CV. Indeed, some ITDs argue that an application form is all that is needed. I disagree. One reason I like to see an applicant's CV is that it is a personal document that is a work sample as well as a collection of information. It gives applicants a chance to expand on the bare facts and to explain items that might otherwise be ambiguous. It is important for you to differentiate yourself from the other applicants, and that is difficult on any *uniform* document. So, my advice is always to include a CV. For internships that do not utilize application forms, I think you should summarize your therapy and instrument competence in your CV using tables. For internships that do employ application forms, use your own judgment about including such tables in your CV as well.

Scholarship and publications. Under scholarship, definitely include all your refereed publications and presentations and label them as such. Also include your thesis and, if you have prepared one, your major area paper, but I suggest you list them under "education" rather than as publications. It is appropriate to list items that are under review, but do not put the name of the journal to which they have been submitted. Do not list articles that are "in preparation" under publications. You may refer to them in describing your future research plans.

In my CV, I have two sections labeled "Notes, reviews and comments" and "Technical reports" in which I include items that have not been refereed. You may wish to include such materials somewhere on your CV as well, but do so in a way that makes it clear you are not trying to pass these items off as refereed publications. If you have publications in other areas, such as poetry or short stories, include them in your CV, but list them in a separate section from your psychological writings.

Opinions differ on including sports, hobbies, and other non-professional activities. While it may be frowned upon in an academic CV, I do not have any problems with it in a CV designed for internship applications especially if it enables you to list an outstanding achievement not included elsewhere (e.g., Gold medal in platform diving, 1996 Summer Olympics). While some activities, such as being a computer hacker, might enhance the perception of your skills, I think the chief value of such material is that it can help the interview get started or assist you in finding some common ground with the interviewer.

Step Three: Organizing Your CV

Your CV should be organized so that readers can easily find the information they are seeking. A well-organized CV gives the impression that you are a well-organized person. The sample CV in Appendix 3 will give you some ideas as to organization.

One key is consistency. If you start with your most recent positions and work backwards in the employment section, then you should do likewise in the education section.

I favor putting all the identifying material up front, including demographics, organizations, and credentials. Once this is taken care of, I find it useful to arrange the CV used for internship applications topically. I suggest that you start with the section on education, and put all the information relating to this topic together.

Begin with your current status, and then add the information relating to your dissertation (including the title, prospectus date, and major professor) first, followed by your major area paper, followed by your master's. Include dates to the left. (If you chose to list your master's under "publications," do not list it here as well. However, I think it best to put it here.)

Next, summarize your undergraduate education. Include any educational honors you have received, unless you have chosen to list them separately under "Honors." (Do not include them twice, although if you graduated with honors you should list your bachelor's as "A.B., *summa cum laude*" or whatever.)

In a separate section, list other educational items such as workshops. I would also include skills under this same general heading.

Next, present your professional experience. Rather than putting everything chronologically, thereby mixing different types of experience, I prefer to use homogeneous subtopics such as "research," "teaching," and "clinical." The order is up to you and is one way you can choose what it is you want to emphasize.

Within each section, first list the positions you have held in reverse chronological order beginning with the most recent in that topic area. As noted above, include your title, the dates, the number of hours worked weekly, the supervisor, a description of your duties and, perhaps, the proportion of time spent on each. Do not include beginning and ending salaries or reasons for leaving in a CV.

Although you may want to put them in a separate section, I suggest that you list your publications immediately after your various research positions. That way everything relating to research is in one section. Combine any sections that are too small (i.e., if you have one refereed publication and two presentations, put them together as "Publications and Presentations").

Similarly, in the clinical section, first list all your positions, then summarize the total number of hours of experience and supervision. Next I suggest that you include the table reporting instrument competence. If you wish, you may add another summarizing the number and the nature of the clients you have seen in various settings.

At the end of the CV, you may include a list of the names, titles, addresses, and phone numbers of all those you have asked to write letters on your behalf.

Step Four: Style and Esthetics

Now that we have dealt with substance, let us turn to style. The most important stylistic issues, overriding all other concerns, are that your resume should be neat, legible, accurate, and easy to read.

Your CV will probably be duplicated for distribution to raters at the internship, so use dark, high contrast typography. If you prepare your CV on a word processing system, and you should, use a high quality laser or ink jet printer rather than a dot matrix. Your department or a copying center should have such equipment available. If you choose to purchase such a printer, it is not necessary to spend a fortune. This entire book including tables, appendices, and figures was printed on an HP Desk Jet 660 color printer that retails for less than $200. However, you should spend the extra money to purchase high-quality, high-contrast paper that is specifically designed for the printer you plan to employ.

Present your data in such a way that the reader can easily follow the sequence and locate things. Use headings, subheadings, and hanging paragraphs to show what belongs with what. Boldface type or different fonts, used judiciously, can also help, but keep it in good taste. A sample CV is provided in Appendix 3.

A common mistake on computer-produced CVs is having an entry carry over a page break. Do not put a heading at the bottom of a page and then have the subordinated material start on the next page, and try not to allow a page break to split a job description or reference. If you cannot get it all on one page, it is better to begin the new entry on the next page. Having generous borders and margins is not only attractive, but it also gives the reader a place to make notes.

While you may elect to employ a copying firm, stay away from the outfits that prepare jazzy resumes for vinyl siding salesmen. The use of different colored inks, "bullets," raised type and other devices utilized by professional resume firms are fine if you are seeking a sales position, but they are a "turn off" when used in a professional resume or CV. Similarly, it is not customary to include a photograph on a CV.

No matter how many times you have gone over it, before you take your CV or any other material to be copied, check for typographical and spelling errors. Do not rely on a computerized spell-checking program. Check everything again when you get it back from the copying firm; do not accept it if there are dark spots or slanted pages. Make sure you check every copy...the one you do not check will be the one with the blank page.

This may seem very basic, but all of these mistakes have been made in the past. Even one error or botched page can give a very negative impression. I recently read a job application in which the candidate misspelled the name of his home state. The fact that the applicant had obviously not bothered to check a document as important as a job application for accuracy made me wonder if he could be trusted to analyze data or prepare research articles correctly.

Mistakes are especially likely to happen when you rely on others to prepare or copy your materials. I speak from experience; before we submitted the manuscript for the first edition of this book, four different people had proofed it in its entirety. However, the cover was prepared by the publishing company. When I received my copies from the printer, I looked at the cover and saw that my name had been spelled incorrectly! The books had all been printed and it was too late to correct it. However, it certainly was an effective illustration of my point that no matter how careful you are, mistakes happen. Let's hope that the publisher gets my name right in this edition, and that you get your CVs right before you mail them to the internships.

CHAPTER 7

PREPARING YOUR INTERNSHIP APPLICATIONS

Once you have formulated your priorities, compiled your list of possible internships, obtained your application forms, and prepared your CV, it is time to prepare your applications. Allow plenty of time, because this will take longer than you think.

Before you actually submit any applications, make sure that everything is square with your ADCT and major professor and that you have the full support of your department. Although some *laissez faire* programs allow students to apply whenever they feel they are ready, most have a formal set of procedures you must follow. These may include checking your transcript and Program of Studies, verifying that you have been admitted to candidacy for the Doctoral degree, review of your practicum evaluations, and formal approval by your ADCT or even, as in our program, a formal review and vote by the full clinical faculty. Your program may also have an established procedure for submitting applications. You may be expected to meet with your ADCT and have your CV and other materials reviewed before you send anything off. Whatever the system is in your department, make sure you follow it to the letter, even if it differs from the advice in this book. You do not want to get a reputation for being a loose cannon at just the time you are asking faculty members to write letters saying how cooperative and responsive to supervision you are.

Let us assume that you have gotten whatever clearances are necessary and have discussed your choices with your advisors. It is now late September or early October and you should have:

1. Compiled a list of places where you plan to apply.

2. Obtained application forms from all of those places.

3. Collected and collated all the information you need to complete the application forms.

4. Prepared a CV or resume, and had it laser printed and duplicated.

5. Contacted the people you want to write letters of recommendation on your behalf, secured their agreement to do so, and asked them to get all their letters in the mail by the Monday before the middle Friday in November (i.e., on or around November 10). The earliest due dates for internship applications used to be around December 1 instead of mid-November, so you may find that some faculty members are accustomed to submitting their letters later in the month. Don't forget to provide your letter writers with the complete addresses of the internships where their letters are to be sent. Also it doesn't hurt to provide them with a copy of your CV.

6. Had transcripts sent to all the places where you might conceivably apply. Since it often takes the Registrar's office a long time to process a transcript request, and since faculty members may put off writing letters of reference, the safest procedure is to request these materials early, even if you have not yet submitted your formal applications.

As I noted earlier, some students worry that transcripts and letters that arrive before the formal application materials are received may go astray. This is probably a needless concern. Every year at this time internship training centers all over the country start receiving application materials. As soon as an item comes in, they check their data base and see if they already have a listing for that person. If so, the material is added to the file; if not, a file is opened and subsequent material is inserted as it arrives. However, to be on the safe side, you may choose to follow Gollaher and Craig's (1994) advice to send a post card advising your selected internships that you plan to apply and asking them to open a file for materials that will soon be arriving. If you do so, make sure you put your complete name and Social Security number on the card, especially if you have a relatively common name such as "Jim Smith" or have had a name change.

Different training centers have different due dates, typically ranging from the middle of November until early January. If you are pressed for time, prepare those with the earliest due dates first, submitting each application as soon as it is ready. However, since most of your references will send the same basic letter to all your sites, it is best to give them the complete list all at once so they can mass produce their letters.

Deciding Where to Apply

Now it is time to bite the bullet and decide where you are going to apply and how many applications you will submit. As I indicated earlier, your application list should include settings that range in competitiveness. By all means apply to those places you are really enthused about, but, if they are very competitive, also apply to some other places that are less popular. Your final selection should include facilities that range from being highly competitive to relatively noncompetitive.

While you are deciding on the internships that should be on your final list, flag some others for a "lifeboat list." These should be internships you would be willing to attend but that for some reason you are less interested in applying to than the others. They should all have relatively late due dates. The APPIC *Directory* lists a few internships that have due dates as late as February. As the name implies, the "lifeboat" list is for emergencies. You will probably never need it, but, if you do, it can save your life. You use your lifeboat list if, midway through the application season, you discover some disaster has wiped out your primary list. This is the backup list you turn to if you only apply to internships in Los Angeles and an earthquake or volcano actually does destroy the city and all your internships along with it.

You have enough anxieties without my listing the various reasons why you might be forced to submit additional applications late in the game. In the one instance where we had to use a lifeboat list, a good student got a poorly-phrased letter of recommendation from his major professor that severely threatened his chances for acceptance at his primary list. He got some interviews but on my advice submitted five additional applications (with a more appropriate letter) to his lifeboat list. After interviewing, one of these backups actually became his first choice and he was accepted there.

Many internships have separate tracks such as child, substance abuse, forensic, and gerontology. In some of these settings, the applications are sorted according to the track specified and candidates are considered by the faculty in each area. When computer matching comes, such internships will submit separate lists of candidates for each of these positions. Therefore, it is vital that you clearly indicate what track you are applying for in such programs. Before you do so be sure you have the qualifications expected for that track. You will have a tough time competing for a child slot, for example, if you have had no experience working with children.

Although other internships may not have track-specific selection, they often must ensure that all their major rotations are covered. The interests expressed by the applicants may be an important selection criterion. Thus, you should be sure your preferences are clearly indicated.

Do not make frivolous applications. This is no time to indulge in ego trips. Do not apply to famous places you have no intention of attending simply to see if you could get in. You may interfere with the chances of other students who are seriously considering the site in question. Also, do not apply to nearby facilities "for practice" so you can use them to test your interviewing technique even though you have no plans to attend. This will give all applicants from your institution a bad name and may interfere with the chances of your fellow students who must stay in the area and who may be very interested in those sites. The bottom line is, "Do not apply any place you are not willing to attend." It wastes your time and the internship's, and in my opinion it is dishonest.

Survey data consistently show that the students who fail to obtain internships on UND are often those who submitted only a few applications in a geographically circumscribed locale (Clay, 1997; Thorne, 1997). This makes sense. Matching your qualifications with internships' preferences is a tricky business. If you are limiting your search to a circumscribed area, especially one that does not have a lot of internships, it is unlikely that you will come up with as many good matches as you will if you have the whole country to choose from. If you are a poorer match than some other applicant, you are more likely to end up on the alternate list. If you limit yourself to an area that is within a day's drive of your university, as many students do, you are more likely to be competing with other students from your program. Since most internships seek variety in each class of trainees, you are further handicapping yourself if you adopt this strategy.

Whether or not your program requires it, you should try to coordinate your applications with those of your fellow applicants. It is all right for two or three people from a single university to apply to the same internship. It is not uncommon for internships to accept two candidates from the same program, although most would balk at three, and after interviewing it is likely that each applicant will end up with a different first choice. Some internships resent getting too many applications from the same school (Belar & Orgel, 1980). Recently, one facility received a carton containing two dozen applications from a single professional school. Apparently, identical cartons had been sent to a number of major training centers, with no attempt to match the individual applications to the resources of the facilities. The ITD sent the carton back by return mail with instructions for the ADCT to select and submit the best application for her internship.

How many applications should you submit?

Plan to submit a reasonable, but not an excessive, number of applications. What is a reasonable number of applications? First, there is no point submitting more applications than you can manage. If you submit two or three dozen applications, you will probably do your chances more harm than good. You can't interview well at that many sites or negotiate effectively with that many ITDs. Once computer matching is adopted, it appears likely that you will be able to include no more than 17 settings on your selection list. Your goal should be to have about ten viable choices after you have completed your interviews

Well, then, how many applications should you prepare and submit? The number varies with the competitiveness of the internships to which you are applying, the reputation of your training program, the number of your fellow students applying to the same internships, the impressiveness of your credentials, and whether you are applying in tandem with someone else.

Perhaps you are enrolled in one of the "less preferred" training programs discussed in Chapter Five, such as a Counseling Psychology program that is not APA-accredited. If so, you will need to submit more applications than someone from a more preferred program, and you will have to target them to centers that are more receptive to Counseling Psychology applicants. If you are an average student, you should apply to more places than if you are the class superstar, especially if you are applying to the same places as the superstar.

Hugely popular internships that receive hundreds of applications are always risky, no matter how strong a candidate's credentials. I never slept well when my students applied to such programs, even though we have a good record with some. If one or more of these programs is at the top of your list, you should back them up with some smaller or less competitive settings. You usually will have a better chance applying to training centers with which your university has strong traditional ties than one that has never before taken a student from your school. Within internships, child and psychotherapy tracks seem to draw more applications than rotations such as chemical dependency or gerontology.

In deciding how many applications to submit, be prepared to delete a couple of possibilities after you visit, because you will undoubtedly find one or more unacceptable for some reason. For example, one of our students who had obviously not done his homework very well submitted an application to a VA hospital that did not even have a Psychology Training Program! If circumstances will prevent you from interviewing in person, submit more applications. Even though they may say telephone interviews are acceptable, most programs favor candidates they have actually seen. As noted above, you should apply to some less competitive as well as some more competitive internships, and it is a good idea to have a "lifeboat list" tucked away in case it suddenly becomes necessary to submit some additional applications at the last minute.

In terms of actual numbers, I have had students who submitted only one application and as many as 26. All in all I recommend submitting 12 +/- 2 applications, a number that is close to the estimated national average (Thorne, 1997). This is one more than I recommended in the first edition of this book, because it seems to me that the competition is getting tougher. However, an intern participating in a symposium at the 1989 APA Convention stated that she had been one of 40 students applying from a free-standing Psy.D. program and that she and her classmates had averaged 22 applications each! This is twice the number I recommend, but we have far fewer students applying each year, and our program is one of those that is considered "preferred" since it is a traditional APA-approved Ph.D. program in Clinical psychology. Ultimately, you must decide what is the best number for *you* to submit; for many applicants, deadlines and fatigue are the final determinants.

Completing the Paperwork

There is an unbelievable amount of paperwork involved in filling out internship applications. You have already taken care of getting transcripts sent, and you have prepared and duplicated a resume, perhaps two if you plan to send out some with and some without tables showing your instrument competence or summarizing your therapy experience. Now the real paperwork begins.

The new APPIC Uniform Application Form is a mixed blessing. The positive aspect is that you will probably not have as many different application forms to complete as students did before it was developed. This means that you may not have to write as many essays and that you can use your computer more effectively. However, it also means that more internships will probably now request application forms in addition to CVs. Moreover, APPIC also adopted other forms that you and your ADCT will have to fill out. In addition to the formal applications, you may also have to submit, or have submitted by your ADCT, the Verification of Internship Eligibility and Readiness form, the Professional Readiness Form, a work sample, and an individually-prepared cover letter.

One general piece of advice applies to all of this material. When you prepare and submit your applications, make sure you comply exactly with the application procedures specified by each program. Failure to do so will show that you do not know how to follow directions, and no one wants a trainee who cannot or will not follow directions. Put your name and Social Security number on each document and make sure that your materials are prepared carefully and attractively. Until you obtain an interview and can visit an internship in person, your application *is* you. This paperwork is all the selection committee has with which to evaluate you, and it must compete with the 70 other applications the average internship receives. If it is sloppy, unprofessional, or poorly prepared, they will assume that you are sloppy, unprofessional, or poorly prepared. If it is late or incomplete, it may not be reviewed at all (Mitchell, 1996).

Verification of Readiness Form

Under the new APPIC procedures, your Academic Director of Clinical Training must submit a "Verification of Internship Eligibility and Readiness Form" for your application to be considered.

In the first part of the eligibility requirement, the ADCT must check one of two statements:

A. This student is ready to go on internship now (has no departmental requirements that would preclude his/her beginning internship), or

B. Needs to complete the following requirements before s/he will be able to go on internship:

_______ Master's Thesis
_______ Comprehensive Exam
_______ Dissertation Proposal
_______ Academic Coursework
_______ Other (Specify)

As I stated earlier, it is essential that your ADCT check "A." All the ITDs I have talked to agree that if there are any outstanding requirements that could conceivably prevent you from going on internship, it is unlikely you will be accepted. Indeed, when they see that your ADCT does not regard you as ready, your application may never get reviewed.

Next your ADCT must indicate the current status of your dissertation and the progress expected as of July 1 of the next year. This will no doubt be done in conjunction with your major professor. The further along you are, the more favorably your application will be considered. No internship wants to risk training an "ABD" who never completes the dissertation requirement, and many, perhaps most, prefer interns who have completed their dissertations. The 1997 CUDCP survey indicated that 10% of the students not getting internships in 1997 were rejected because their dissertations were incomplete and 8% because they had clinical training deficits (Thorne, 1997).

The last part of the Eligibility and Readiness document has the following statement:

> This applicant possesses the emotional stability and maturity to handle the rigors of the internship experience. S/he possess the theoretical/academic foundation necessary for effective counseling/clinical work. S/he possesses the skills necessary for translating theory into integrated practice. S/he demonstrates awareness of, and practices according to, the current standards of ethics for professionals. S/he demonstrates the capacity to participate in supervision constructively and can modify his/her behavior in response to feedback.

Letters of recommendation

Opinions vary on the importance of letters. Studies of ITD decision-making consistently rank letters as being among the most important criteria (Lopez, Oehlert, & Moberly, 1996; Stedman et al., 1981), but others maintain they are of little value (May, Rice, & Birckhead, 1990). Most letters are overwhelmingly positive, prompting some writers to ask whatever happened to the lower 90% of the student population (May et al., 1990; Miller & Van Rybroek, 1988). May et al. (1990, p. 39) concluded, "...training directors will only see letters as informative if they 'damn with faint praise.' Letters are apparently used more often to lower an applicant's ranking than as a general discrimination factor," and a recent survey by Lonigan (1994) confirmed that negative letters are weighted heavily.

In my opinion, the more work that goes into preparing a letter of recommendation, the more likely it is to contribute to the decision-making process. I spend a great deal of time on composing each letter. I begin by reviewing the student's transcript, CV, academic folder, and my notes of my interviews with the applicant regarding internship. I read all the letters of recommendation sent by undergraduate mentors prior to admission to our program, and the quarterly ratings made by clinical supervisors, noting quotations I can use in my letter.

I then integrate all this information into a three- or four-page summary of the candidate's individual characteristics. This is descriptive rather than evaluative, although I do my best to put things in a positive light. For example, if a candidate has been in the program for an eternity, I emphasize his maturity and experience, whereas one who is applying early and has relatively few hours is praised for her youthful energy and drive. If there are deficits, I acknowledge them and try to explain what the problem was. ITDs can forgive candidates for some bad grades if they know they were ill or going through a divorce at the time and the problem is now resolved. Whenever possible, I try to include concrete behavioral examples to illustrate points made in my evaluation. ITDs often report that they find these individualized letters are helpful in evaluating candidates, especially when they are attempting to compare several applicants from our program. Since our candidates appear to do pretty well, these frank appraisals evidently do not hurt their chances, perhaps because the information is accurate and placed in context.

Whom to solicit for letters. You should submit at least three letters of recommendation. One should be from your major professor, one should be from a current or recent clinical supervisor, and one must be from your ADCT. Only solicit letters from people with appropriate professional credentials who are in a position to evaluate your skills as a psychologist. Character references from clergy or civic leaders have no place in an internship application.

Your major professor's letter should focus on your academic qualifications and research. In addition to all the other good things your major professor discusses, there must be a statement that you will definitely finish your dissertation and obtain your doctoral degree in the foreseeable future. No one wants an intern who will be an "ABD." When I was ADCT, I asked our major professors to evaluate students in absolute rather than relative terms. I preferred a letter that said a student is "excellent" to one that stated he or she is the "best." The reason is that comparative statements implicitly put down other students from our program who might also be applying. When I had several major professors each claiming his or her student was the "best," or even in the "top 5%," I felt they all lost credibility. (You and I both know that a large proportion -- perhaps even 50% -- of the students who apply each year are actually *below* the median, but not according to any of the letters that will be written.) However, some jaded ITDs report that they scan letters seeking such superlatives.

The second letter should be from someone who is familiar with your clinical work and who has supervised you recently rather than in the distant past. If you have had recent experience in a couple of different settings, it is a good idea to have letters from both. Before listing anyone as a reference, make sure you ask his or her permission. If someone does not feel comfortable in recommending you, or is going to be away when the letters are due, it is better to find out early and obtain other references.

It used to be necessary that the third letter came from the ADCT. This letter constituted the program's formal endorsement of your application and it certified that the student was in good standing academically and clinically prepared for internship. This is now accomplished by the certifications signed by the ADCT, so you can have someone else prepare the third letter if you choose. However, I still recommend your ADCT unless he or she has little knowledge of your qualifications.

Other letters. In addition to these three "must" letters, it is wise to solicit a fourth "wild card" letter as well, preferably from someone who thinks you are terrific. This letter can help balance a perfunctory ADCT letter or one from someone who for some reason "damns you with faint praise." It can also fill in if one of the others is late arriving. Some programs may not evaluate any folders until there are at least three letters; your "wild card" letter will allow it to go forward without delay.

You may be applying to some places where someone on your faculty has a "special relationship" with someone. Perhaps they were colleagues some place, or maybe one of your faculty members was the ITD's major professor. If so, it may help to have that faculty member write or call his or her friend on your behalf. Check first with your ADCT, and do not ask a faculty member to make a special appeal on your behalf unless you are very interested in that setting. If, after such a call, you decide not to attend that internship, it will be embarrassing for both your faculty member and his or her friend.

The reciprocal situation is when some faculty member, like "Prof. Buck Muledeer", assures you that, if you give the word, a single phone call to his former student, Dr. Carrie Boux, will ensure your acceptance at Moosehead Medical Center. If this occurs, thank the good professor and *check with your ADCT*. If Moosehead is your first choice, *and* your ADCT approves, you may decide to let Prof. Muledeer call. However, do not burn your bridges to other training centers.

When Prof. Muledeer heard that one of his graduate students, "Bambi Gazelle," was applying to Moosehead Medical Center, he offered to intervene on her behalf. Unfortunately, he swore her to secrecy because he surmised, correctly, that I might not approve. Ms. Gazelle agreed, and a few days later he assured her that she would definitely get a slot at Moosehead. Bambi took Prof. Muledeer at his word; when ITDs from other internships called her, she thanked them for their interest and told them she planned to accept the offer that would be forthcoming from Moosehead. There was one slight problem, however. The younger stags had taken over at Moosehead and, a week before UND, Bambi was informed she was out of the running. By the time she finally came to me, she had almost destroyed her chances of acceptance elsewhere. With a lot of abject phone calls to other ITDs, we managed to get her into a good program, albeit not in her preferred rotation. Muledeer was right about one thing, however; I definitely was upset. The moral of the story is that you should always keep your ADCT informed.

Professional Conduct Form

APPIC has also devised a "Professional Conduct Form" that you will probably be required to sign and submit along with your formal applications. It asks you to respond "Yes" or "No" to the following four questions:

1. Has disciplinary action ever been taken against you by a supervisor, educational or training institution, health care institution, professional association, or licensing certification board?

2. Have any complaints been filed or are any currently pending against you before any of the above bodies?

3. Have you ever had a civil suit brought against you relative to your professional work, or is any such action pending?

4. Have you ever been suspended, terminated, or asked to resign by a training program, practicum site, or employer?

If you answer "yes" to any of these questions, you are instructed to attach an explanation regarding the circumstances. You should do so. As a general rule in such matters, covering up has worse consequences than acknowledging such difficulties and explaining what happened. As Richard Nixon and countless others have discovered, the consequences of a cover-up are often worse than those associated with the initial transgression. Indeed, making false statements on an application form is a criminal offense in most jurisdictions. If you have had such difficulties, you should acknowledge them and explain what happened, because the next section of the form gives the agency broad powers to investigate you and your behavior and to dismiss you without incurring any liability if they decide that you concealed or misrepresented the facts on this form or in the rest of your application.

Formal applications

Many programs will require you to fill out a printed application form. Some are unbelievably complicated and time-consuming to prepare. "Why," you might ask, "do they need all this information?" They don't. Extremely complex applications are a test of your motivation, designed to screen out anyone who is not a serious applicant.

As I have noted, APPIC is developing a Uniform Application Form ("UAF") that will be ready for use beginning in the Fall of 1997; copies will be available at the APPIC Web site or on disks from the Central Office in Mac, Word for Windows, and WordPerfect for Windows formats. This will make completing applications much simpler; no longer will it be necessary to find a typewriter that still works and buy a gallon of correction fluid and a paint roller. However, be warned. APPIC members are not obligated to use the UAF. They can continue using their own forms or add questions to the UAF, such as a section asking candidates to indicate which of the agency's rotations they prefer.

There is some ambivalence among APPIC members over the new forms. Obviously no uniform format will please some ITDs as much as ones they devised themselves. Some programs fear that making the application process easier will encourage frivolous applications. May et al. (1990, p. 38) reflected many internships' dissatisfaction with such standardized applications when they wrote, "The advent of the word processor has led to 'mass produced' applications that are frequently not very revealing....Disadvantages [of standardized application forms] include a tendency to homogenize applicants and a possible increase in applications from candidates who are not serious but wish to 'hedge their bets'."

The VA has been experimenting with uniform application forms for several years, and the pilot data they have collected suggest that their use did not increase the number of applications. Although they experienced a 36% increase in the number of applications from 1994 to 1996, the increase was the same in those centers that had adopted the uniform application and those that had not (Cantrell & Garfield, 1997).

Before filling out any application, it is advisable to make extra copies of the forms in case you make errors. For non-uniform application forms, try scanning the form into a computer. In general, you should try to limit your responses to the space available on the form if you can do so without distorting the information you provide. If you have more honors than the space permits you to list, you can scan or retype the form into your computer and then make your list using a smaller font. However, do not make the type so minuscule that it strains the eyes of the readers; use a continuation page if necessary. Knowing that they have dozens of applications to review, you do not want to make their task any more difficult than it already is.

After reading dozens of similar responses, reviewers take note when one turns up that has some originality or humor. Late one night, a student who had been preparing applications all day encountered a form that asked him to "list his strengths." He impulsively wrote down, "I have never been arrested," and went on to the next item. After he had mailed the applications, he regretted his flip answer and figured he could write off that placement. To his surprise, when he interviewed, everyone at the agency was eager to meet the one intern applicant with a sense of humor, and he was treated like visiting royalty. (Of course, if you all start using his response, it won't appear original anymore.)

Personal statements and essays

Because of their dissatisfaction with the information contained in application forms and letters of recommendation, many programs will also ask you to submit a personal statement or essay. Typical topics include a mini-biography ("Who are you?"), a discussion of why you want to be a clinical psychologist, an essay on why you want to attend their particular internship, or a statement on what you plan to be doing after you get your degree. The current APPIC UAF asks the following four questions and gives you an inch of space to respond to each:

1. Please list your short-term and long-term career goals in Psychology:

2. Describe your interpersonal strengths and weaknesses:

3. Describe the clinical strength you would bring to us:

4. Describe the clinical skill areas in which you feel you lack adequate experience and should emphasize during internship training:

You should give these questions some thought before responding. Even though your written answers will necessarily be succinct, it is very likely you will be asked to amplify upon them when you are interviewed. Question 4 is especially important. Mitchell (1996, p. 91) noted, "an application is...weakened when a candidate fails to identify specific goals for the internship year."

Next, the UAF asks you to amplify on your goals for your internship training by answering the question, "How do you view our training program being able to meet your needs and goals for internship training?" It notes that this answer, which is limited to 400 words, should differ according to the site and the training it offers. I believe that this question will be one of the key items discriminating successful from unsuccessful applicants. Those who take this injunction to heart and prepare a unique response for each internship site will make a much better impression on the selection staff than those who send the same standard answer with every application. Your answer should show that you have done your homework, studied the characteristics of that particular training center, and given careful thought to how they fit with your particular attributes and needs.

Some internships, of course, will not use the UAF. If they do not, I suggest that you make a brief outline of how you would have answered this question had you been asked to do so. Include these points in your cover letter.

It is up to you to prepare your own essays. I suggest that you be positive, realistic, and professional. Mitchell (1996) has made a number of valuable suggestions on preparing personal statements. She suggested that you be specific. Instead of using a vague label to identify your theoretical orientation, for example, specify what that label means and how it influences the way you approach a case. She also advised referring to significant life events that may have influenced you. Do not, however, use a personal statement or biography as a a confessional. I have read biographical statements that began, "It was only after I accepted the fact that I am an alcoholic and that I had ruined the lives of my family that I realized I had been chosen to save others by becoming a clinical psychologist." I am rarely eager to hire such people.

Mitchell (1996) also has advised that you be honest and resist the temptation to give the internship what you think it wants to hear. She noted, "Selection committees eye with suspicion the applicant who claims that their training site is perfect given his or her career goals, yet nothing in his or her previous work or practicum experience confirms this stated interest" (1996, p. 91). Or as one of my students less elegantly remarked, "Don't suck up too much."

In addition to the personal statements, one internship is reported to be experimenting with an addendum to their standard application that asks candidates to prepare responses to questions in the areas of professional ethics, assessment, and interventions that are modeled after state licensing examinations (May et al., 1990). If this catches on, applications will include what amounts to a take home examination. Daehnert and Carter (1987) reported that MMPI scores were the best predictors of internship performance, but so far I do not know of any site that uses them for selection.

In addition to being a test of your motivation, essays and personal statements are evaluated on the basis of style and literacy as well as actual content. Writing is an important part of any psychologist's job, and these compositions show raters whether you can write clearly and cogently. Make sure you revise and edit these essays, and check them for style and spelling.

Work samples

Unless you are required to submit a clinical work sample, I would not do so. A clinician can always find something to criticize in someone else's work sample. If there is a perceived flaw, you will get marked down. If it is flawless, they will assume your supervisor is responsible. Either way, it is a no-win situation. Many ITDs agree that work samples may do you more harm than good.

If you are asked for a work sample, try to ascertain if it is *required*. If it is not, you are probably better off without it. I was surprised to learn from one ITD whose hospital supposedly requires a work sample that applicants who do not submit one are not penalized. In fact, he noted, it seemed to work the other way -- the students who *did* submit work samples tended to draw more negative ratings from faculty because the clinical faculty had something concrete to criticize! I have raised this issue with other directors and they concur.

If a work sample is definitely required, by all means prepare one. Many settings will not review an "incomplete" application. One of my students advises sending two samples from different settings, explaining to the internship that they represent the approaches and styles of different supervisors and placements. She maintained that this demonstrated her flexibility and responsiveness to supervision.

A request for a work sample can also raise ethical issues regarding confidentiality and informed consent. Obviously all materials must be disguised to protect the client's identity, but you should also get the client's permission to share these materials with a third party. One student felt that obtaining a release after the fact would violate his understanding with clients he had previously assessed, so he asked if he could substitute a report he had prepared for a class on projectives using data provided by the instructor, who had procured it from a consenting client. Although most ITDs understood his concern and allowed the substitution, one insisted that he provide a work sample with tests he had administered personally. This led the student to question that ITD's sensitivity to ethical issues and, eventually, to withdraw his application at that program.

A safer course of action is to perform an evaluation expressly for your application, using a legally competent volunteer who has had the purpose of the assessment explained, given informed consent, and signed a release that will allow you to share the data and the report, suitably disguised, with internship selection personnel. Not only will this permit you to select a battery that will best highlight your skills, but it should also enable you to avoid some of the ethical difficulties associated with seeking an after-the-fact release from a client you have previously evaluated.

If you do submit a work sample, attach a note indicating why you chose this particular work sample, the circumstances under which it was obtained, and what it illustrates about your work.

Cover letters

Although no agency will list this as a requirement, by all means include a one-page cover letter. This cover letter will be the first thing the reviewers read, and it is vital to making a good first impression. The cover letter gives you a chance to emphasize the points you are trying to make in your resume and personal statement. Indicate who you are, what position you are applying for, what is included in your application, whose letters of reference they can expect to receive and, in a couple of sentences, why you are applying to this particular program and why they should select *you.* This is one sure way to make your application stands out from all the rest, especially since many of your competitors won't bother to send *any* cover letter.

It is much easier to submit the same cover letter and personal statement to all your internships. It is also less effective. Adapt your cover letters and personal statements to each individual internship, indicating the specific people and programs that attract you and why you feel there is a good match between your abilities and needs and what the program offers. Of course, it requires a lot more work to individualize your applications, but everyone wants a hardworking intern.

Remember, most selection committees are faced with the task of selecting a small number of outstanding and congenial people from a large number of applicants, most of whom are qualified. Unless an application catches their attention from the start, there is little incentive to wade through it all or to invite the applicant for an interview. Raters are most likely to notice applicants who have done their homework and whose letters and personal statements show they are familiar with the program and how it meshes with their qualifications. Many internships will decide who to interview based only on your application materials. If you don't make the cut, you don't get invited for an interview.

Other issues

Unrequested materials. Determine program policy about submitting unrequested materials such as reprints, prospectuses, or copies of term papers. If you have a published reprint, I would definitely include it, but I would hesitate at a typewritten preprint that makes the folder bulky, and I would not include academic papers unless specifically told to do so.

Spelling and style. Until and unless you are selected for an interview, your application *is* you. Make sure it is complete, clean, and correct. Sloppy applications suggest you have sloppy standards. Check for typographical errors and misspelled words. Do not rely on your computer to catch spelling mistakes. A spell-checking program will approve both "form" and "from" even though one will be incorrect in a given context; you do not want to report that you are familiar with the Revised *From* (sic) of the MMPI.

Submitting Your Applications

Finally you have all your application materials completed. For each application you should have an individualized cover letter, a copy of your CV, completed application forms, personal statements or essays, work samples if required, and any other material you are submitting such as reprints. Make copies of everything and file the copies in a separate folder for each internship, along with the internship's brochure. Plan on taking the folder along with you to internship interviews so you can review what you said the night before your interview.

Next assemble each individual application. Make sure that each is complete and correct, accurate and attractive. Make certain that you have the right materials in each application and that each document has your name on it. If you have prepared individualized cover letters, essays, and personal statements, as I have advised, make sure they are going to the correct place. It will not help your cause if the extremely behavioral internship gets the letter in which you express your interest in dynamic psychology and learning more about Rorschach interpretation, while the analytic institute receives the statement indicating you hope to become a radical behaviorist. Similarly, double-check your addresses, and make sure the name of the training director matches the internship and the address on the envelope matches the one inside. Finally, don't forget to sign the letters. After you have sealed each completed application, take them personally to the Post Office, have them weighed, put on the correct postage, and send them off.

If all has gone according to schedule, you should have completed this by the middle of November. For the next couple of weeks, there is not much to do on the internship front. Use the time to catch up on your academic work and get reacquainted with your family. Take a few days off for rest and relaxation. And don't forget that flu shot.

Following Up

It is *your* responsibility to ascertain that your application has been received by the internship facility and is complete. (Some programs will request that you include a stamped self-addressed postcard for this purpose.) After a reasonable time has passed to allow the applications to be logged in and filed, check to make sure your application is complete and that all your letters of recommendation have been received.

Don't get annoyed if the internship staff is not able to give you an immediate answer as to whether or not some vital document has been received. Remember that APPIC reported that 37,107 applications were received in 1995-1996 and that I estimate that over 2,800 students each apply to about 12 sites. If each application involves at least seven documents (cover letter, transcript, application form, CV, and three letters), that means that over 260,000 documents have to be logged into data bases and filed into approximately 33,600 folders in a two-month period that includes the Thanksgiving, Christmas, and Chanukah holidays. Moreover, you are not the only person calling. This is why so many Internship Training Directors and their staffs get so hassled every winter. If they can't find something right away, don't get hysterical. If you make yourself truly obnoxious to the harried clerical staff, someone may make sure that your folder really does get lost and that it stays lost. It is one way to make sure you won't be bothering them all next year.

When you get an answer, if your folders are complete, tell them that you hope to interview, and start working on your travel plans. If you are told your folder is incomplete, don't panic. Perhaps the training center has misfiled something. This is especially likely if you have recently changed your name. Your transcript will probably have your former name, while you are using your new name. If you use a hyphenated name, such as "Eggs-Benedict," have them look under "B" as well as "E." Similarly, if you have an Hispanic name such as "Guillermo Huevos Rancheros" and you go by "Huevos," see if some material has been filed under "Rancheros." An Asiatic name such as "Egg Foo Young" could lead to materials being filed under "E," "F," or "Y" depending on how knowledgeable the clerk is with regard to Eastern customs. Finally, if you have a fairly common name, such as "Jim Smith," it is possible that more than one person with your name has applied, and some of your material may be in the other person's folder.

Assuming the missing material cannot be located, take steps to resubmit it. You should have copies of all the material you submitted. If a letter is missing, find out if it was ever written or mailed; if so, have a duplicate copy sent. If not, get on the party's case. Find out how urgent the time constraints are, and fax or Federal Express material if necessary.

You may be told that it is too late and that nothing more will be accepted. Send it anyway, then ask your ADCT to call the ITD or, failing that, call the ITD yourself. Messages like this are usually the result of overzealousness or misunderstanding on the part of a lower echelon clerical person. ITDs, on the other hand, do not wish to offend any university training programs unnecessarily. If even this does not work, thank the powers that be you have discovered how rigid and autocratic that place is. You certainly would not have enjoyed interning there! Remember, you agreed back in the beginning of this book that no internship is worth pursuing as if it were the Holy Grail. Moreover, you have just saved yourself some travel money. To save more, proceed to the next chapter.

CHAPTER EIGHT

TRAVELING TO INTERNSHIPS: HOW TO SURVIVE AND STAY SOLVENT

Your next step is visiting the internships to which you have applied and interviewing. I am a firm believer in the importance of the on-site interview. Although it may not be required, I feel it greatly enhances your chances of being accepted. Some ITDs use the interview as a motivational test. At a recent APPIC meeting, one remarked, "If they don't care enough to interview, they won't be interested enough to accept." Moreover, interviewing in person affords you an opportunity to evaluate a setting and its personnel before deciding if you want to spend a year of your life training there. Chapter Nine deals with all aspects of the interview process. This chapter focuses on travel; if you cannot afford the trip or if you get stranded en route to the internship, all the interview skills you have acquired will be wasted.

Travel is the biggest single expense associated with applying for internships. It can also be a major hassle. The purpose of this chapter is to help you save time and money traveling to internship sites and maximize your chances of actually getting to your intended destination on or about the time you planned, with your luggage and your temper intact. This, despite the fact that you will be traveling at the worst time of the year from the standpoint of air fares, weather, and crowds.

In the pages that follow, I will offer a great deal of unsolicited advice about traveling to internships, most learned the hard way. Unfortunately, this will also make me sound like your mother. However, if you want to save money, avoid hassles, and stay healthy on the road, heat up a cup of chicken soup, find a comfortable chair, and get out your highlighter.

Join the club(s)

As soon as possible, join the frequent traveler programs of the airlines you are likely to be using, the AAA automobile club, the "preferred renter program" of the major automobile rental companies, and the "honored guest" programs of the major hotel chains. The AAA charges an annual fee; most of the others are free.

Airlines. The main purpose of the airlines' frequent traveler programs is to build customer loyalty by reinforcing you for flying with them. The more you fly, the more "frequent traveler miles" you earn; these "miles" can later be redeemed for upgrades or free travel. You typically get a bonus of several thousand "miles" for joining, and then at least 500 miles credit for each "flight segment." For example, if you fly from Charleston, SC, to Chicago, IL, and back, changing in Atlanta, you may accumulate four "flight segs" or 2,000 miles. If you fly from Charleston to San Francisco, again changing in Atlanta, you may get 500 miles for the Charleston to Atlanta flight seg, and the actual mileage (2,139) for the Atlanta to San Francisco segment. The total round trip "miles" would be 5,278.

The basic mileage credits are just the beginning. Promotions occur that will award you double or triple mileage if you travel through certain cities, fly at certain times, stay at certain hotels, or pay for your travel with certain credit cards. In addition to rewarding you with free travel coupons after you accumulate enough miles, the frequent traveler programs also entitle you to reduced rates or upgrades at cooperating hotels and car rental agencies. Their monthly publications also announce special discounts and bargains that might help you save money.

Like air fares, the number of incentive points awarded and the amounts needed for various rewards wax and wane. When the last edition of this book was published, 15,000 miles could be redeemed for a free ticket for your companion when you bought a regular price coach ticket, and 20,000 miles earned you an off-peak round trip coach ticket anywhere in the United States. Currently it takes 25,000 miles to get a round trip coach ticket. Who knows what the premiums will be worth the next time I rewrite this chapter? The point is that if you are traveling by air, you might as well take advantage of the freebies. The mileage credits I accumulated while researching this book helped me "buy" round trip tickets to London for me and my wife and our five children.

Automobiles. The AAA automobile clubs do more than provide emergency road service. They will give you free tour books listing selected hotels and motels and their rates in the places you will visit. They will also supply you with free state and city maps that will help you find your way from the airport to the training center. An AAA card also entitles you to discounts at major car rental agencies and many hotels. They also provide travelers' checks free of surcharge.

The major car rental firms such as Avis and Hertz have preferred renter "club" cards. There is no charge for joining; you simply fill out an application with credit information and a profile of your preferences in automobiles, insurance coverage, and the like. You have a special "800" number to call for reservations, and you no longer have to wait in line and then fill out a lengthy rental agreement at the airport. When you arrive, your car is waiting for you. Although you do not accumulate "miles" the way you do with airlines, from time to time you will receive coupons that entitle you to an upgrade or some special package.

Hotels and motels. Most hotel and motel chains also have their own travel clubs. These include the Marriott "Honored Guest" program, the Hilton "Honors," the Holiday Inn "Priority Club," the Radisson "Key Rewards," the Hyatt "Gold Passport," and even the Days Inn "Inn-Credible" Card Club. Some, like Hyatt, charge an annual fee; others assess a one-time initiation fee. Most are free.

Compared with the airlines programs, the hotel and motel preferred guest programs take considerable time (and expense) before you build up enough credits to qualify for an award such as a free weekend. They typically give you a point for every dollar you spend. You may prefer to have the credits applied to your airline account. Their main value is that they often entitle you to certain perks such as an "800" number for improved reservation service, a special check-in line, discounts, a free breakfast, a room upgrade, or a morning paper.

The March, 1995, *Consumer Reports Travel Letter,* summarized in the April, 1996, issue of *Consumer Reports* magazine, evaluated a number of hotel discount programs. For an annual fee, you get a card that entitles you to a reduction in the cost of a room at thousands of North American hotels and motels. The best buy appears to be the "America at 50% Discount Program." A fee of $19.95 entitles you to 10% to 50% reductions at a number of budget to mid-priced hotels and motels. You may do just as well with your AAA card, but call 800-828-5004 for information. You can find out more about this and other ways to save money on travel by getting the most recent *Consumer Reports Best Travel Deals* at your local bookstore.

Saving money on air travel

As you know, since deregulation, air travel costs can vary wildly and seem to have no rational basis. Most travelers are accustomed to costs being based on mileage... the longer the trip, the more it costs. Not so in air travel. I once flew from Tallahassee, FL, to Toronto, Ontario, for *less* than it had cost me to fly from Tallahassee to Fort Myers, FL, the previous week. The overhead involved in air travel... salaries, gate rental, insurance, aircraft...is so high that once the airline gets a plane in the air, the distance it flies is a negligible aspect of the total cost.

Air fares are driven by the need for the airlines to fill as many seats as possible to break even. They will offer all kinds of inducements and discounts to fill the empty seats on the less popular flights, while charging the highest fares possible on the heavily subscribed routes. This leads to some strange paradoxes. I don't know what rates will be when you read this book, but I have encountered or read about some bizarre fares. For example, the fare from San Francisco to Dallas, a very popular route, was $360, but there was a cheap flight from San Francisco to Kansas City, changing in Dallas, for $195 (Gavzer, 1992). Book the Kansas City flight, carry your luggage, get off at Dallas, and pocket $165.

Or you may discover that the whole is greater than the sum of its parts. Gavzer (1992) reported that when a direct full-fare ticket from Los Angeles to Dallas cost $330, by taking the cheapest flights from LA to Albuquerque ($95) and from Albuquerque to Dallas ($92) you could make the trip for $187, thus saving $143. This "split city" scheme would be terrific if you wanted to visit an internship in Albuquerque; otherwise you may have to waste a lot of time there waiting for your cheap flight to Dallas.

It is essential that you consult a knowledgeable expert who is willing to work with you to take full advantage of differential fares and discount rates. Remember, travel agents work on a commission. For them, time is money. So the more time they spend saving you money, the less they make. A good one who values your repeat business and enjoys finding you a bargain can be very helpful, but do not expect that every one will automatically give you that level of service. Ask around and shop for a good agent.

If you have access to a computer with a modem, you can be your own travel agent. Subscribe to a gateway service such as America On Line, Prodigy, or Compuserve, and you can access American Airlines' "EASY SABRE" system, see for yourself what flights are available at which fares on the dates you wish to fly, and book your own reservations on line. You can also choose how to receive your tickets. A nice feature of the system is you can request that it present you with the options available according to the fares, beginning with the least expensive. Or you can surf the Internet to the various airlines' Web sites and find special promotions that no one, not even travel agents, can book for you.

Whether you use your computer or a travel agent, be prepared to invest a fair amount of time and effort planning your trip to obtain the lowest prices. When I was ADCT, I looked for every opportunity to visit my students on internship who were scattered all over the U.S. When I had a meeting in Chicago, I decided I would use the occasion to visit a student who was interning at the University of Rochester School of Medicine. Looking at the map, it seemed it would be easy to fly from Tallahassee to Rochester, NY, visit our intern, fly on to Chicago, attend my meeting, and return home. Not so. Thanks to the "hub" system, none of the airlines serving Tallahassee flew from Rochester to Chicago; I could go to Rochester and return from Chicago on an "open jaws" plan for about $500, but getting from Rochester to Chicago on another carrier would cost $350 for a total of $850.

Since one usually saves money by staying with a single carrier, I tried again, plotting a zigzag route that had me going from Rochester to Chicago via the hub in Cleveland. That pushed the total to over $1,000. It seemed I would have to abandon my plan to visit Rochester, so I asked the round trip fare from Tallahassee to Chicago; $168 I was told. On an impulse, I asked the round trip fare from Chicago to Rochester and return on the other carrier, and found it was only $178. That's right; they charged $178 round trip but $350 one way! Apparently many more people want to go from Rochester to Chicago than vice versa. So, by buying one round trip from Tallahassee to Chicago and another round trip from Chicago to Rochester, I was able to do the whole trip for $346 instead of the $850 I was first quoted. Although I saved $500, it required at least a half a day to work everything out.

As a general rule, you can save a great deal by booking early and paying promptly, but you often must pay a penalty of as much as 100% if you cancel or make any changes. For example, when Eastern Airlines was flying, the unrestricted round trip coach fare from my home city to Los Angeles was $1,020, the restricted excursion with a 25% penalty ranged from $400 to $460, and the restricted excursion with a 100% penalty was $350 to $410 depending on the time of day and so on. However, if I made my arrangements properly, I could stop off at Dallas or Houston for very little extra or go on to San Francisco on an "open jaws" itinerary for about $100 more.

Airlines compete heavily for discretionary travel. Flights in and out of tourist areas are apt to be more heavily discounted than flights catering to business people who have to fly regardless of cost. If you consult the travel section of your Sunday paper, you may find deeply discounted fares to popular tourist areas such as Atlantic City, NJ, or Orlando, FL. If you find some bargains such as these to cities near where you will be interviewing, it may pay to book the cheap flight and rent a car. Indeed, sometimes a rental car will be part of the package.

On the other hand, air fares are excessive in and out of cities served by only one or two carriers or where the economy dictates there will be a high proportion of business travelers. Many of the travelers in my home town of Tallahassee travel on state business and have to fly no matter what the fares are. Since our major carrier, Eastern, collapsed, there is little competition, so fares are now extremely high. When my wife and I recently flew to Phoenix, another state capital, we saved $500 each on air fares by flying out of Jacksonville instead of Tallahassee. We felt the three-hour drive was worth it. If you are in a similar situation, check air fares out of neighboring locales.

Most business travelers return home for the weekend. To attract the discretionary traveler, airlines often offer deep discounts on trips that extend over a Saturday night. when I had to fly from Tallahassee, FL, to Austin, TX, on business. I found that the air fare was $600 less if I stayed over Saturday.

Regardless of the number of seats sold, transcontinental airlines have to get the planes they flew to the West Coast during the day back to the East Coast by the next morning, in spite of the three-hour time zone differential. In order to fill otherwise empty seats, they often offer reduced "night owl" or "red eye" fares on overnight flights from West to East.

Those of you who are "night people" may also save in another way. During the day, the airlines' booking agents are very busy. Their calls are monitored, and they are evaluated by how many calls they can handle in an hour. That is why you often get a busy signal when you dial their toll free "800" numbers. In the early morning hours, however, the 24-hour "800" numbers have very little traffic, and the bored agents can spend much more time working with you. We have obtained some incredible travel bargains, such as a $198 round trip Miami to London fare, during these conversations at 2:00 or 3:00 AM.

Whether you call at night or during the day, do not assume that the price you are being quoted is definitive, or even correct. Not only do different airlines have different rates subject to different restrictions, but booking agents differ in their knowledge of the system and their willingness to ferret out bargains. Each flight has only a limited number of discounted seats available, and, of course, full-fare passengers have first priority for any available seats. Thus, the availability of bargain fares varies. You may be told on Monday that a low fare is unavailable, but if you book at a higher rate, don't expect anyone to notify you if there is a cancellation on Wednesday and the lower rate you initially requested becomes available.

Booking agents can make mistakes computing fares. A newspaper did a study in which they called agents and general managers at several different airlines inquiring about the cost of certain flights. They reported that the rates quoted differed substantially, not only among carriers, but also among agents computing fares for a particular flight. In short, if you do not like the rate you are being quoted, hang up and try again later. You may get quoted a lower price. If so, take it. Once you have made your reservation, your fare is locked in. (The exception to this is if there is a general fare increase. In that case, your fare is protected only if you have already been ticketed.)

It may be possible for your ADCT or your support group to negotiate a special group rate for your internship class. One year the sales manager at Eastern Airlines waived certain restrictions for my internship applicants, such as giving them the over Saturday rate even if they did not stay over. The rationale was that this group of students, who would be doing a great deal of travel on limited budgets, would soon experience a marked increase in income, and it was an excellent way for the airline to build customer loyalty. Unfortunately, Eastern went bankrupt the next year.

Getting there is half the hassle

The combination of high holiday volume and poor weather make December and January bad months to travel. Unfortunately, that's when you usually must interview. Do not schedule tight connections in hub cities, and keep your luggage in your possession. Do not wear casual clothes, such as warm up-suits or shorts, while flying, unless you are prepared to interview in that outfit.

Flight delays. A flight is considered "delayed" if it is 15 minutes or more late in departing from the gate or arriving at the destination gate. (Mechanical problems and weather are not counted, so as to avoid the temptation to fly an unsafe plane.) In 1991, Department of Transportation data showed that 17.5% of the flights in the U.S., involving an estimated 80 million passengers, were "delayed" (Gavzer, 1992). Every month the FAA publishes a "list of shame" in which it reports those flights that were delayed more than 80% of the time during the previous month. One month, USAir Flight 326 from Boston to Washington was late *100%* of the time, with the delays *averaging* 77 minutes. Airports are also evaluated. Among the five worst are La Guardia, Newark, Chicago/O'Hare, Kennedy, and San Francisco (Weiner, 1990). If you are traveling on an airline or through an airport with frequent delays, allow extra time for your connections or consider changing your itinerary.

Losing luggage. Although you should plan to carry your luggage on the aircraft, the airline personnel at the gate may require you to check it. This is most apt to happen if your bag cannot fit under the seat, if you have more than two pieces, or if the overhead compartments are full, which is often the case around Christmas. If your bag is checked, it may get lost or items may be stolen from it, whether or not it is locked. Do not pack anything you cannot afford to lose in a bag that may have to be checked. Dress nicely, and carry a small survival kit with essential toiletries and a change of underwear in your briefcase or purse. It also helps to bring along your sense of humor.

Getting "bumped." Airlines often overbook at peak seasons, such as December, and at prime times, such as late afternoon. When more people with reservations show up than the computer predicted, they are in what they refer to as an "oversold condition." More prosaically it means someone is going to get "bumped."

The best way to avoid being bumped is to have your boarding pass and to arrive at the gate early. Select your seats when you buy your tickets, and get your boarding passes issued at the time of ticketing. Then check in *at the gate* early...at least 45 minutes before flight time. It is the folks arriving at the last minute who have not had their boarding passes stamped who are most likely to be stranded.

It can pay to volunteer. Before bumping anyone, the agent will make an announcement that the flight is oversold and will ask for volunteers. If your schedule is loose or you are on the return leg, it may be to your advantage to volunteer to be bumped. At the very least they should offer you a free round trip ticket anywhere in the system that is good for a year. (Check the fine print...it may black out certain dates or be "subject to availability" (i.e., only good for standby.) The more oversold they are, the more incentives you may be offered. Perhaps they will offer to make the free ticket good any time or, as they get more desperate, offer a free companion ticket or even cash in addition to the ticket. There can be a stampede of volunteers, so decide early.

One student on his way home volunteered and was given a free unrestricted round trip ticket for anywhere in the U.S. and a seat on another carrier's flight departing an hour later. He actually arrived at his destination several hours sooner than the passengers who remained on the original flight since it developed mechanical difficulties and had to turn back.

If you are bumped, voluntarily or otherwise, you are entitled to certain perks. The airline will usually notify people waiting to meet you at your destination, either by telex or by letting you use the phone. If the next flight out is after a normal mealtime, ask for a free meal ticket so you can have lunch or dinner at their expense. Most airlines have clubs or VIP rooms. If you ask, the gate attendant may give you a card allowing you to wait there. If you have to spend the night, you should ask for lodging at a nearby hotel and meal checks for dinner and breakfast.

Canceled flights. Nice clothes, a polite manner, and a frequent traveler card may also help you get better treatment from harassed ticket clerks if your flight is canceled and you have to be rerouted (as occurred to me on three out of four flights one miserable December). Remember to keep on your person a list of the names and phone numbers of the people you are supposed to see so you can notify them when your plane is canceled or delayed. (See the Travel Planner in Appendix 4.) A long distance telephone credit card or, even better, a cellular phone, and a supply of travelers' checks are other helpful travel accessories.

While the airlines are obliged to provide meals and lodging if you are bumped, this may not apply if the flight has to be canceled, especially if the cancellation is due to weather. Under Industry Rule 240, they must get you to your destination, either on an alternate flight or another airline, but there is no guarantee *when* you will get there. You will be competing with everyone else who was on your flight for a limited number of seats, and if weather has closed the airport, no one will be going anywhere until it reopens. That is why every winter the newspapers feature photos of stranded passengers sleeping on their luggage.

To lessen your chances of being stranded by a canceled flight, give your airline a number where you can be reached the morning of your flight, and arrive early. Airlines may know several hours in advance that a flight will have to be canceled. If they have your number and/or you arrive early, they can put you on an earlier flight or on another airline.

If you are late getting to the airport and miss a flight, you may have to switch to another airline that may not accept deeply discounted or complimentary tickets. Or if your airline goes bankrupt, as one seems to do most every year, other carriers may be reluctant to accept any tickets issued by the insolvent airline. Have a credit card with a high enough credit limit or enough travelers' checks to pay for a new ticket if necessary. If you charged your ticket on the bankrupt airline to a major credit card, the charge should be canceled. Otherwise you are just one more creditor (Gavzer, 1992).

Jumping ship. Sometimes a flight's departure is delayed interminably, supposedly to correct mechanical problems. This can be a subterfuge. An airline that has two partly-filled flights, both going to the same city an hour or two apart, may be tempted to board the first flight, delay it for an hour, then transfer the passengers to the second so they can fly one full flight instead. To accomplish this, they stall the passengers seated on the first flight by assuring them the difficulty will be corrected momentarily. Eventually they announce that the "bad news" is the problem can't be corrected but the "good news" is they have another flight to the same city that is just about to depart and they have room for almost everyone on this other flight. Then everyone scrambles off the first plane and engages in a footrace to the second one in order to be one of the "lucky" passengers who secures a seat.

Of course sometimes there actually is a mechanical problem. Your first hint of trouble may be a note on the departure board to "see agent." Or you may surrender your ticket, board the aircraft, and find that ten minutes after the scheduled departure time the door is still open and everyone is standing around. Eventually you may be told that they are awaiting a new crew or checking a possible leak in the framistat.

If it is important that you get to your destination on time, don't just sit there. Try to find out what is going on. Perhaps, looking out the window, you see that the ground crew has disassembled one of the engines and are quizzically scratching their heads as they gaze at the parts scattered over the tarmac. The flight attendants are sitting down and working on their nails. If you are on a tight schedule, consider taking another flight. Experienced air travelers carry a copy of the *Official Airline Guides North American Pocket Flight Guide (OAG)* that is published monthly and is available in major airports. For every destination in North America, it lists every flight on every airline from every city. If you are on the ground in Los Angeles waiting for your flight to O'Hare to depart, consult the *OAG Guide.* You will see there are about five dozen other flights going from "LAX" to "ORD" every day. The people you see grabbing their luggage and heading for the door when a mechanical problem is announced are hurrying to get on one of these other flights. Consult the *OAG*, and, if you have a phone, call the other airlines to see if they have seats available on their flights to your destination. If they do, book the flight, take your luggage, get your ticket back from the agent at the desk, and go catch your new flight. If you don't have a phone or an *OAG,* you can still debark and try to switch to another flight, but it is much more difficult.

In the event your destination city is socked in by weather or the delay is caused by a "gate hold" at your destination, changing planes won't help. However, a cellular phone can still come in handy. When a flight that normally serves dinner was held at the gate well past the normal meal time, one ravenous passenger called Domino's and had a large pizza delivered to his seat on the plane.

Gate attendants are human, and, like all of us, they respond better to people who are polite and considerate. *They* didn't cause the overbooking, cloud the skies, or break the framistat, so don't take out your frustration by berating them. Be firm, however, and, if the delay is going to ruin the rest of your life, let the agent know. Although you should not get hysterical, a quavering voice and a controlled tear or two may help.

Car rentals

The only practical way for you to get to some internship centers in distant cities will be to fly there and rent a car at the airport. You will find that rates and amenities vary tremendously. Like the airlines, the car-rental agencies have a glut of customers during the business week and fewer on weekends. They establish their rates to encourage discretionary travelers.

To rent a car you need to have a valid driver's license and be over the minimum age established by that company. However, I would not rent a car without having a major credit card. Without one, you will be required to leave a humongous cash deposit to guarantee you will return the vehicle. Reserve an automobile in advance, and shop for the best deal. If you work for a state agency or university, you may be able to get a government rate. One might assume that firms whose names emphasize their frugality (i.e., Budget, Dollar, Thrifty) would give you the best rates. That may not be true, especially when you factor in hidden costs. Check out the major firms as well. If you ask, your travel agent can usually find the best rate and reserve a car for you.

Find the package that is best suited for your needs on this particular trip. In addition to the daily cost, ask whether there is a mileage fee. If you are not driving very far, a lower daily rate with a 100-mile-a-day allotment may be best; on the other hand if you are going to be logging a lot of miles, a higher daily rate and unlimited mileage may be more economical.

Insurance is a major factor in renting a car. Many companies make as much from the insurance as they do from the rental. If you already have auto insurance, check with your carrier. If you are covered while driving a rental car, and almost everyone is, refuse the added coverage. (Remember your AAA membership probably covers any emergency road service.)

Make sure you know the renter's policy on gasoline. Are you expected to bring the car back with the same amount of gas as you found in it, fully fueled, or what? How much will they charge you if they have to refill it? Not knowing these details can easily add $10 or $15 to your costs.

In choosing a car-rental agency, consider whether it is located at the airport or in the boondocks. The greater convenience of the airport location may offset the price differential, especially if you are on a tight schedule. Being stuck at an off-brand car rental office waiting for their one van to take you to the airport while your plane takes off without you can ruin the best-planned trip.

Make sure to ask if there are discounts available. You may qualify for a discount by virtue of belonging to AAA or some other organization, because you flew in on a certain airline, or by virtue of staying in a particular hotel. I was once given an unexpected discount because I was in uniform when I returned the vehicle... a Scoutmaster's uniform! Make sure you take along all your membership cards and don't forget your driver's license. Also bring along any discount or upgrade coupons you have received from your airline flyer's club or AAA. In winter, especially, having a larger car may be very helpful.

When you pick up the car, look it over for obvious damage. If you see anything wrong, get another car or have it noted on your contract so they do not charge you for it. Similarly, check to make sure you have a spare tire. If you don't, ask that one be provided, or, if you feel daring, make sure the absence of a spare is noted on your contract so you don't get accused of selling it. If you are not sure how to get to the internship, ask for a map and directions, and make sure you know how to get to the place where you must return the car. In fact, if I know I am going to be in a hurry to make my flight on the way back, I check out the location of the rental return area before I leave the airport to make sure I know how to find it.

Renting and returning a car is much simpler if you belong to their "club" and have a prearranged rental number. Most companies have programs whereby you fill out an application form that lists your preferences in vehicle, insurance options, driver's license number, preferred mode of payment, discounts you may be eligible for, credit card numbers, and so on. They will issue you a card, which the clerk puts in a computer and the rental contract emerges printed correctly. If you are in a hurry when you return the car, you merely have to record the mileage, insert the papers in a time clock, and drop it in a slot. The bill will be mailed to you.

Lodging: Reducing the "rack rate"

The least expensive lodging is, of course, to stay with a relative or friend. Often a fellow student from your school who is currently interning at the place where you are interviewing will put you up. If you hope to visit someone, you should check well ahead of time, before you have booked your tickets.

Realistically, unless you have a large extended family or are only applying to places close to home, you will have to spend some nights in hotels or motels. If you are driving to internships or if you rent a car, you will have many more options than if you are relying on public transportation. This is where the AAA tour books come in handy, because you can use their spotter maps to locate hotels in the vicinity and then check the rates that are listed. Be advised, though, that the AAA book does not include all the motels in an area, and the fact that a place is not included does not necessarily mean that it is unacceptable.

If you look at the hotel maps for most cities, you will see that there are generally three clusters that have a high density of accommodations: 1) the "downtown" area, especially in the proximity of a civic or convention center; 2) the airport; and 3) near the exits to an Interstate or "beltway" around the city. Typically the downtown area is the most expensive, catering to commercial travelers who use their room to conduct business and who can put a $100 to $200 room on their expense account.

Next most expensive is the airport area, especially the chains such as Hyatt, Marriott, and Sheraton. However, there are often smaller places that may lack such amenities as a pool or a lounge that are less expensive (i.e., in the $39 to $49 bracket). These are the motels airlines use for stranded passengers. They often have the code word "Inn" in their names: Comfort Inn, Days Inn, Fairfield Inn, HoJo Inn, Red Roof Inn. However, this is not an infallible sign, so make sure you negotiate the rates.

Least expensive, typically, are the places near an Interstate exit. Many cater to automobile travelers who are looking for a place to sleep and little else. Since motorists are, by definition, mobile, they can shop for bargains, and these motels must be economical to compete. If you have wheels, you can often save money by staying at one of these places on the edge of town and driving in to the medical center instead of booking a room across from the hospital. Of course, the cost is even lower if you team up with another applicant to share travel and lodging expenses.

Although everyone knows you can shop for air fares, fewer people are aware that hotel rates are very negotiable, especially at the more expensive places. No matter where you stay, *always ask for a lower rate*. When you book your room, ask the price. Whatever they quote you, respond, "Oh, that must be your rack rate," and ask what discounts are available. ("Rack rate" is a key phrase, and it shows you know the ins and outs of the hotel business.)

You can probably qualify for a discount on the basis of some group to which you belong. Obviously, if you joined one of the hotel discount clubs described in the *Consumer Reports* articles I mentioned earlier, you should start with that. Even if the motel you are negotiating with is not listed in the book you got with your membership card, try asking anyway. Different hotel chains join and drop out of these programs faster than the books can keep track of them. APA membership entitles you to special rates at Holiday Inn, Howard Johnson, and Sheraton. AAA membership is worth a 10% discount at participating hotels and motels. If you are a state employee, such as a Teaching Assistant at a state university or a psychology trainee at a state hospital, try asking for the "government" or "state" rate. You may be told to be prepared to show government ID or a letter of authorization on state stationery when you arrive. However, the only place I actually have been asked for my government ID is in the District of Columbia. Again, being well-dressed helps at the check-in desk. If the government rate does not apply, ask for an educational or student discount. You will soon learn which chains cater to which groups. Or your travel agent may be able to book a combination package that includes air fare, hotel, and car, all at a discount.

Many major medical centers have negotiated special medical or hospital visitor rates with one or more local hotels and motels. Ask the secretary who books your interview. If the secretary does not know, simply ask for a hospital rate when you make your reservation. Because I was a hospital visitor, Hilton recently charged me only $39 for a $120 room.

Each hotel has only a limited number of discounted rooms, so the earlier you book, the better your chances. The nice thing about hotels, in contrast to airlines, is that you do not have to pay in advance and there is no penalty for canceling your reservation.

Other things are also negotiable. You might be able to get a free breakfast, for example, especially if you belong to the hotel chain's preferred guest program. Other perks can include a room upgrade, a complimentary cocktail, concierge service, and a morning newspaper. If you prefer a nonsmoking room or a king size bed, ask for it. If you are a woman traveling alone, mention this and ask for a secure room. Not only will this lessen the likelihood that you will be followed across the parking lot by some polyester-clad creep from the lounge, but it may also get you upgraded to a superior room at the same price.

The time to negotiate discounts and special perks is when you book the room, not at midnight after you have arrived, tired and disheveled, from the airport. If you are trying to get a discount, it is best to call the hotel or motel directly, rather than the 800 number, The person answering the 800 phone may not have the necessary authority. If you cannot get what you want, ask for the Assistant Manager. If they still will not budge, try someplace else. (As a general rule, the better the hotel and the more they are geared to business travelers, the greater the discount you can get.)

Even with all these maneuvers, if the hotel is heavily booked, the best you may be able to do is the "corporate" rate. That gets you a nice room, but it is very expensive. It is best to try somewhere else, but if you must stay at that hotel, take that rate and ask to be put on standby for the lower government or educational rate. When you check in, ask the clerk if the lower rate room opened up, and you may be pleasantly surprised. Most airlines have arrangements with major hotel chains, so you may get additional frequent traveler miles when you fly in on that airline. Ask for a coupon at the desk, fill it out, and leave it with the clerk.

Whatever the rate you manage to negotiate, make sure you obtain and record a confirmation number or name. No matter what your expected arrival time, it is a good idea to guarantee your room for late arrival by providing a major credit card number. If for some reason you cannot make it, call and cancel before 6:00 PM or you will have to pay for your (unused) room. Make sure you get a cancellation number, and later examine your credit card bill to make sure the charge does not appear.

Like airlines, hotels sometimes overbook, especially when there is a big convention or a major sporting event in town. Also, in many states, guests are not legally required to leave when their reservations expire. If the airports or highways are closed because of bad weather, many guests will stay on and new arrivals are out of luck, even though they have guaranteed reservations. If you arrive after all the rooms at your rate have been occupied, the desk clerk has three choices: 1) check you into a better room at the same rate if one is available; 2) get you reservations at another hotel (and have the van take you there); or 3) shrug and express regrets.

If you were a desk clerk in this situation and you were confronted with: 1) a polite, well-dressed young person who is a member of your "Honored Guest" program, 2) some smelly slob who is clad in shorts and a stained tank top, or 3) an arrogant SOB who is calling you names and pounding the counter, which one would *you* discretely signal to come back in 20 minutes and then upgrade to the Presidential Suite? (If you want to try overkill, you might mention to the desk clerk how much you admire his or her ability to deal with such contentious people and offer to fetch the poor harassed person a cup of coffee or a soft drink while he or she works on your problem.)

Even with all these discounts, travel is very expensive. If your parents or relatives inquire about a suitable Christmas gift, you might mention a go-anywhere ticket if they ever again become available, or they may be able to provide you with some free travel if they have saved up some frequent traveler coupons. If you can cadge a first-class upgrade coupon, take it by all means. Luggage and clothing are also quite acceptable. If you have not purchased a new suitcase or garment bag in the last three years, you will be amazed at the advances that have been made.

Dressing for travel and interviews

You may need to add to your wardrobe. You will have to dress professionally when on internship, so you might as well get the clothes now. Assuming you are going to be on the road for several days, I would suggest you take at least two complete outfits, preferably ones you can mix and match. A solid color navy blue business suit and a light or medium gray one in compatible fabrics (preferably 100% wool in a climate-suitable weight) can provide at least four outfits as you swap your jackets with your slacks or skirts. Dark brown and tan provide another compatible combination. Women have a greater range of colors to mix and match, such as red, black, or white. Or consider a solid color suit and sports coat/slacks outfit for men, and suit or blazer/skirt outfit plus a business dress for women. (Stick with solids when you are building your wardrobe. Patterned materials are much less versatile and hence less cost-effective.)

Think of your jacket as a frame for your blouse and scarf, or shirt and tie. Only one item should be patterned. If you wear a patterned suit or jacket, keep the other items plain. If your jacket and the shirt or blouse are solid, then you can have a patterned tie or scarf. Men should stick with white or light blue shirts. Jewelry should be understated and complementary to the overall outfit. Remember, you want people to focus on you and not be distracted by excessive or clashing accouterments.

Sweaters and slacks/skirts will probably be appropriate when you are working at most internship agencies (although some insist on coat and tie for men and a suit or dress for women), but I feel this is too casual for interviewing. Nevertheless, take along some "nice" informal clothes such as dress jeans for going out in the evening with the present interns. Be prepared for cold or inclement weather. Now is the time to invest in that tan all-weather coat with the removable lining.

Remember that you will be doing a lot of walking, so take well-shined leather shoes that are attractive but comfortable. This is not the time for five inch stiletto heels (especially for the men), but don't go to the other extreme and wear running shoes or (shudder) sandals. Gender-appropriate hose is a must.

Murphy's Law applies with a vengeance when it comes to traveling. To paraphrase the bumper sticker, "Spills Happen," usually the first day out, so avoid those light colored fabrics that do not blend well with tomato sauce. Familiarity with the operation of a sewing needle and an iron (both of which will be available where you stay) may prove useful. If they aren't in the room, call Housekeeping. You can minimize difficulties by taking the time to check for loose buttons, wobbly eyeglass frames, and frayed shoelaces before you pack.

What to take

Prepare for internship travel as you would for a backpacking trip in the Andes. Include "emergency equipment" such as spare glasses or contacts, a sewing kit (with extra buttons), a styptic pencil, nail clipper, band aids, spare shoelaces, extra pantyhose, (and clear nail polish to repair the pantyhose) in your travel kit. You may never need them, but if you do, you will *really* need them. "Traveling light" is fashionable, and there is no need to carry excessive amounts of heavy items such as shampoo, but it is important to take everything you might need. This is not the time to conduct an empirical test of whether that new deodorant really does last 72 hours without replenishing. Which is worse, carrying along an extra four ounces or asphyxiating the internship selection committee?

Invest in a box of Ziploc freezer bags and, after squeezing the air from bottles of liquids, seal the bottles in bags. (Liquids expand and leak at altitude.) Instead of loading up your luggage with huge and heavy bottles, just take a small container with the minimum necessary amount of each item. If you cannot find 2-oz. travel sizes, buy small plastic bottles at the nearest discount drug store and decant the appropriate amount of whatever therein.

Is this beginning to sound like a Scout Manual? Well, as a matter of fact, I do carry a Swiss Army knife in my permanently-packed travel kit; it has reattached the handle of a briefcase, repaired eyeglasses, sharpened pencils, and opened innumerable soda bottles. A mini-flashlight that stays beside my bed in case of fire also helps me find my way around a strange motel room in the dark. Don't forget a small travel alarm, and remember to reprogram it as you change time zones.

Interviewing and travel are both stressful, so don't be surprised if your body turns on you. Even if it functions with the regularity and precision of a Swiss chronometer at home, it can go totally out of synch on the road, especially if you have jet lag to contend with. Take along whatever you use to deal with bodily emergencies such as gastrointestinal distress, allergies, headaches, hemorrhages, cramps, etc.

Go to AAA and get maps of where you will be visiting. One year an applicant got hopelessly lost, gave up, and returned home without interviewing. After turning South instead of North more often than I care to remember, I added a small compass to my kit. In addition to helping me orient myself when I leave an airport or a subway, it can be invaluable in finding my way around strange hospital corridors, many of which seem to have been designed with minimal spatial cues to thwart patients bent on leaving.

Don't forget to take along the material you will need for interviewing: copies of your application, including extra CVs for interviewers, and brochures issued by the centers where you will be interviewing, along with any notes you might have made about questions to ask. And of course, bring along this book with a paper clip marking Appendix 6 on questions to ask.

Before you depart, make arrangements for staying in touch with your home base. Other internships may call while you are off interviewing, so your friends and ADCT should know how to reach you. If you take a cellular phone, leave a message with its number on your telephone answering machine. Answering machines can be invaluable, especially those that automatically "time stamp" your messages and from which you can retrieve your calls by phone while you are on travel status. However, do not rely on them. Tapes can get overloaded, especially if you have some "friend" or former lover who feels it is amusing to recite poetry or play music into your machine. Power outages can erase your messages. Most important, from the time you send in your first application until the week after Notification Day, remember that your future Internship Training Director may be calling. If you have "amusing" or "entertaining" messages on your machine, ask yourself if this is really how you want to impress your top-choice ITD. Selection staff at internships have told me that one of their greatest frustrations is repeatedly listening to "cute" messages on applicants' answering machines. That aggravation may determine whether or not they call back. (Some students have told me that this advice alone is worth the price of this book.)

Other tips

Six weeks or more before you leave for interviews, get a flu shot. Except for a test tube, which it rather resembles, an airplane is the best place in the world for exchanging air-borne viruses with people from all over the world. If you are visiting hospitals, remember that they have lots of sick people and therefore more than their share of germs. If you don't pick up something while traveling, you will from one of your fellow applicants. By Groundhog Day, many of the intern applicants who didn't get their flu shots will be sick.

CHAPTER NINE

THE SITE VISIT AND INTERVIEW

The personal interview and visit to the internship facility is the most time-consuming and expensive part of the internship-seeking process. Applicants and training staffs alike often get little else accomplished during the six- to eight-week long interviewing season. The mean expense reported in a recent poll was more than $1,000 per applicant (Thorne, 1997), and some applicants spend twice that (Fox, 1991). Despite all this effort, there is no evidence that interviewing improves intern selection. Rickard and Clements (1986) compared the interns selected during the years when their training center interviewed candidates with those chosen the years they did not; on all the objective performance criteria they examined, the two samples were virtually identical.

Nevertheless, interviewing has become an accepted part of the selection process. Although a few programs do not interview candidates, the vast majority request an interview if only as a test of applicants' motivation. Fox (1991, p. 34) reported, "Some programs apparently use the interview as a screening device by indicating to applicants that interviews are optional, but that willingness to appear for a personal interview will be viewed as an index of strong interest in their program."

Training centers' policies with regard to scheduling interviews vary greatly. Some centers grant interviews to all who request them; others adopt a "first come, first served" policy," granting interviews for the first 20, 30, 40, or whatever candidates who ask and then not scheduling any more. Many internships now interview only by invitation after they have screened the written applications. As a result of these differences, one Northeastern internship interviewed only ten applicants for three vacancies, whereas another interviewed 95 to 100 candidates for five slots (Plante, 1987).

To add to the confusion, some internships conduct interviews whenever applicants can arrange to visit, some confine interviewing to a two- or three-week period, and some require all applicants to present themselves on a specific date with no exceptions permitted. Some allow telephone interviews; others do not. Plante (1987) described the plight of one student who had to make two round trips from Kansas City to Boston to interview at two neighboring internships because one only conducted interviews in December whereas the other would only interview in January. Her cost in air fare was equivalent to 20% of the stipends offered by the internships. As Fox (1991, p. 34) remarked, "Some directors are understanding and flexible in responding to the realities of students' life circumstances, others are embarrassingly rigid and callous."

If at all possible, make an effort to go to the training center to see it for yourself and interview in person. Not only should it enhance your candidacy, but it is your single best opportunity to obtain the data *you* need to evaluate the program and its personnel. As I noted earlier, every year some students change their opinions radically after actually seeing the internship settings and meeting the people. I personally find a site visit indispensable in sizing up a place.

An exception is when the facility has rigged the situation so that you are deprived of an adequate opportunity to evaluate their program. One of my students traveled over 2,000 miles at considerable cost and personal inconvenience to sit in a cafeteria with 50 other applicants on a Saturday morning listening to the ITD read the program's brochure to them. After a brief tour of the grounds, they were sent on their way. While he was understandably indignant, he had learned enough about the program's attitude to cross it off his list.

In the middle of December, after you have submitted all your applications and before you start traveling, there will be a lull during which you can catch your breath, regroup, and get ready for the next phase. This is a good time to prepare for interviewing.

One of the best ways to get ready is to read the advice of previous students who have been through the process and written about their experiences. I recommend the accounts by Burt (1985), Kingsley (1985), Gollaher and Craig (1994), and Jacob (1987). These first-person reports by actual survivors have an authenticity that cannot be duplicated. They will help prepare you for some of the mood swings you will experience and give you the concrete practical advice that can only be provided by someone who has been through the process, such as taking advantage of every opportunity to go to the bathroom because you never know if you will get another chance.

Their accounts are also full of "war stories" about the strange things that can happen and the peculiar people you might encounter.

Fox, who was an ITD before becoming an ADCT, complained about "... the high-handedness, arrogance, unprofessionalism and plain rudeness which a number of our students encounter each year in their dealings with some of our colleagues in some internship programs" (1991, p. 35). Fox is correct. I have been out there myself and experienced it firsthand, so don't think this behavior is reserved for students. Some training personnel are equal-opportunity jerks. Fortunately these turkeys are in the minority, and, as Fox noted (1991, p. 35), "We all have our bozos." Nevertheless, attitudes like this rankle and are an added aggravation at an already difficult time in your lives. So, during your travels, if you think you have wandered into the Twilight Zone, recall these accounts. It may not be reassuring to realize that this is reality, but at least you will know others have survived similar insanity.

Also helpful are articles by Internship Training Directors on how they view the interviewing and internship selection process. I recommend the articles by Belar and Orgel (1980), Grace (1985), and Monti (1985), all of which can be found in the book edited by Dana and May (1987). May et al. (1990) reported that many ITDs rely on the interview as their primary selection device. They are as interested in intangible aspects such as rapport, a sense of humor, and flexibility as they are in the actual content. Maintaining eye contact and shaking hands firmly may be as important as what you say.

Hersh and Poey (1985) have provided a convenient and concise outline of questions that ITDs may ask you and that you can ask them. They also suggested some questions you should *not* ask. Appendices 5 and 6 provide you with questions asked by interviewers and other questions you can ask them. Study this material, assimilate it, and then integrate it into your own personal style. Often it is a good idea to role-play or practice interviewing using a fellow student or your major professor as the interviewer. Then switch, and you try taking the ITD's role. You will find it greatly increases your understanding of what the person on the other side of the desk is looking for.

Scheduling interviews

As I have noted before, I recommend that you visit all the sites you are considering if it is at all possible. This is for your own benefit. More than once an applicant has walked into a place and immediately sensed, "This is not for me."

Policies on interviewing differ. Whereas some internships will simply not consider any applicant they have not personally interviewed, at least one internship refuses to interview anyone. Because they are located in a remote area, they reason that interviewing would give local applicants an undue advantage because travel to and from the facility is so difficult and expensive. If applicants insist, the Training Center does set aside two Saturdays when candidates can visit the facility and listen to lectures on the various rotations. People who have participated reported that this was not a worthwhile expenditure of time and effort.

Most internships will interview anyone who requests an opportunity, either in person or by phone. Indeed, not interviewing is often seen as a sign of disinterest, and, as I noted in Chapter Two, perceived disinterest is deadly to your candidacy. Some internships set aside a couple of specified weekends for interviewing, and others make individual arrangements with each candidate. As the number of applications increase, more internships are first screening the overall pool of applicants and inviting only a select subgroup. The safest strategy is for you to take the initiative and call requesting an interviews.

Realistically, however, you may not have the time or money to interview everywhere. This is especially true if your top priority is a particular type of internship experience, such as a children's hospital, since such facilities are scattered all across the country. Do not write off a place because it will not be possible for you to interview there in person. Our students who have participated in telephone interviews have reported that they got a good feel for the facility. They have been accepted at very competitive programs and had good experiences at these internships. In my opinion, telephone interviews usually help the site in selecting students more than they do the students in evaluating the sites.

You should recognize that the internship-selection process, including interviewing, can place a great strain on a training center. The present interns are nearing the end of their first rotations and being evaluated, and the training personnel must continue to deal with their regular clinical duties throughout internship-selection season. After they have interviewed dozens of bright well-qualified applicants, staff can be forgiven for not being enthusiastic about seeing more. Therefore, it behooves you to request an interview as soon as possible. Not only will it help you make more economical travel arrangements, but latecomers may simply be told that there are no appointments left.

Winiarski (1986) noted that you can begin to get a feel for a place when you first call requesting an interview. "Does the secretary greet you warmly, or are you put on hold for 30 minutes? Are you offered lodging with other interns...or are you told, 'See you at the office at 9:30 Monday' and then expected to fend for yourself?"

If your request for an interview is refused, check with your ADCT. As a student, you probably had to deal with a secretary or executive assistant, but your ADCT will have access to the Internship Training Director and can find out directly what the problem is. It may be that your folder appears incomplete. If there is a perceived problem with your application or your apparent credentials, your ADCT can find out. If there is some misperception involved, your ADCT may be able to correct it. It could be that someone simply made a mistake. One year an ITD told me that his secretary had misinterpreted something he had said and had denied interviews to anyone who called after January 1. Whatever the reason for your refusal, your ADCT may be able to arrange an interview for you by dealing directly with the ITD.

If not, being denied an interview is not the kiss of death, as discouraging as it may be. On Notification Day, one of our students actually received an offer from an internship that had earlier turned down his request for an interview. He enjoyed telling them that he had already accepted a position at a rival training center.

Winiarski (1986) recommended that, if possible, you arrange to visit your lowest ranked choices first. "This will benefit you in two ways. First, if you flub up some early interviews, the damage won't be as great, and you can learn from the experience. Second, you'll have more data going into the more important interviews, and therefore know more about what to look for and have better questions to ask." His advice, of course, assumes that your motivation will remain constant. If you wait too long, you may be burned out and no longer care what sort of an impression you make. Perhaps the best advice is to schedule yourself some rest days so you can recuperate between visits.

When you make an appointment for an interview, make sure you know *exactly* where you are supposed to report and how to get there. If you are going to be driving, ask about the availability of parking. If possible, find out to whom you will be talking so you can learn more about them before you interview.

Preparing for the interview

Before visiting a site, make sure you do your homework. Review the facility's program descriptions and brochure. One of my recent students *outlined* the brochure, noting questions in the margins, the night before the interview so it would be fresh in her mind the next morning. She would take the outline with its questions along with her and refer to it during the interviews. Whatever technique you use, you need to be focused. Arrive at the internship with a clear picture of what their program offers and what information you need to help you evaluate it. Staff get turned off when applicants ask questions that show they have not done their basic homework and are not familiar with the basic program. If you are interested in children, don't ask, "Do you have a child rotation?" If you have read the brochure, you should know that there is a child rotation. Instead inquire about what sorts of training experiences are available on the child rotation or how interns get chosen for that experience.

The *Directory of the American Psychological Association* (APA, 1993) is a useful tool in learning more about the internship personnel. Usually the internship brochure will list the key faculty members, but if not, the *Directory's* geographical index will provide the names of those people who listed the training center as their address. By looking up the names of the training personnel, you can learn where they got their degrees, their credentials, where they have previously been employed, and their interests as reflected in the divisions to which they belong. Your reference librarian can guide you to other directories such as the *Who's Who* series, but the APA *Directory* should suffice.

Using 3 X 5 inch cards that you can quickly review before an interview, make notes on salient aspects of their careers. If you are familiar with where they did their graduate work and where they interned, you may be able to identify some mutual acquaintances. Perhaps they know some other students who graduated from your university, or they might know someone on your faculty.

As you know, *Psychological Abstracts* in both its written and computerized (PsychLit) forms have author indices. Take the time to look up the people you will be meeting, identify some of their writings, and obtain them from the library. Not only will this help you evaluate the setting and the caliber of personnel, but you can impress the interviewer with your knowledge of his or her research. This is also a time to recall those papers presented by internship personnel that you observed at professional meetings or workshops.

You don't have to be profound. Just say, "I was interested in the work you did with Fibula Fistula on peptic ulcers; have you done anything further in that area?" (Of course, be prepared to respond intelligently when you are asked, "What aspect of that study interested you?")

Going to the interview

When you travel to the internship, make sure you take along all the materials you will need. Take copies of all your notes, lists of specific questions to ask at each internship, and the internship's brochures so you can review them before starting your round of appointments. Also take a duplicate copy of your completed application forms in case a part of your application has been lost (they will say "never received"). Don't forget your Travel Planner and the 3 X 5 cards on the people you will probably be meeting. If you have business cards with your name and phone number(s) on them, take them along too.

Always take extra copies of your resume. The internship may not be sufficiently well-organized or have the resources to provide every person you see with a copy of your CV, and it is not realistic to expect that everyone has taken the time to review all the CVs in a central file cabinet, especially if it is one of those "interview everybody" weekends. So bring along extra copies to give to the interviewers.

Allow plenty of time to get to your first appointment. Indeed, if you get in the night before, I recommend you do a reconnaissance trip and locate exactly where it is you will be going the next morning. Count on getting lost. When I visited internships, I always had one of our present interns drive me in from the airport and half the time *they* got lost, even though they had lived there several months. Even if you do not get lost, parking is usually a terrible hassle at any major medical center. This may be a good time to spend a few extra dollars on a taxi; while the cab drivers usually manage to get lost too, at least you don't have to worry about the parking.

One advantage of visiting each internship is that you can observe how they deal with you and the other applicants. Some places will be very well-organized. You will be given a schedule of appointments, you may be escorted around by one of the present interns, arrangements will be made to provide you with lunch, and, as you go from office to office, you will note that the people you meet have copies of your CV and have taken the time to read it. At other places, none of these nice things will happen. You may be one of a herd of applicants who is lectured to and then marched from place to place on a cursory tour. The people you meet may be harassed and act like seeing you is just one more annoyance in another difficult day. These observations can tell you a lot about a setting and its attitude toward students.

After a while, as you travel from place to place, your perceptions of the various sites will begin to blur. After visiting a site, take 20 minutes to write down your impressions while they are fresh. (Later share them with your support group.)

Questions you may be asked

The interview process is a time for mutual evaluation. You will be evaluating the personnel and the setting, and they will be evaluating you. This means *everyone,* including the current interns who may be showing you around or taking you out for pizza. They will probably be asked for their impressions shortly after you leave for your next visit.

Be prepared to answer why you feel this internship would be good for *you.* This is a natural question and does not infringe on any APPIC rules. Instead, it provides you with an opportunity to sell yourself to the staff by focusing on your particular abilities. Use this opportunity to comment on your expectations so that you can validate them. One student applied to a facility because of its superb inpatient child/adolescent unit; when the applicant mentioned this, she was told that it had been closed the year before. As disconcerting as this was, it would have been a lot worse to find out after accepting an offer.

You will no doubt be asked why you are applying for this particular internship position. Be reasonably frank. That is, do not say, "My ADCT insisted I apply to one fourth-rate place so that I can be sure of getting an offer somewhere." Instead focus on programmatic elements and particular personnel with whom you would like to work. This is a good opportunity to mention any favorable comments made by previous interns from your school. It not only helps remind the person that your predecessors have done well there, but finding a mutual acquaintance is often a major turning point in an interview.

You can also comment knowledgeably on the research being done by the training staff. Having previously located and read their publications, you can discuss their work with insight (and admiration). This will convince them that you are a very intelligent and discerning individual.

After reciting all the professional reasons, do not be afraid to mention other, nonprofessional, reasons why you are applying, such as climate or geography. The fact that you want to be near aged or infirm parents, or that you hope to locate in the area, are perfectly valid considerations. They should not be the *only* factors, but Internship Training Directors listen for such comments since they suggest you are likely to accept an offer if it is made.

As Hersh and Poey (1985) pointed out, you may well be asked detailed questions regarding your professional experience, theoretical orientation, or preference in personality tests. You may be asked to conceptualize a current case or to describe the populations with which you have worked. If so, don't get annoyed because much of this information is in that resume you so carefully constructed. The interviewer simply wants to hear a sample of your professional verbiage. Can you discuss a case coherently or give the rationale for a therapeutic intervention? Underneath, the interviewer is asking, "If I send this person on a consult to Ward 22, will our service be embarrassed?" So use this as another opportunity to impress the interviewer with your ability to think clearly under stress and to formulate cogent responses. Give them a sample of what they can expect from you in a case conference if you attend that facility.

Remember, you are applying to a *training* facility, so they should not expect you to be a fully-qualified professional. Be honest about your experience, indicating what your areas of competence are and where you need additional training. Remember your self-analysis and the reasons why you applied to this particular internship.

During your site visit be prepared to back up the claims you made in your application. One year I mentioned in my letter of recommendation that a non-Hispanic applicant with a Polish surname was fluent in Spanish. Sure enough, one interview was conducted entirely in Spanish.

You may be asked some questions that stump you. If so, it is better to confess to your ignorance of that topic than to try to fake expertise. Winiarski (1986) recalled that he had mentioned having a course that dealt in part with multiple personality disorders. When the interviewer asked him if he was familiar with that literature, he gulped and replied, "No, not really, just what I heard in class." The interviewer then presented Winiarski with a comprehensive review of the literature on multiple personality disorders he had just published. Winiarski (1986) noted, "My interview would have been over immediately if I had pretended knowledge I didn't have."

One of the disadvantages of applying for a psychology internship is that you spend a lot of time being interviewed by psychologists. Some of them feel compelled to act "psychological" and approach the interview with a clinical or diagnostic mindset. So don't be dismayed if some ask questions about personal matters. One applicant was asked to report the most negative thing she could think of about her father; when she stated she thought he was a fine man who had put all of his children through college under very difficult circumstances, she was accused of resisting. Another was interviewed by six psychiatrists who sat in a circle taking verbatim notes. She was quizzed about everything except her masturbation fantasies, and they seemed likely to start on that topic when time ran out.

You do not have to answer intimate questions. If interviewers begin getting too personal, you can ask them why they think this information is relevant or simply declare that it is none of their business. Remember that in normal employment interviews the interviewer is not even supposed to ask your marital status, much less pry into your personal life.

Once in a while, perhaps out of boredom, someone might toss in an off-the-wall question to see how you react to the unexpected. One interviewer liked to ask candidates what it was they most hoped he would *not* find out about them. (If someone tries this, tell them you hope they won't discover that you are a workaholic.) The nastiest question I have ever heard of was in an interview jointly conducted by several psychiatrists, one of whom asked the applicant to tell a joke. The candidate thought a moment and responded with a story about a young woman who discovered she was pregnant shortly after her boyfriend, who was a psychiatrist, had dumped her. She chose to have the child without telling him. When the psychiatrist eventually found out, he told her that he would have married her had he known. She replied that she was aware of that, but she and her parents had decided that having one bastard in the family was enough. After a pause, during which no one laughed, the interviewer commented, "That was a very hostile story." The candidate replied, "That was a very hostile question."

I doubt if anything this bad will happen to you, but if something of this nature does occur, maintain your equanimity. Deal with the question or request as best you can, asking for clarification if necessary, and simply note that this place, too, has its share of bastards.

Asking questions of the interviewer

Each person you talk to wants to get to know you. Most will ask if you have any questions. This is their way to be helpful and to learn more about you. Nothing is tougher on the interviewer than the person who simply says, "No." As one Internship Training Director remarked with exasperation, "It is inconceivable that a person seriously planning to spend a year of his or her life here has no questions."

Even if it has been a long day, when the final interviewer asks you if you have any questions, don't reply, "No, the others already answered them all." If you do this, you will spend the rest of the time staring at each other. Recall some questions from Appendix 6, or ask where the interviewer interned. Obviously it was at the current site or somewhere else. If the interviewer actually interned there, you can ask how often interns take positions on staff and launch into all the questions you normally ask current interns, as well as ask for comments on how life changes once you obtain your degree. If the person interned somewhere else, you can ask how this internship compares with the place the interviewer attended. Such a comparative approach often provides new perspectives, and you can be sure the answers will not be ones you have already heard. The point is not to shut off the dialogue. Ask questions that require elaboration rather than a simple "yes" or "no." Remember you are being evaluated in part on the basis of *your* interviewing skills.

Your interviews will probably be with a variety of people: staff, present interns, and the Internship Training Director. Use your interviews with different people to cross-check information and get data on different aspects of the program, such as the clientele, working conditions, the relation of psychology to psychiatry (always important at medical centers), number and nature of colloquia, and so forth. How does the staff's perception of how rotations are assigned or the balance between training and service agree with the students'? What is it the staff seeks in an intern?

You might also ask for additional written information about rotations or programs that interest you that goes beyond what is included in the brochure, especially at a consortium where there are several different agencies. Some internships will also have information pamphlets available that describe the area and its amenities. You can also ask if the internship or the community have

Web sites you can access. (One recent applicant referred to this display of interest as "Sucking up in a dignified manner.")

The only thing worse than asking no questions is asking a really stupid question. For most Internship Training Directors, one of the stupidest questions you can ask is for a "general description" of the program. This tells the interviewer that you did not read the brochure they went to such pains to produce. As one ITD said, "A student must be pretty dumb to come all the way here to apply for an internship when he doesn't know anything about the program."

Prepare *specific* questions in advance. As in any job interview, the interviewer will be more impressed by inquiries relating to professional matters, such as the nature and extent of supervision, than with questions about the number of days off or the frequency of coffee breaks. How you phrase a question can be important. The interviewer will be more impressed with your eagerness to learn if you ask how many seminars are "offered" as opposed to how many are "required." If you think certain training experiences are important, this is the time to determine whether they will be available.

Don't be afraid to ask about living conditions in the area. Rather than being considered "unprofessional," it tells the ITD that you are seriously considering what is involved in moving to this locality. One of our applicants was a single mother with a ten-year-old child. She was very concerned about such things as school districts, day care facilities, and drug use in the schools. One ITD she grilled on these subjects later called to tell me how impressed he was with this woman's professional maturity, sincerity, and commitment to being a good parent. He made her an offer and was truly disappointed when she chose to go to another city that she felt would be better for her son.

Dealing with beverages

A word about coffee and other beverages. When you are touring internships, you will soon find that offering a visitor coffee or some other beverage is part of the etiquette. *Don't accept.*

Whatever the beverage, it is rarely available in the interviewer's office. If you accept, the interviewer is obliged to go down the hall to wherever the beverage area is, locate a reasonably sterile receptacle, and mix the beverage from whatever ingredients are at hand. The only thing you can be sure of is that it will not be the way you prefer it.

Often the coffee center is in the secretarial pool and there will be a sign indicating that coffee is $ .25. You fumble for change, the interviewer assures you that it is not necessary, and the secretaries glare at you. Then you return to the office with 15 minutes of your allotted 30 dissipated.

So there you sit, with your cup of coffee in one hand, your portfolio for collecting handouts and reprints under one arm, and your notepad in another hand. As you reach for your pen, you suddenly realize you have one hand less than you need. So you must, gracefully of course, park something somewhere, while attending to the interviewer's every word and formulating cogent answers. What is the fate of the beverage? Well, you can always spill it. If you do, it is a toss up whether it is better to spill it on the interviewer's desk or on yourself. (See "Packing for travel.") Or, you can hold it clutched in one hand until the interview is over.

The question then arises what to do with the cup. Do you leave it behind for the interviewer to clean up? Do you take it with you? (Hint: if ceramic cup, leave it; if Styrofoam, take it.) You then have to cope with shaking hands with the next interviewer while holding your portfolio, clipboard, pen, and coffee cup. However, you do have a ready answer to the next interviewer's question of whether you would like a cup of coffee.

Of course, it is possible that you might actually manage to consume the beverage during the interview. If so, you will proceed to the next interview wondering how to deal with a) an empty coffee cup, and b) a full bladder. In short, unless you are being asked to join a group in the coffee shop, for which refusing would be antisocial, skip the coffee.

A lawyer who read this told me that she had been advised to always accept a beverage because failure to do so would be considered antisocial. When interviewing at a prestigious New York firm she had a series of six consecutive half-hour interviews with male partners of the firm, each of whom offered her a cup of coffee which she dutifully consumed. By the time the last interview was completed, she was bursting at the seams. She asked the secretary for the location of the nearest women's room, was given a key, dashed to the designated door, and headed for a stall, only to discover in the worst possible way that she was in the men's room, which was being used by three of her erstwhile interviewers. (She maintains that she was set up by the secretary, which leads us to our next topic.)

Charming the executive assistant

By this point in your training you must have learned that every office has a key person who gets things done. Usually a woman, she may have a title ranging from "executive assistant" to "secretary." She usually has an office next to the titular head who is called the "Chair" or the "Director." Although the ITD may think he or she is in charge, nothing much gets done without the executive assistant's input. She is responsible for much of the work of internship selection. She is the person who makes sure that your application and supporting materials are filed correctly and that the training staff gets their ratings made. It is she who will probably answer your phone calls requesting information or making appointments.

If possible, meet this person and charm her socks off during your visit. Whatever you do, don't alienate her. The surest way to do so is by being patronizing. A friendly executive assistant can be incredibly helpful, especially as Notification Day approaches, and a hostile one can misplace your folder so it never sees the light of day. (Or give you the key for the wrong rest room.)

Evaluating the setting

While visiting, take the opportunity to get a feel for the atmosphere of the facility: the degree of structure, friendliness, caring for the intern's experience, attitude toward clients, and all those other intangibles. Is it fast paced or laid back? Is morale high, or do people seem disgruntled and harassed? How do the offices and the patients' areas look to you? How do they *smell*? Will you be treated as a colleague or a serf? Try to talk to the present interns, but remember they are probably rating you too. If you do not get a chance to talk to them, ask for their home phone numbers so you can call them later.

If possible, check out the town. What would it be like to live there? Get a newspaper and see what the rents are like. Drive through the areas where interns typically live. Will you need to invest in a bulletproof vest if you go for a walk? In short, before you leave, make sure that you have enough information to evaluate each setting on those factors that are most important to you. Also, if others are coming with you, check out the aspects important to them.

At some point review Chapter Three, in which I discussed the aspects of the internship to consider in deciding on priorities, especially those dealing with morale, interdisciplinary relations, collegiality, quality and quantity of supervision, and the like. At that time, you constructed what amounts to a template of your ideal internship. How well does this internship match that template?

On honesty in communication

At the 1988 APA Convention, we had a panel discussion on interviewing for internships. Everybody, Internship Training Directors, university directors, and, especially, graduate students who had been through the process agreed that the three most important things to remember in interviewing are HONESTY, HONESTY, and HONESTY. This applies to all parties: students, the internship staff, and the university faculties. However, over the years it has become apparent that different parties may attach different meanings to the word "honesty." For students and their ADCTs, "honesty" means abiding by the rules, especially those that state, "Internship programs may not solicit information regarding an applicant's ranking of programs or his/her intention to accept or decline an offer of admission until after that offer is officially tendered." For Internship Training Directors and their staffs, however, "honesty" is more likely to refer to applicants keeping their word when they pledge that they will accept an offer on UND. Whenever possible at the annual meeting of the American Psychological Association, I try to attend the meetings of both the Council of University Directors of Clinical Psychology (CUDCP) and the Association of Psychology Postdoctoral and Internship Centers (APPIC). At CUDCP, tales abound of students being pressured to reveal their rankings or to promise they will accept an offer if it is made, while down the hall at the APPIC meeting, ITDs are complaining about students who "burned" them by putting them on hold or declining an offer they had promised they would accept.

As a student, you might say it serves the ITDs right for forcing the applicants to reveal their rankings in the first place. However, it appears that under the pressure of the shortfall in the number of positions, most students in the 1996 and 1997 selection derbies voluntarily informed their "first choice" placements of their Number One ranking without any overt pressure being applied. Whereas Constantine and Keilin's (1996) anonymous poll showed that 30% of the students reported that one or more of the settings asked them to reveal their rankings, Thorne's (1997) poll indicated that 81% of the students reported voluntarily revealing their rankings to their first choice placement.

One ITD, who scrupulously does not ask his applicants for rankings (or disclose his own until UND), told me that one student had started calling a year before UND to assure him that his internship ranked first. These calls continued on a monthly basis right up until UND, but the ITD, sticking to the rules, did not disclose to the student the fact that he would get an offer on UND. On UND, the ITD made an offer to the student and it was declined! Noting the widespread reports of violations of the APPIC rules, Zimet (1988), a former Chairman of the APPIC Board of Directors, suggested that every student should assure all the ITDs who asked them for their rankings that their internship was their first choice. In time, Zimet reasoned, the ITDs would learn that the question did not discriminate applicants from one another and would stop asking it. However, it is a sorry situation when you are advised to begin your professional career with such unprofessional behavior as lying to your future ITD.

In Chapter Two, I described the new APPIC policy that requires all parties involved, ITDs, ADCTs, and you, the students, not to discuss rankings. Although we will discuss this in more detail in Chapter Ten, I strongly advise you not to discuss your rankings with any internship staff while you are interviewing. There is no reason in the world why you should be expected or required to indicate anything more than sincere interest during the interviewing phase. How can you rank settings until you have seen them all? The people you are visiting would certainly feel you had abused their hospitality if you came to an interview having already made a commitment at a previous site. By the same token, it is unfair to everyone else on your list to rank the agencies until you have seem them all. So, be noncommittal. Even if you are enthusiastic about a setting, don't indicate that it is your first choice. Your opinion may change before the selection season is over.

I hope that the new APPIC rules whereby internship sites must agree not to solicit, accept, or use information about rankings will decrease pressure on students to reveal their rankings during interviews. However, I doubt that it will eliminate it entirely; most of your interviews will be with internship faculty members and present interns who may not be aware of the stringent new prohibition. If you are pressed, I suggest that you tell the person that, under the new APPIC policy, your ADCT made you sign a pledge that you would not reveal your rankings and stressed that doing so would be unethical. You might even bring along a "To Whom It May Concern" letter from your ADCT that says she or he has pledged to God and APPIC that you will be dismembered if you discuss rankings. This should shield you during the interview phase. If you do experience pressure, inform your ADCT.

During the close-out interview, especially if it is with a member of the selection committee, you may ask how well they feel you fit their needs. If you do, be prepared to respond with *your* perception of the goodness of fit. This is an appropriate question. Be honest and use this as an opportunity to reiterate the message you want to get across; for example, you might say you think you would fit in because of these reasons, you were impressed with these aspects of the program, the people were real nice, and you think you could get good training there, especially if you got your favorite rotation. However do not say anything that can be construed as a commitment. At the other end of the spectrum, don't write a place off prematurely. Keep an open mind and make your decisions after you have surveyed all the options and returned home.

Finally, remember that everyone you meet will be evaluating you, just as you are evaluating them. Some may try to "break your cover." Beware of the intern who, taking you to the airport after your last appointment, casually asks how it went and whether you think you will come if accepted. It is likely that your response will be reported to the Internship Training Director. Be honest, but not naive or ingenuous.

Following up

Your mother no doubt taught you to write "bread and butter" notes after visiting friends to thank them for their hospitality. After you return from interviewing, you should send such notes to all the places where you interviewed. (Indeed, Gollaher and Craig (1994) advised sending notes to *every individual* you talked with.) After the interviewing season is over, a major problem for Internship Training Directors is how to determine which interviewees are still interested. A friendly, albeit noncommittal, note, thanking them for their hospitality and repeating that you were impressed with the program, is a good way to communicate the fact that you are actively considering their program. In fact, ITDs who do not get a note such as this may conclude that you are not interested. If you have some remaining questions, you can use this opportunity to ask them. This will put you in a good position to begin the "Endgame" (Chapter Ten).

NOTES

CHAPTER TEN

THE ENDGAME

When you first return from interviewing, you will probably feel relaxed and confident. You got through it and you survived! You held your own in professional interactions with top psychologists away from your home base. It is a heady experience, and you will probably be eager to swap war stories with fellow applicants. Enjoy this feeling while it lasts. Get reacquainted with your family and major professor. Soon you will be entering the most difficult and distressing stage of the internship-selection process, the "Endgame." The Endgame is the climax of the whole seemingly interminable process that began back in the Fall. This is when the training centers finally decide on their selections, and the applicants rank their choices. It culminates with Selection Day. It is a time of uncertainty and tension for all involved, especially in the light of recent events.

The effects of recent events

For the next few years, these final phases of the internship-selection process are going to be even more muddled and confused than usual for three reasons. First, the shortfalls will continue. As this is being written in the summer of 1997, the latest data from the Clearinghouse indicate that there are 150 unsuccessful candidates from 1996-1997 who are still seeking positions (Williams, personal communication, May, 1997). Only eight vacancies are listed. All have been on the board for several months now, so I imagine that they are undesirable. My guess is that they are unfunded slots at non-accredited internships, or maybe even some of the "paid positions" sponsored by professional schools in which the interns pay the internship center for their training. Although various surveys are being undertaken and a conference on supply and demand is scheduled for October, 1997, it is anybody's guess how many students will apply for internships in 1997-1998, much less in 1998-1999, 1999-2000, and beyond (Stedman, in press). However, it seems clear that their numbers will be augmented by those who failed to obtain internships the previous years and that there will not be enough positions to go around.

Second, in response to widespread accusations of ITDs "cheating" by asking candidates for their rankings during the 1996-1997 selection season, the APPIC Board adopted a new policy in April, 1997. As I advised you in Chapter Two, under this new plan the internships pledge that they will not, "... solicit, accept or use any ranking-related information from any intern applicant prior to Uniform Notification Day," and you, the applicants, promise that you will not, "offer information or respond to questions about ranking-related information to any internship site prior to Uniform Notification Day." Moreover, the ADCTs vow that they will not, "...offer information or respond to questions about ranking-related information regarding an intern applicant to any internship site prior to Uniform Notification Day...," and that they, " ...will prohibit intern applicants from their doctoral programs from offering information or responding to questions regarding ranking-related information to any internship site." I will simply refer to these new provisions as "The Rule," using capital letters to differentiate them from the previous APPIC Guidelines.

There is no way of knowing what effect The Rule will have. As this is being written, the internship centers are just learning about it, and virtually no ADCTs have yet been informed, much less any students. Conceivably the APPIC members could revolt, depose the Board at the Annual Meeting, trundle them off to the guillotine, and rescind The Rule. This is unlikely. In the past, most APPIC members have followed the rules, but many have not. This pattern will probably continue in the future. What remains to be seen is how the ADCTs and students respond. As we have seen, APPIC has only limited power to enforce rules among its own members. It has absolutely no authority over non-members such as ADCTs and students. APPIC or no, the First Amendment is still in effect, and if students or ADCTs insist on disclosing first choice or ranking information, all the ITDs can do is cover their ears, try not to hear, and strive not to be influenced by the information if they do hear it.

Third, computer matching is on its way. It will not arrive in time for the 1997-1998 selection year, but it is conceivable that it could be in place by 1998-1999. Computer matching is supposed to be like having John Wayne and the entire Seventh Cavalry ride over the ridge to our rescue, solving all our problems just in the nick of time. In the meantime, we will have to circle the wagons, do the best we can, and listen for a distant bugle.

Given all these changes, past, present, and future, it is difficult for me to predict how the game will be played in the years to come. In the pages that follow I will describe how the Endgame has worked in the past, because some players will continue to play their cards according to the old rules or by their own rules. If you encounter these folks, you need to know what to expect. Others will play by the new rules, so we will discuss how they are likely to affect the game. Computer matching, when it comes, will fundamentally change the game for everyone; in the next chapter, I will discuss how computer matching will work.

Back to the poker table

When you applied for college and, later, for graduate school, you filled out your applications, went for your interviews, and then waited for the results. Eventually you learned where you had been accepted and made your choice. The final stages of the internship selection process are quite different; be prepared to be an active participant instead of passively awaiting the outcome.

As Notification Day approaches, there will be considerable jockeying for position, negotiating, and second guessing. Applicants and internships alike will be poring over their lists, trying to decide on the best matches. Even though the intent of The Rule is that each party should ignore the other's rankings, inevitably both the ITDs and applicants will be trying to guess how they stand with each other, like courting couples pulling petals off daisies and reciting, "S/he loves me, s/he loves me not... ." The internships will do their best to ensure that their favorite applicants rank them highly, and the applicants will do their utmost to promote their candidacies at their top-choice programs. Some will no doubt bend or break the rules; others will do their best to abide by them. The fact that ADCTs and students are now supposed to be pledged not to reveal choices to internships will make the game even more uncertain, if only because there are no precedents to go by. If the past is any guide, rumors of violations will swiftly spread, but the many instances in which players abide by the rules will be overlooked. In the past, some ADCTs have acted as mediators, facilitators, or referees. Under The Rule they will be defining new roles for themselves. The only people who enjoy the Endgame are investors who own stock in the various long distance telephone companies.

While you were interviewing, you probably had some experience of the internship "poker game" you read about in the early chapters. Unless strict adherence to the spirit of the new Rule is more universal than I expect, you have learned firsthand that some ITDs and their staffs are interested in how you rank their internships. They may have been more discreet about it than they were in the past, but you have no doubt discovered that some would like to get a glimpse of your hole card. Continuing the poker game analogy, at this stage of the game, the cards have all been dealt, some players have dropped out, and those remaining have finished the first round of betting. Now it is time for you to examine your hand and see if it can be improved.

Discarding and drawing. Once you have reflected on the internships you visited and discussed your reactions with friends, relatives, and advisors, review your list. Are there any internships that you would definitely not attend, even if they were the only offers you received on UND? If so, discard them, especially if a fellow student is very interested in that placement. Send them a polite note withdrawing your application.

Discarding internships you have no interest in attending is to everyone's advantage. It saves the internship staff the trouble of having to decide how to rank your application and leaves them free to pursue more promising candidates. Your frankness can create goodwill that may later help you professionally. Perhaps you do not want to work in that particular setting now, but circumstances change, people move around, and it always helps to have a network of professional contacts who think well of you.

Once you have discarded any internships that you would not attend under any circumstances, reexamine your hand. If your list has gotten too short, and you are doubtful about your chances for acceptance at the remaining institutions, you may want to draw some more cards by submitting another application or two to those centers with late due dates on your "lifeboat list." At this stage of the game, the thought of filling out more applications and going on more interviews will probably be very aversive, but, if your list is truly too short, it is better to do it now than through the Clearinghouse after Notification Day.

Ranking your selections

In late January, ready or not, the actual selection process begins. It is time for you to rank your choices, and the sooner you do so the better. Using the lists of priorities you established back before your reconnaissance, match your template of what you are seeking in an internship with your perception of what each program offers.

In the process of establishing your final rankings, you should consult with other people. These include your ADCT and other faculty members who may have additional information about certain programs, alumni of your program who may have interned at places on your list, your fellow applicants, and family members and friends who may be involved in your decision. You may discover you need more information in order to make your rankings. Maybe one of your classmates heard a rumor of a key program change at a certain site. Perhaps your ranking of another setting depends on your chances of getting a particular rotation or working with a specific individual. Now is the time to check these details. Call the ITD and ask. This also serves to communicate to the ITD your continuing interest and provides the program with some indication of what your concerns are.

Shuffling the deck. Once you have obtained all the information you need, it is time to rank your choices. It will probably be easy to sort the centers into "A," "B," and "C" lists: one or two top choices, another two or three second echelon choices, and some others that you wouldn't mind attending but that for one reason or another you find less attractive than those on your A and B lists. However, this isn't good enough. When computer matching comes, and it will, you will have to rank each and every choice on your list before you submit it. Until then, you will still need an absolute rank order so you will know how to respond to offers from any agency on UND.

The more compulsive you are, the more difficult this can be. The simplest technique is to write the name of each site on a 3 X 5 inch card and try placing them in order from most preferred to least preferred. You will probably experience the most difficulty in the middle of the list. Using cards makes it easier to shuffle the order around than it is when you are writing numbers on a list. As you perform this exercise, you will see why I advised you that applying to 25 or 30 sites is counterproductive.

Using a grid. Some students find the card method is too simple. Some facilities are better on some factors, such as location, while others are stronger on other characteristics, such as rotations. If so, go back to the list of priorities you formulated at the beginning of this process. Reconsider the list. In the light of your experience interviewing, you may want to add some categories and delete others. For example, Stedman, Neff, Donahoe, Kopel, and Hays (1995) discovered that one of the factors that differentiated intern applicants' highest, middle, and lowest choices was an intangible "gut" feeling about how well they fit in with the program. If this was not one of your original categories, you might want to add it to the list. In the course of dealing with ITDs, you may have found some to be very honest and forthright, whereas others seemed more devious. If so, you might consider adding "integrity" as a category.

On the other hand, you may have discovered that some factors that you thought would be important at the outset have diminished. Perhaps that "Significant Other" that you felt you had to be near has dumped you because you have become so obsessed with internship-seeking that you have been miserable company recently. If so, rejoice! You have one less factor to worry about.

Once you have your final list of categories, you can use some of the attitude-scaling techniques you learned about in Social Psychology to help you make a decision. Jacob (1987) advised making a "grid" or spreadsheet with columns for each factor and rows for each internship. You can then evaluate each internship on each factor. You can do this using five or ten-point, Likert-type scales. An even better procedure is to use the 3 X 5 cards and rank order the settings on each factor. This forces you to compare the sites. But maybe you still have trouble ranking all your sites.

Stewart and Stewart (1996a) went one step further and advocated a formal paired-comparison technique in which you consider every possible pair of sites and choose which one of the two is better; thus you would compare Site A with Sites B, C, D, ...N, and next compare Site B with Sites C, D, ...N, and so forth until each site has been paired with every other site on each variable. You then tally up the number of times each site was chosen and compute a score for each setting on each factor. See Stewart and Stewart (1996b, Figure 1) for a detailed example. They reported that comparing ten sites on eight factors took about and hour and a half, which is less time than many students spend obsessing over their global rankings.

In the Stewarts' (1996a) paired-comparison technique, each factor was weighted equally. However, if some are more important to you than others, you can include weights that reflect this fact. So if "work prospects for spouse" is twice as important to you as "estimated work hours," you simply multiply the scores on that variable by two. Or you can do this implicitly by including several variables that represent different aspects of the same general factor. "Climate," "proximity to family," and "urban area" are all aspects of "location." There is no end to the complexity of the schemes you can use to help you evaluate the settings.

When you complete this exercise, you will end up with scores for each setting that you can convert to ranks. The results may surprise you. You may find that some sites rank higher or lower than you would have expected. Give them some further thought, but don't be *too* compulsive. If your favorite site ranks fifth, for example, and you still feel you like it best, then make it your first choice. How you get your rankings is not important. What *is* important is that you have all your sites ranked.

The Endgame from the Training Directors' perspective

While you are sorting out your cards and deciding how to play your hand, the Internship Training Directors and their Selection Committees are doing likewise, albeit on a larger scale. Their decision process is complicated by the fact that they must often consult with consortiums and committees, and consider local policies and politics in formulating their lists, satisfying as many colleagues as possible. Some will also be trying to balance their classes with respect to gender, ethnicity, academic program, and similar factors. As in Maslow's hierarchy, concern for basic survival takes priority over fulfillment of higher order needs. So, their first goal is to eliminate any applicants they feel are unqualified or unsuitable for various reasons. At this stage, they are more concerned with avoiding candidates who are incompetent, paranoid, psychopathic, or unethical than they are with selecting those most likely to win APA "Early Career Achievement" awards.

Given a pool of acceptable applicants, they want to:

1. obtain the best possible intern class, according to whatever criteria they deem most important, and

2. avoid "being burned" by not filling all their positions.

Strategic considerations may strongly influence who they select. Most Internship Training Directors believe that the first hours of Notification Day are critical. Obviously, they would like to get an immediate acceptance from each candidate. Failing that, however, it is far better to get an immediate rejection from someone who ranks their program last than it is to be put on "hold" by candidates who rank their programs second or third. The ITDs know students typically apply to a dozen or more places each and that some accept the first good offer they receive. Their alternate list can be melting away while their offers are being held by applicants who may eventually decline. This is why many ITDs seem obsessed with ascertaining how their applicants rank their facilities.

First choicing

Much of the anxiety and stress during the Endgame has come from some candidates' feeling pressured by some settings to reveal their rankings or to "first choice" (i.e., to assure their preferred settings that they were the applicants' first choices and that their offers would be accepted on UND) (Carifio et al., 1987; Constantine & Keilin, 1996; Johnson, 1986; Zimet, 1988). As we have seen, this pressure comes from the ITDs' fear of making offers to uncommitted candidates who may then "hang them out to dry" by "holding" an offer for a lengthy period of time and eventually declining, during which time the applicants on the internships' alternate lists all decide to go elsewhere (Stedman, 1983, 1989). As long as the Uniform Notification procedure requires ITDs to make binding commitments and limit the number of offers to the number of slots they have, the ITDs will have an incentive to make offers only to candidates they can be certain will accept them. Indeed, a few may decide not to make an offer to a "superstar" who seems likely to go elsewhere and call only those applicants who they are reasonably sure will accept. They will be more likely to risk making an offer to a candidate who may not accept if they can be sure the applicant will decide promptly and not hold the offer interminably.

It is for this reason that most ITDs, especially those at sites that do not have a 100 or more applicants, weigh the likelihood that an applicant will accept when they are deciding to whom they should offer positions. It is a short step from *considering* whether they will accept to *asking* them, either directly or indirectly, and unfortunately some ITDs or members of their staffs cross this line, perhaps by saying to an applicant, "You are in our top group and we would love to have you join us. Where do we stand with you ?" (Johnson, 1986).

Students generally have not objected to informing their first choices of this fact, especially if it appeared to enhance their chances of acceptance. Indeed, as we have seen, surveys show that in recent years approximately 80% of the applicants "first choiced" their favorite setting (Constantine & Keilin, 1996; Thorne, 1997). However, many felt they were being pressured to make such commitments. Constantine and Keilin (1996, p. 313), reported, "A number of applicants described the high degree of pressure and confusion they experienced related to this obligation to disclose, particularly in terms of their fears about whether or not they would still be considered as viable candidates by their second- or lesser-ranked sites."

That, of course, is the rub. If I freely tell my first choice that they are Number One, what do I tell my second choice?

In the last edition of this book, I wrote:

> The new [1991] APPIC rules forbid internships from asking you outright if you rank them first or if you will promise to accept an offer if one is made. Nevertheless, this can happen. If it is your clear first choice, you will probably agree, but if it is number two, then you are in a dilemma...
>
> You may be tempted to assure two or more ITDs that they are your "first choice" and promise them both that you will come if invited. **DON'T**. Doing so is a serious mistake. Besides being dishonest, it can blight your career once you are found out. It is pretty obvious that you were lying when you "first choice" a program and later turn down their offer
>
> One ITD told me about an applicant who had volunteered that her internship was his first choice, and that he would definitely accept an offer. On Notification Day, he "unexpectedly" received an offer from a place he regarded as more prestigious, and went there instead. He still practices in that area, but, as far as this ITD is concerned, he is an unethical person who will never, in his entire life, get any cooperation from her, whether it involves applying for a job, referring patients, asking for subjects, or trying to place students (Megargee, 1992, p. 194).

A 1997 applicant wrote, "The main problem for applicants arises in deciding how to communicate our preferences to our second, third, and fourth choice sites...its difficult to realize that being honest with our second and third choice sites about where they stand... might be costing us an offer there" (D. Gill, personal communication, 1997).

ITDs who try to stay within the letter of the guidelines have an analogous predicament. Although they may have decided who they are going to call first on UND, they cannot be sure that they will all accept, and so they have to keep their second-choice candidates interested for the alternate list. This is called "stringing along." Some do this by talking in code. Recently one student who had made a first-choice commitment to an internship got a call just before UND. The ITD told him that on Selection Day he should, "Just sit tight. Don't do anything foolish." He understood this to mean that he was going to get an offer. When he told his major professor, she said it sounded as if he was on their alternate list and they were stringing him along. She advised him to call his lower-ranked selections and tell them he was still interested. The student demurred; he had made a first-choice commitment, the ITD was very nice, and he was sure he would get a call on UND. He did. It was the ITD saying he was sorry, all their slots were filled but that the student had been their "first alternate." When he called all his other choices, they too had filled.

The commitment letter. In order to enhance their chances, many students in recent years have chosen to make a unilateral commitment to accept an offer from their first-choice setting. As an ADCT, I felt it was hazardous for my students to make a unilateral commitment to an internship without any safeguards. I knew from experience that many programs played strictly by the rules and disregarded such pledges. Others, who had had students lie to them, no longer trusted first-choice commitments. I also feared that if some ITDs did believe the students' promises to accept an offer, they might feel they could safely place them on an alternate list while they pursued more attractive uncommitted applicants on UND. (This is probably what happened to the student who was "strung along" in the above example.)

In those days, before The Rule, ADCTs and ITDs could share ranking information, so I told my students who wanted to make such a commitment to tell me first. I would discuss the potential hazards with them, and if they insisted on making a commitment, I would call the ITD at the internship, ask how my student ranked, and ascertain whether or not a first-choice commitment would make a difference. If the ITD was not concerned with how the applicants ranked the internships, or if my candidate's ranking was so low that an offer was unlikely, then I would advise my student to look elsewhere. However, if the ITD said my student was a viable candidate and that such a commitment would make a difference, I would advise my student to go for it. To ensure credibility, I backed up the student's commitment letter with my personal promise to the ITD that if the student was offered a *fully funded* position by *10:00 AM CST* on Uniform Notification Day, he or she would accept it and definitely attend. I also promised the ITD that if the student reneged, he or she would be dismembered and his or her body parts sent to the training center at the time the internship was scheduled to begin. (Fortunately, this was never necessary.)

An example. Let me describe a case that took place several years ago, before ADCTs were specifically prohibited from discussing rankings with ITDs. I told all my applicants to give me their final lists because I expected some ITDs would be calling and I needed to know how they stood in order to represent their interests effectively. One student, "Ginger Curry" had been having great difficulty making up her mind because her partner could not decide what city would be best for him or, indeed, if he wanted to go along at all. I did not know this, however, and, when Ginger turned in her "final" ranked list of choices, I had no idea that they were actually changing from day to day according to her partner's moods.

Ginger and two other students, "Herb Dill" and "Corrie-Ann Derr," had applied to the "Caraway Consortium." Ginger and Herb had both ranked it first, but it was Corrie-Ann's sixth choice. The ITD at Caraway, "Dr. Laurel Bayleaf," was a good friend and graduate of our program who had accepted several of our students in previous years.

Late in January, Dr. Bayleaf called me to discuss our applicants, as ITDs often did in those days when two or more of our students had applied to the same program. She first asked about Corrie-Ann. Since Corrie-Ann had ranked Caraway sixth and was well-regarded by her first choice, I advised Laurel that she had a better chance of recruiting Ginger or Herb. Ginger fit their needs better than Herb, but both had made a good impression, she said. After the Selection Committee met, Laurel called me again to tell me that Ginger would be on the first list and Herb on the alternate. Since both had ranked Caraway number one, I said either would accept.

The Friday before Notification Day, Ginger's partner announced he would go with her only if she attended an internship in the Pacific Northwest where he could fish for salmon. The only salmon near Caraway were in cans, so Ginger came in with a new list with Caraway ranked near the bottom. I was sure that Ginger would get an offer from Caraway; if she turned it down it would damage our relationship with the internship and undermine Dr. Bayleaf's credibility at her program, so I told Ginger to call Dr. Bayleaf and indicate she was having second thoughts. Dr. Bayleaf had to be called out of the final selection committee meeting, but Ginger was able to get the information to her in time. Although disappointed by Ginger's ambivalence, Laurel was very impressed with her honesty. Over the weekend, Ginger realized she really wanted to go to Caraway, with or without the salmon fisherman, but figured she had irretrievably blown her chance. However, on Notification Day, Caraway made offers both to her and to Herb Dill, and they both accepted. After completing her internship, *Dr.* Curry stayed on at Caraway, where she became the chief assistant to Dr. Bayleaf, who had been promoted to Chief Psychologist.

In addition to illustrating how some ADCTs and ITDs negotiated in those days, this story also illustrates the importance of ranking your choices and keeping your ADCT informed. Even though ADCTs and ITDs are not supposed to discuss rankings under the new Rule, ITDs can, and no doubt will, continue to call ADCTs to learn more about the candidates from their programs, especially when two or more have applied. It is not unlikely that some ADCTs who are asked to compare students from their programs will be more likely to evaluate an applicant who ranked that internship at the top of her list as being a "good match" than someone who ranked it eighth or ninth.

The 1997 rule change

The 1996 rules stated, "Internship programs may not solicit information regarding an applicant's ranking of programs or his/her intention to accept or decline an offer of admission until after that offer is officially tendered" [on UND]. The new Rule goes much further by forbidding ITDs from "accepting" or "using" ranking information. It also enjoins students and ADCTs from disclosing or discussing rankings with the internships. As you can see, this "rules out" the kind of negotiations that we have been discussing.

The new Rule should help protect you from feeling obligated to reveal your rankings to any internships. The Rule states that you must not disclose your rankings; moreover your ADCT is supposed to prohibit you from doing so. It might be difficult for you not to inform your favorite internship that it is your first choice, but if you do so it now means that *you* are operating outside the guidelines. If The Rule has its desired effect, you as an applicant can concentrate on making your selections on their merits without worrying about which internships rank you highly. They should not ask you to rank your choices, but if they do ask, you can just tell them you will accept the best offer you get on UND. The UND rules are consistent with this strategy because you can still choose to accept, reject, or hold an offer.

The Rule will make Selection Day more difficult for those ITDs who have relied on "first choice" data in making their selections. The fact that they must "turn their cards over first" puts them at a disadvantage, at least until computer matching arrives. As long as there is a tactical advantage from knowing which applicants are most likely to accept, there will be a temptation for ITDs to try to ascertain or guess which candidates are most likely to accept. However, The Rule should inhibit flagrant attempts to solicit such rankings, especially if candidates state that they are ethically bound not to disclose such information. Ideally, the ITDs should only be concerned about selecting the best applicants for each slot, without regard for the likelihood that they will accept. When computer matching is finally introduced, there will be no advantage to having "first choice" information. Then, perhaps, the ideal will become a reality.

Countdown to Notification Day

After Early Notification and Computerized Matching were voted down, APPIC drafted a more detailed and stringent set of rules governing the Uniform Notification. A copy of the latest "June, 1996" revision is included in Appendix 1 of this book, and you should review these rules as Notification Day approaches. Each year the current Policy Statement is reprinted in the APPIC *Directory* and included in each internship's packet of materials. Check these sources to determine if there have been any changes in the rules or in the time Notification Day begins or ends.

The courtship. During January and early February, the internships' selection staffs pore over their lists, looking not only for the most talented students who best fit the needs of their programs, but also for those who are most likely to accept their offers. In previous years, this is when things would get very intense. The rules then, as they do now, forbade internships from asking applicants to rank their programs before Notification Day, but there was no rule forbidding applicants from *voluntarily* informing programs that they ranked first. So interns got calls designed to give them an "opportunity" to express their enthusiasm.

Consider the following scenario: "Tom Cod," an intern applicant, might get a call from "Dr. Almondine Dover-Sole," the Training Director at "Halibut Hospital." She asks how Tom is and whether there is anything more about Halibut's program he needs to know. Then Dr. Dover-Sole says, "We are going into a meeting now to decide on our first choices, and I just want to tell you that we are really impressed with your application and we really think you would fit in well here." After a long pause for Mr. Cod to respond, Dr. Dover-Sole might have pushed it one step farther and say, "We certainly hope you like us as much as we like you." Tom would have had to decide whether to reply that Halibut was his first choice or equivocate in some way. Unfortunately, any equivocation can be interpreted as a rejection. As in a courtship, when one party is so bold as to say, "I love you," or even to ask, "Do you love me?" any response other than "Yes" may be interpreted to mean "No."

The Rule forbids ITDs and applicants from asking or answering those loaded questions. Nor can the ADCT act as an intermediary or marriage broker. Although The Rule states that internships cannot solicit, accept, use, or communicate to applicants any information about rankings, they are certainly going to be interested in what you think of them, just as you will be curious about how they regard you. So we all play games. After it is over, many applicants look back on it as being similar to dating (Gollaher & Craig, 1994). Unlike casual dating, however, you and the internships both know that these interactions will soon result in a binding commitment. Therefore, I think an old-fashioned, fairy-tale type courtship is a better metaphor. In this scenario you are the blushing maiden, the Princess if you will, and the ITDs are your suitors. Your goal is to get one or more of them to propose on UND. You hope that it will be your special favorite, Prince Charming, who asks for your hand, but in case he doesn't, you need to keep the others interested. If the Prince doesn't come through, you don't want to end up staying in the drafty old castle with your stern father, the King (i.e., your ADCT), for another year.

Unfortunately, there is an overabundance of fair maidens in the kingdom, so the Prince and his colleagues won't lack for ladies who will accept their proposals on UND. Your task is to make yourself more attractive than the others and induce Prince Charming and various other suitors to propose when the time comes, but not before. However, your father has prohibited you from disclosing your true feelings to the Prince or anyone else. You must keep your distance to maintain your innocent reputation. Similarly, the suitors are enjoined from telling any of you how they feel. Imagine a very proper, white-glove, debutante ball with wall to wall chaperones; you may dance, at a discrete distance, and talk with the various suitors, as long as you don't talk about what is really on your minds. No doubt it will seem very constrained and somewhat artificial, but the purpose of the rules is to safeguard your virtue until UND.

In the weeks leading up to UND, you need to keep in communication with the internships that interest you. Some will call you. In January, this may be to "answer any questions" and to determine whether you are still interested, but as Notification Day approaches, the courtship gets more serious. Even though they are supposed to wait until Notification Day to "pop the question," what some really want to know is if you will accept a proposal. To preserve your honor, you must fend them off, but do so in an inoffensive way that lets them know you are still interested. You may fear that without some encouragement, Prince Charming will never propose, but at the same time, you do not want to get a reputation of having promised yourself to everyone in town. This is a confusing time.

The thing to remember is that any proposition before UND is invalid; none of the suitors are obliged to come up with a ring or a real proposal on UND. However, if you go "all the way" and agree to "first choice" Prince Charming, you are morally if not legally, committed. As long as you are engaged to Prince Charming, you can't date his cousin Prince Almost-As-Charming. Although you regard yourself as betrothed, you can be left at the altar. If the pressure to commit starts getting intense, consult the King; maybe your ADCT can help sort things out if the ITDs are overstepping their boundaries, especially if they are asking you to disclose ranking information you are pledged not to reveal.

While you are coping with ITDs who may be calling you, be advised that many ITDs feel it is inappropriate for them to call applicants. They may be waiting for you to call them, and, if they do not hear from you, they may assume you are not interested in their programs. If a program does not call, do not assume that you are out of the running. Find reasons to contact them to reassure them of your interest without overstepping the boundaries imposed by The Rule. Gollaher and Craig (1994) advised sending personalized thank-you notes to the people with whom you interviewed, making specific reference to some topic you discussed. Other methods of expressing your interest include calling to introduce yourself to someone you were not able to see when you interviewed, or requesting more information or literature on some topic. However, don't call so often that you make a pest of yourself.

Notice of exclusion. According to APPIC Rule 2, "Internship program directors must inform applicants who are excluded from consideration as early as possible in the process, and no later than one week before selection day." The big programs that receive 100 or more applications for ten positions or so, can easily afford to notify 50% or 60% of their applicants that they are out of the running. Less popular programs may be reluctant to exclude many. If they could be certain that all their top-ranked applicants would accept, then they could afford to advise the rest to seek other positions. Lacking this knowledge, they will probably not want to exclude, or even discourage, lower-ranked applicants because they may need these people on their alternate lists. Such fears may lead some training centers to "string along" applicants who do not have a realistic chance of being accepted.

Some programs adopt what is referred to as a "2-X" strategy; that is, they try to come up with a list of viable candidates that is twice the number of slots they hope to fill. If they have six slots, they try to identify 12 strong candidates. Some centers are more cautious; one recently used a "5-X" strategy, telling 30 candidates they were in the running for six slots. Stedman (1989) reported that one well-regarded program informed numerous applicants that each was "first alternate."

If you receive an exclusion notice, do not be devastated by the news. As I stated in the beginning, rejections are inevitable, and not everyone fits a program's needs. An exclusion notification simply means that this program is honest and secure enough to follow the rules rather than string you along. Most will probably send out form letters, but if they call, don't get angry or give in to the temptation to say something nasty. Instead, be gracious, and show them that you are a class act. Thank them for the information, express your disappointment, and wish them well. Inform your ADCT, and encourage the other placements on your list.

The fact that you have not received an exclusion notice does not necessarily mean that you are a strong contender. If you are really interested in a position, especially if it is your first choice, you should keep in touch with that training center prior to Notification Day.

The final week. As Notification Day approaches, the pace speeds up. Selection Committees are making their final choices and deciding which candidates to call first. ITDs may be calling you and your ADCT. Some last minute bargaining may go on...for example, you may be asked how important a given rotation or track is for you. This is particularly apt to occur in facilities that have track-specific selections. If the strongest candidates are all seeking a certain slot and another rotation has few applicants, they may try to see whether some candidates are willing to change.

It is essential at this stage that you stay in touch with your ADCT and with your fellow applicants. You must also remain accessible for ITDs who might call you. One of the major frustrations of Internship Training Directors is that graduate students are hard to find, especially during the daytime. Make sure the Directors of the places you are most interested in know how to reach you. Answering machines and fax receivers can be very helpful. Again, make sure you have erased any "cute" messages, ribald songs, and so forth from your machine and replaced them with something more appropriate and businesslike.

As UND approaches, make sure the internships you are especially interested in have the number where you will be on UND, as well as any back up numbers such as a fax or cellular phone. You might also want to find out what number you should call if you want to contact them on UND; Gollaher and Craig (1994) pointed out that internships on Pacific time might not be open at 9:00 AM CST on UND, so the central number you have been using may not be operative. This is also a good way to reassure your top-ranked internships of your continuing interest.

Uniform Notification Day

Notification Day finally comes on the second Monday in February. It is absolutely essential that you have a clear rank-ordered list of your preferred placements. Calling is supposed to begin no sooner than 9:00 AM *Central* Time. This is 10:00 AM in the Eastern Zone, 8:00 AM in the Mountain Zone, 7:00 AM Pacific Time, and 6:00 AM in Hawaii. (I have had students in the East who thought it started at 8:00 AM EST and were suicidal after they received no calls in what they thought were the first two hours.) Follow these rules:

1. Get everything ready early, such as taking a child to a sitter or day care, getting your list near the phone, and so on. Some programs jump the gun and call early.

2. Stay by the phone and keep the line clear. If possible, have a back-up phone that you can use to call out.

3. Do *not* call friends who are also applying. They need to stay by their phones and keep their lines clear. However, it helps to have someone with you who can hold your hand, run errands, deliver messages, and answer the phone while you use the bathroom.

4. If you are going to need to consult with someone else such as a partner or your ADCT, make sure the arrangements are in place and you know how to contact this person. Time is of the essence. However, by this time, you should have your decisions made, and the need for consultation should be minimal.

5. When you are made an offer, you must respond that you will "Accept," "Reject," or "Hold" the offer. If you decide to hold, you have until 1:00 PM CST to respond. After that time, the offer is automatically rescinded if you have not accepted. (Any internship that will make you an offer only if you agree to accept immediately is violating APPIC guidelines. Tell them so.)

6. Once you accept an offer, this is a binding commitment. You cannot under any circumstances accept any other offer. Notify all the other programs that you applied to that you are no longer available. If you are holding an offer, notify that program first.

7. You can hold only one offer at a time. If you are holding an offer and a lower-ranked program calls, decline. If your first-ranked placement calls, accept and then release the program whose offer you are holding. Similarly, if a higher-ranked program that is not your first choice offers you a position, tell them you will hold it, and immediately release the lower-ranked program whose offer you had been holding. (It is all right to hold the two offers for the brief period it takes to notify the lower-ranked facility, as long as you do so immediately.)

8. If you have not been contacted by your first-choice or other higher-ranking programs after a reasonable time, such as 30 to 45 minutes, don't just pace the floor waiting for the phone to ring. Call them and determine your status. You can now tell your first-ranked program that if they make you an offer, you will accept. Your call may precipitate an offer. If they have already filled, call your second-ranked setting and tell them you will accept.

Whether you accept or decline, do not expect any lengthy conversations with the internship personnel when the initial offers are being made on Selection Day. Their time is at a premium, and most communications last less than a minute. A typical conversation might go like this:

> "Hello, Mr. Tom Cod? This is Dr. Almondine Dover-Sole at Halibut Hospital. Have you accepted an internship position anywhere yet?" (This question is required by Rule 7-b.)
>
> "No."
>
> "Excellent. I am pleased to offer you a predoctoral psychology internship in our substance abuse track for next Fall. The stipend is $15,000, and the internship begins September 1."
>
> "I accept."
>
> "Wonderful. You will soon get a letter of confirmation. Good-bye."

The selection period officially ends at 1:00 PM, CST. That is 2:00 PM Eastern Time, 12 Noon in the Mountain Zone, 11:00 AM Pacific Time, and 10:00 AM in Hawaii. According to Rule 4-d, "Any offer that has not been accepted is void as of the ending hour of selection day." If you are holding an offer, it disappears at that moment. As the minutes tick away, you are in a classic approach-avoidance conflict. On the one hand, you do not want to lose the offer you are holding; on the other, if you have been waiting for a slot to open at your preferred site, it may soon become available.

Everyone who is holding slots is in the same boat, sitting on an alternate list waiting for a more preferred slot to open. As the time gets closer and closer to 1:00 PM CST, some will decide to accept the offers they are holding. This can precipitate a domino effect, as the alternates waiting for those slots discover they are unavailable and accept the offers they are holding. If the person who is holding the slot you are waiting for decides to accept that offer, the position you were waiting for disappears, so you should then accept the next-best slot that you are presently holding. The problem is the timing; if you have not accepted it by the tick of 1:00 PM, CST, you have lost it and the ITD may reoffer it to someone else.

Of course, if you hang in there and the person holding the slot you are waiting for does not accept it, then it will become open at 1:00 PM. The ITD at your first-choice internship can then make you an offer, but he or she is not obliged to do so. You may not be the only alternate. If you are caught in this sort of situation, you should determine your exact alternate status at your first-choice internship at least a half hour before the close of the selection period. Can you get the ITD to guarantee that you will get the offer if the slot becomes available? If so, can you believe the guarantee? If you have fax capability, I would try to get it in writing. Of course, the ITD can not guarantee that the person presently holding the offer won't accept at the last instant.

If you are caught in a gridlock situation of this type during the last hour of UND, consult with your ADCT and those affected by your decision. If the offer you are holding is for an APA-accredited, fully-funded internship, I would advise you to take it. If you end up on Selection Day without an internship, the odds are strong that you might not get one at all this year. Remember back on page 62 you agreed that you were too cool to think that there was any such thing as a perfect internship. The disappointment of not getting your top-ranked internship is much less than that of not getting one at all.

After Notification Day

If you have accepted a position, you should write a formal letter of acceptance in which you state your understanding of the agreement that was reached. Specify details such as the stipend level and any agreed-on rotation. Moreover, within 72 hours after the close of Notification Day (i.e., by the following Thursday), the Training Director at your internship is supposed to send you and your ADCT letters confirming all the details of your appointment. If your understanding agrees with the ITD's, you have a "done deal." If not, you and your ADCT should get in touch with the ITD and discuss the differences. For a contract to be valid, both parties must agree on the terms; the time to discuss any discrepancies is as soon as they are perceived, not when you report to the internship the following September.

For most candidates, Notification Day signals, at long last, the end of the seemingly interminable internship application season. It has consumed months of your life. At last it is over, and you will be surprised how soon it fades from memory. It never failed to amaze me how applicants who were pacing in agitation the week before Notification Day assured their younger colleagues that it was a breeze when they reported their experiences at our annual internship panel discussion a week later.

What to do in case of disaster

What should you do if disaster strikes? I hesitate to discuss this subject because it might induce a panic reaction in the more obsessive readers. At the same time, there is information you should have in case of an emergency. If I could, I would have this section published in a separate glass box that you could break open and read only in case of emergency. Instead, just skip over this section and read it only if something dreadful happens. If you ask, "What does he mean by dreadful?" it is obvious that it has not happened, so you do not need to read this section. It will just make you anxious.

Now that we have gotten rid of the lurkers, I can concentrate on those of you who need help. The first thing to remember is not to panic. Bad things sometimes do happen, but everything usually gets sorted out, and, more often than not, things seem to work out for the best. One reason why things work out is that after Notification Day, everyone is on the same side. Up to now you may have seen only the competitive side of the ITDs; after Notification Day they can resume their normal role as educators trying to give you the best training possible. APPIC, with which you have had minimal contact so far, can be extraordinarily helpful if something goes wrong. If the problem is something you and your ADCT can't deal with, APPIC often can and will.

Failure to obtain a position. For some applicants, disaster means not getting offered an internship on Notification Day. What should you do in this eventuality?

As soon as the official UND period ends, all the unclaimed slots revert to the ITDs who can reoffer them to whomever they choose. Inform your ADCT that you do not have a slot yet; there will be a lot of communications flying around via fax, phone, and e-mail during the afternoon. I often had ITDs with vacant slots call me wanting to know if I had any students who had not found a suitable placement. Your ADCT may well receive such calls.

Meanwhile, start calling the various internships on your list to see if any still have openings available. If you were assured that you were the "first alternate" somewhere, call and see if they can now make you an offer. If you were holding an offer when the clock ran out at 1:00 PM CST, call and tell them you will accept if it is still open. If you declined an offer from your ninth-ranked site so you could hold one at your second-ranked setting, see if number nine has filled yet. In short, see if you can still secure a site, because those that are still vacant are likely to go fast.

Assuming these efforts are unsuccessful, you are going to feel devastated. If you are a graduate student in psychology, you are used to succeeding. You may not have experienced a significant failure before, and it will take some effort to work through. Take some time to cry or do whatever you do when you have had a major disappointment. When you are ready to deal with it, discuss the situation with your ADCT or other mentor and diagnose what went wrong. Together you can review your application materials and credentials. Your ADCT may be able to call some programs where you applied for feedback on your application. It may be that, professionally or personally, you are simply not ready to go on internship and this fact was evident to the Selection Committees. If this is the case, painful as it may be, it is probably best that you did not get chosen this year. You need to concentrate on remedying whatever deficits you have so you will be ready at some future date. This may mean additional courses, completing your dissertation, obtaining additional practicum experience, or perhaps getting some personal therapy or counseling.

If you were adequately prepared, perhaps you applied to a poor choice of internships, ones that for some reason were not suitable for a person with your credentials. Perhaps they expected more practicum experience than your program affords. It may be that your credentials did not stand out from the rest, or that you limited your applications to very prestigious institutions with high selection ratios. Maybe you applied for specialized tracks for which you lacked the necessary credentials. Perhaps you refused to apply to places that did not meet your exact specifications. Maybe one of your references had doubts about your abilities, or you didn't interview effectively. The point of all this is not to ruminate obsessively about what went wrong, but, with the help of your ADCT, mentor and, perhaps, even some of the ITDs who rejected your application, to decide whether or not to continue to seek an internship this year. It may be better to spend another year working on your academic goals and building up your credentials.

If you and your advisors decide that this is indeed the best time for you to go on internship, the next task is to match you with one of the remaining unfilled slots that will meet your needs. The most efficient procedure is to access the APPIC Clearinghouse, which opens at the conclusion of UND and continues operating until August. The basic procedures for using the Clearinghouse are described in the *Directory*. They were changed in June, 1997, so make sure you use the current copy. Previously, ADCTs having unplaced applicants after UND would list their programs and the number of students available with the Clearinghouse. Similarly, the ITDs having vacancies would list their availability. All communications with the Clearinghouse were by e-mail or fax.

Under the new procedure, which will begin in 1998, training programs having vacancies after UND will list their vacancies on the APPIC web site. ADCTs will not need to list their programs or the number of unplaced applicants. Instead, students still seeking internships after UND can simply access the web site, see what programs still have openings, and contact the ITDs directly.

The sooner you access the Clearinghouse the better. Although the number of vacancies always used to exceed the number of qualified candidates, in recent years the Clearinghouse has definitely been a sellers' market. In 1996 and in 1997, there were approximately 150 applicants and only a handful of internship vacancies listed with the Clearinghouse after the purge and throughout the summer.

The disappearing internship. If you obtained an internship on Notification Day, and you are nevertheless reading this section reserved for people experiencing disasters, then your emergency may be that you got an internship and it disappeared. Nobody ever told you that this could happen. In fact, this is extremely rare, and we usually do not mention it because we are afraid that already apprehensive trainees would get absolutely hysterical if they heard about disappearing internships. That is why I did not let the others read this section. But now that it has happened to you, how do we deal with it?

This topic was not covered in the first edition of this book because, until 1991, I had never heard of an internship disappearing. That year, I encountered four cases. While this is an infinitesimal proportion of the 2,400 plus internships awarded annually, it is extremely upsetting to those concerned.

Internships can disappear by acts of God, which are called "natural disasters," and by acts of humans, which logic demands we term "unnatural disasters." In my sample of four cases, unnatural disasters outnumbered the natural kind three to one. We will not draw any theological or philosophical conclusions from this, but simply report on the unnatural kind first.

In 1991, Dr. Kathie Larsen, who was then Chair of APPIC, reported to the membership, "As a number of states are in dire financial straits, training budgets have sometimes been a target of budget cuts. In three cases which came to our attention this summer, internship programs had funding withdrawn or frozen, months after they made offers to interns on calling day" (Larsen, 1991, p. 1). Hiring freezes and layoffs, or, as the British term it, "redundancies," are phenomena more common in the 1990s than in recent decades. Ask Bob Dole.

Larsen (1991) reported that APPIC intervention was successful in restoring the stipends in two of these cases. The third program was not a member of APPIC and declined intervention. Moreover, Larsen (1991, p. 1) noted, "The attorneys for this program maintained that acceptance letters specifying dates and the stipend amounts were necessary for the offers made on calling day to be considered binding. The program had not written such letters."

There are several instructive lessons to be drawn from Larsen's comments:

1. Only do business with an APPIC internship;

2. After acceptance, send your internship a letter stipulating your understanding of the conditions of employment, including the dates and stipend;

3. Insist on receiving a formal letter from the Internship Training Director specifying the conditions of the appointment, as required by Rule 11 of the APPIC regulations; and

4. If you are later told your position is frozen (or if the conditions of employment do not conform to those stipulated in your letter), notify APPIC and ask for their assistance.

If something like this should occur, you will find that the internship's ITD and the training faculty will be on your side and will do whatever they can to assist you. They want you as an intern, and they will be utterly appalled and abashed at any abrogation of their good faith agreement by bureaucrats or administrators. They should welcome the APPIC intervention and anything else that can be done to restore the original agreement.

Apart from some budgetary problem, could an internship change its mind after you have accepted an offer? No. Acceptance is binding on the training program just as it is on you. Once you have received the letter, you have an enforceable contract. There is only one possible circumstance that I can imagine whereby an internship might be able to rescind an offer; that is, if you submitted a false or fraudulent application. What would constitute fraud? Misrepresenting your education or employment history, forging a transcript or letter of recommendation, concealing a felony conviction if asked... these are the sorts of things that could conceivably lead an internship to reconsider and prevail in the event of a lawsuit (Hollander, 1990). If a candidate has honestly supplied all the information required, then the internship's acceptance letter makes it a "done deal."

But what about natural disasters? Well, these do occur. Hurricanes, tornadoes, floods, and other natural disasters can strike internship facilities just like anything else. However, even such catastrophes can sometimes work out for the best. One year, one of my students seemed to have nothing but bad luck. A thoroughly congenial chap, "Hard luck Sam" had excellent credentials and superb letters. He should have had no difficulties, but unfortunately his first choice was a VA Medical Center that receives well over 100 applications. Admission there always requires good luck, and Sam's seemed in short supply. The ITD was most supportive and told Sam that he had been one of the first alternates; there were simply not enough slots available to make him an offer.

Sam was disappointed, but he accepted a position at his second choice, another VAMC, and made the best of it. Some months later Sam called me in a panic. As he and his family were packing to move, he had received a call from his internship; there had been a natural disaster and much of the institution had been badly damaged. The patients were being transferred elsewhere, and the facility would be closed for at least a year for repairs.

I called the ITD at Sam's first choice and told her about his latest hard luck. I reminded her of all the positive things she had said about Sam and suggested that it might be possible for her to arrange to have Sam transferred to her program along with his stipend. It took some doing, but eventually it was all worked out. Thanks to the natural disaster, Sam ended up at his first choice where he had a superb year.

Reflections and projections

If you are well-prepared to go on internship, choose your sites well, and play your cards as I have suggested, the odds are that you will obtain an internship that is good for you. Don't discard your application materials -- next year you will probably need them when you apply for a post-doctoral fellowship or a supervised clinical position leading to licensure. Of course, if you obtained a Gainesville model two-year internship, next year is already taken care of.

Keep working on enhancing your skills and credentials. As you will soon discover, the present oversupply of psychologists is not limited to internships. It also extends to the marketplace, especially for those who want to devote their careers to psychotherapy. Remember to view yourself as a product that you will have to sell (Spruill, 1997). Since HMOs are not convinced that Ph.D.s or Psy.D.s in psychology practicing psychotherapy are any better than master's level licensed social workers or counselors, it is difficult for doctoral level clinical or counseling psychologists to justify charging higher fees. As a result, many psychologists who have specialized in the practice of psychotherapy have fallen on hard times.

As you prepare for internship, keep the issue of supply and demand in mind, and prepare yourself to fill a less crowded niche in the marketplace. My personal opinion is that more psychologists ought to return to their roots and focus on assessment and research. However, I am biased because that has been my career path. If you want to specialize in an area that has less competition from master's level practitioners, consider behavioral medicine, pediatric psychology, neuropsychological assessment, the assessment of developmental and learning disabilities, and forensic psychology.

During the course of the internship-selection process, you may have observed or experienced behavior that you felt was inappropriate, objectionable, or prohibited under the APPIC guidelines. You may have wondered what can or should be done about it. In the final chapter, I will discuss the frequency of such violations and review the APPIC procedures for dealing with such behavior. Everyone hopes that the advent of computer matching will reduce, perhaps even eliminate, the incentives for such behavior. I will conclude by describing the forthcoming computer-matching system and how it is likely to transform the internship-selection process.

CHAPTER ELEVEN

RULE VIOLATIONS AND COMPUTER MATCHING

Although I have alluded to various rule infractions that can occur during the internship selection procedure, we have not dealt with how extensive such behavior is or what APPIC can or will do about it. I will address the problem of rule violations and sanctions in the first part of this chapter, and then take up computerized matching, a new method of pairing intern applicants with sites that we hope will decrease such violations.

Sins and Sanctions

After the 1997 internship-selection season ended, Carl Zimet, the Chair of the APPIC Standards and Review Committee ("ASARC"), announced that it had been an "epic" year for allegations of selection rule violations by APPIC members. The clamor was so great that the APPIC Board took the highly unusual step of unilaterally changing the intern selection rules by adding the new "don't ask, don't offer, don't accept, don't use ranking information" Rule. Before you seek an internship, we should discuss rule violations and the APPIC sanctioning process.

How frequent is rule-violating behavior?

Paraphrasing Charles Dickens, 1997 was, "...the best of years... the worst of years..." with respect to the reported frequency of alleged rule violations. Depending on the source one consulted, violations reached either an all-time high or an all-time low. Reading e-mail bulletin boards and listening to the tales told by various participants in the process, chicanery and duplicity reached pandemic proportions. ADCTs and students complained about the deceitfulness of internships, and ITDs deplored the mendacity of applicants. Survey data presented a somewhat different picture; although respondents reported unacceptably high levels of rule-violating behavior, the frequency was considerably lower than one would expect on the basis of the anecdotal evidence. Finally, the number of *official* complaints filed with ASARC in the weeks following UND reached an all time *low* (Zimet, 1997).

Anecdotes and rumors. It seems possible that some of the recent increases in infractions may have been more apparent than real. As more and more psychologists share information via the Internet, there has been increasingly wide dissemination of reports and comments regarding the internship selection process. As with any other type of gossip, people are more interested in misbehavior than in conduct that follows the Guidelines. This book is no exception. Most of the stories I have included are about things that went wrong and people who behaved inappropriately, despite the fact that most of the students I have guided through the internship application process have had minimal difficulties.

Next time you are in a group, bring up the subject of air travel. Everyone will compete to tell their favorite stories of the worst possible airline trips you can imagine. Listening to them talk, you will get the impression that none has ever had a safe or comfortable trip that arrived on time; if they did they certainly would not admit it. The same principle applies to internship applications. When I was an ADCT, my internship applicants and I always got together for a debriefing session when it was all over. Most of the stories we swapped dealt with awful things that had happened and the gross behavior of some internship staff, as applicants tried to top one another in their tales of misfortune. If anyone told about a visit that went exactly as planned, no one would listen. Boring!

I noticed the same phenomenon while monitoring the electronic bulletin boards during the 1996-1997 selection season. One could easily get the impression that all ITDs were wolves in wolves' clothing, lurking in their lairs to abuse helpless applicants. On one board, a lynch mob mentality began to develop as some correspondents who were apparently ADCTs proposed vigilante action, namely publicly posting the names and settings of ITDs who had allegedly violated the rules. The frenzy escalated until an ITD suggested that if this policy were adopted, the internships should respond by posting the names of students who behaved unethically or inappropriately, along with the names of *their* ADCTs and *their* academic programs. They could begin with those who stated (or implied) that an internship was their first choice and later turned down or "held" an offer when it was tendered. This suggestion led to some concerns over due process, which, of course, was the ITD's point. The board soon turned to a new topic.

Survey data. Although I have certainly been critical of APPIC and the internship selection process on occasion, I don't want you to get an exaggerated impression of the nature or extent of rule violations. So let's examine some survey data that may put the issue in perspective. Using data collected a decade ago, Carifio et al. (1987) reported that 53% of the 90 students they polled felt that one or more programs violated one or more Guidelines. Unfortunately their survey used admittedly flawed sampling methods (Carifio & Grace, 1992) and was conducted before APPIC had adopted their current system for dealing with alleged violations. Perhaps the most common violation, reported by 64% of the students, was that some programs did not notify alternates once they had filled all their slots; since then the rule on this issue has been tightened up to stipulate that programs *must* (rather than *should*) notify other applicants by phone as soon as possible. Other frequently-reported transgressions were that 40% of the applicants felt pressured to commit before UND, and 25% reported they had received an offer before UND (80% of whom felt good about it). (Parenthetically, one successful 1997 applicant who had made a first-choice commitment complained about the fact that internships waited until UND to notify successful candidates they had been accepted; he felt that candidates should be notified as soon as the selection committee decides to accept them. This, of course, would move the clock back to the days before APPIC when internships could and did make offers whenever they chose.)

A more recent and carefully-conducted survey of ITDs, ADCTs, and students after the 1994-1995 selection season found that 73 of the 185 applicants (40%) who responded to the survey reported they had experienced at least one violation of APPIC Guidelines (Constantine & Keilin, 1996). (If we phrase it the other way, this means 60% perceived no problems.) These 73 students reportedly experienced 154 violations, an average of 2.1 per reporting student (or 0.83 per student for the entire sample). If we assume that they each applied to about a dozen internships, these data suggest that the vast majority of the internships they had contact with were seen as operating within the Guidelines.

Constantine and Keilin (1996) also ascertained the nature of the alleged violations. They classified the complaints into 16 different categories and reported, "...ten of the 16 types of violations reported by applicants were actually not violations of APPIC Guidelines, even though they may have been perceived by applicants as uncomfortable or inappropriate" (1996, p. 310). These pseudo-violations included asking applicants personal questions in interview, asking them what other sites they had applied to, ITDs calling applicants before UND, perceived favoring of minority candidates over whites, giving candidates who were not being considered a "courtesy" interview, giving applicants negative feedback about their interviews, and rudeness. These allegations represented 20% of all the perceived violations; the other 80% were in fact infractions of APPIC rules. Of the actual violations, 62% involved pressuring applicants to reveal rankings, followed by telling an applicant to expect an offer on UND, not properly notifying applicants of their status prior to UND, extending offers before 9:00 AM CST on UND, and "leading on" applicants about receiving offers. These findings suggest that while there is an unacceptably high incidence of rule violations, some reports of the frequency or extent of infractions may be exaggerated by the inclusion of behaviors that are not actually prohibited. This is borne out by an examination of the charges officially filed with APPIC.

Official complaints. The APPIC Standards and Review Committee was established in 1988 and began receiving complaints in 1989. Over the years few formal charges have actually been brought against APPIC members. Twelve complaints were filed with ASARC in 1990, five in 1991, 12 in 1992, and ten each in 1993 and 1994 (ASARC, 1994). In 1996, ten complaints were received, but only five complainants actually filed charges (Zimet, 1996). Zimet and Lamb (1992) reported that half the accusations received are either not within the jurisdiction of APPIC, because they involve academic programs, students, or other non-members, or are complaints that are unrelated to the selection Guidelines, such as someone not returning a phone call or an applicant being reimbursed for a trip.

The remaining charges are investigated following ASARC procedures, and some result in sanctions being imposed against the offending party, the most serious of which to date appear to be "Notices of Public Sanctions" being published in the APPIC *Newsletter.* The 1994 ASARC report to the APPIC membership listed the following alleged violations in the period 1990 - 1994:

1. Site did not notify remaining candidates that all slots were filled on UND (11)

2. Site did not notify candidates they had been excluded one week before UND (9)

3. Site made calls before 9:00 AM CST on UND (9)

4. Site unduly pressured applicants holding an offer to accept or reject (9)

5. Program made an offer and then withdrew it (5)

6. Program asked applicants to rank their choices (4)

7. Program communicated acceptance information to candidate before UND (4)

8. Improper notification of alternate status (4)

9. Solicitation of applicant's response prior to making offer (2)

10. Applicant did not receive confirmation letter within required time period (1)

Obviously, the number of formal complaints is vastly lower than the unofficial reports of infractions that are informally discussed by ADCTs, students, and even other ITDs. Some students are naturally fearful of the possible repercussions of leveling charges against a senior professional such as the head of an internship center. Zimet (1996) noted that a letter had been received that made various allegations regarding selection violations. However, the university faculty and students who had signed the letter stated they would not file a formal complaint because they feared retaliation. Zimet (1996, p. 16) noted, "...fear of retaliation is being heard more frequently by the ASARC Committee, yet not a single incident of retaliation has come to ASARC's attention since its existence. However, that anxiety is understandable given the imbalance between the number of intern applicants and the number of intern positions." ASARC urged individuals who had experienced violations to report them.

Quite apart from repercussions, pursuing an official complaint is an involved and cumbersome process. By the time things are finally adjudicated, the results will have little or no impact on the life of the student, so few are motivated to make the effort after UND is history. In Constantine and Keilin's (1996) survey, of the 73 applicants who reported they had perceived at least one infraction, only 12 (16%) had reported it to anyone. Of these 12, five reported it to their ADCT, five to their major professor or some other professor, and two did not specify whom they told. Most significant, none reported it to ASARC.

Some ADCTs may also discourage students from complaining because they do not want their students to be labeled as "whistle blowers" or "troublemakers" (Zimet, 1997). They may feel that such a reputation would make it more difficult for future students from their programs to get accepted. Three of the 29 ADCTs in Constantine and Keilin's (1996) survey reported that at least one of their students had told them about an alleged violation of APPIC policy. One of these ADCTs reported the violation to the internship and to ASARC, one reported to ASARC only, and the third did not report it to anyone.

The APPIC sanctions process. The procedures for filing a complaint are laid out in great detail in each issue of the APPIC *Directory*. I will summarize them here to give you an idea of the complexity of the official sanctions process.

The first step when a possible violation is noticed is to attempt an informal resolution of the problem. Rules 12, 13, and 14 of the APPIC Guidelines provide that people who become aware of apparent rules violations should contact the alleged offender(s) directly, bringing the problem to their attention and asking them to comply with the rules. (See Appendix 1.) You will recall that this is how I handled the situation described in Chapter Ten in which an internship staff member asked one of my students whether he would accept an offer. It is only if the people involved in the matter cannot sort things out for themselves through consultation that a violation should be filed with ASARC.

To make the process clearer, let's trace a hypothetical case. On page 137, I described the case of "Bambi Gazelle," who had been assured by "Prof. Buck Muledeer" that Muledeer's former student, "Dr. Carrie Boux," the ITD of the "Moosehead Medical Center," would make sure Bambi was accepted at Moosehead. The real Bambi actually got a notice of exclusion from Moosehead the week before UND and was able to find a place elsewhere.

Let's suppose instead, however, that Bambi got a phone call from Moosehead the week before UND that she thought confirmed Muledeer's assurance that she would be accepted. Instead, let's further suppose that late on Selection Day, Bambi got a call from Dr. Carrie Boux saying that Moosehead was filled. Since Bambi had burned her bridges with the other settings to which she had applied, she was left without a slot.

At this point, Bambi finally tells her ADCT everything that has happened including the fact that she got a phone call that seemed to confirm that she had nothing to worry about. Following the Guidelines, the ADCT calls the ITD and explains the situation. Dr. Boux says that her assistant, Dr. Ann T. Lope, did call all the applicants the week before UND, but it was only to verify their phone numbers for Selection Day. She regrets any misunderstanding, but Moosehead is full and there is really nothing that can be done.

Bambi and her ADCT are frustrated and angry. They decide to complain about the shabby treatment Bambi received. They call APPIC and report the whole sorry business. Although Prof. Muledeer is responsible for much of what happened, APPIC has no jurisdiction over non-members, but they are told they can file a complaint against Moosehead. They are sent a standard complaint form by registered mail. The form requires Bambi to identify the agency (Moosehead Medical Center) against whom the complaint is being filed and to grant ASARC permission to identify her as the complainant. Many potential complainants balk at being identified, but as Zimet and Lamb (1992, p. 28) pointed out, "...it is necessary and consistent with due process that the person filing the complaint be identified, so that the accused can respond to the complaint." The identity of the individual making the complaint is revealed only to the accused party and to the members of the ASARC and APPIC Boards.

In the rest of the complaint, Bambi would explain what happened and what policies she feels were violated. She might write that on January 28th at 9:00 AM she received a call from Dr. Ann T. Lope of Moosehead Medical Center, which Bambi thought promised her an offer. After being told that Moosehead thought very highly of her, she was asked if she would be at her home number on UND. Then Dr. Lope allegedly said, "I can't tell you that you will be receiving an offer on Selection Day, but your husband should start looking for jobs in Moosehead City." The form asks what APPIC rules were violated, and Bambi answers Rule 3a, which prohibits internships from extending veiled offers prior to UND. Bambi would also have to describe the attempts to handle this informally, indicate what the outcome was on UND, and return the form, preferably by registered mail, by April 1.

Within 15 days of receiving the complaint, the ASARC Chair would send a registered letter to Bambi acknowledging it has been received. Since Moosehead is a member of APPIC, the ASARC would have jurisdiction, and the Chair would assign the complaint to a "case coordinator." In this case, the coordinator is "Dr. William E. (Billy) Gote." Dr. Gote is one of four APPIC members appointed to serve on the ASARC by the APPIC Board of Directors. He is the Chief Psychologist at the Unicorn University Counseling Center and, like other APPIC officials, donates his time and services to the organization. His task is to conduct a low profile investigation and present his findings to the ASARC at its next meeting. Since Unicorn is located in a different state from Moosehead Medical Center, he will conduct most of his investigation by mail or on the phone.

Following the ASARC "Procedures for Handling Grievances and Violations of APPIC Policies," which is reprinted in the APPIC *Directory*, Dr. Gote first notifies the ITD that a complaint has been filed against Moosehead in the matter of Bambi Gazelle and provides her with a copy of the allegations. Dr. Carrie Boux has 30 days to respond. She replies that she had Dr. Ann T. Lope, a member of the selection committee, call all the Moosehead applicants to verify where they would be on UND and ask if they had any questions. She states that Dr. Lope recalls that during the call, Ms. Gazelle volunteered the information that Moosehead was her first choice. Dr. Lope said she told her that she was delighted that Ms. Gazelle held Moosehead in such high regard and that she and the rest of the selection committee were very impressed with Ms. Gazelle's credentials. However, she couldn't tell Bambi whether she would receive an offer on Selection Day. When Dr. Lope asked her if she had any questions, Bambi had inquired about job opportunities for her husband in Moosehead City. On learning that Mr. Gazelle is a machinist at the John Deere Tractor Company, Dr. Lope told Bambi that there are few manufacturing or factory jobs available in Moosehead City. Bambi asked if he should start looking for work now, and, according to Dr. Boux, Dr. Lope recalls answering that it is never too soon to start investigating job opportunities at a potential internship site. Dr. Lope recalls she concluded the call by telling Bambi that Dr. Boux would be calling on UND. Dr. Boux added that this was true because, following her understanding of the APPIC Guidelines, she calls *all* the applicants on UND to notify them of the outcome.

Upon receiving Dr. Boux's response, Dr. Gote might decide that he needs more information. He might want to talk to Dr. Lope to verify Dr. Boux's account of the conversation. The ASARC procedures state that if Dr. Gote wants to contact Dr. Lope or any other Moosehead personnel, he must first notify the ITD. The idea is to keep the investigation as confidential as possible until the allegations have been verified. He might also call Ms. Gazelle, who denies asking about job opportunities until *after* Dr. Lope suggested that her husband should start looking. When his investigation is complete, Dr. Gote would present the information and his comments to the ASARC at its next meeting. If the ASARC is not scheduled to have a face-to-face meeting for some time, the complaint could be considered by means of a conference call.

The ASARC can make one of three decisions: 1) there was no violation, 2) they need more information, or 3) there was a violation. If they decided there was no violation, Ms. Gazelle would have 30 days to renew the complaint if she could provide new information. If they decided they need more information, Dr. Gote would continue his investigation. If they concluded that a violation had occurred, they would pass the complaint on to the APPIC Board of Directors and recommend possible courses of action, taking into consideration the apparent intent of the offending party, the number of such violations that Moosehead may have committed in the past, and the consequences to the individuals involved and to the profession.

The APPIC Board of Directors then decides what should be done. The Board can vote to uphold, review, or change any of the ASARC findings or recommendations. APPIC policy permits a wide range of possible actions, both private and public. Private actions include a "directive," a written statement directed only to the ITD that serves an educational function; a "reprimand," which is addressed to the ITD and to his or her supervisor; and a "reprimand with monitoring" in which ASARC monitors the program for up to a year. Public actions include "censure," a statement addressed to the ITD and his or her supervisors accompanied by printed announcements in the *Newsletter* and *Directory;* "probation," which includes censure plus monitoring the program to assure compliance with the Guidelines; and "expulsion" from APPIC. In addition, APPIC could refer the matter to various state or national associations or accrediting bodies.

After the parties have been notified of the outcome by registered mail, either side has 30 days to file an appeal. In that event, the rules provide for further reviews by the Board or by specially appointed re-hearing committees until the Board makes a final determination of the case. The procedural rules further stipulate that the cost of the investigation and the time spent by the Board are borne by APPIC, but if either Dr. Boux or Ms. Gazelle wants to present her case to the Board at one of its scheduled meetings, she has to pay her own travel expenses.

Enforcement of the APPIC Guidelines. Despite the elaborate procedures I have just summarized, you can see that APPIC must rely on the voluntary compliance and cooperation of its members to promote adherence to its rules governing intern selection. Sanctions can be imposed only after an elaborate, painstaking set of procedures is followed. These procedures are designed to ensure due process and to safeguard the rights and reputations of the parties to the dispute, as well as to protect the APPIC Board from lawsuits from people who may be unhappy with the outcome. After this long tedious process, a case like that of Bambi Gazelle and Dr. Boux may boil down to two people having different recollections of what was said during a telephone conversation. Unless there was a repeated pattern of similar complaints leveled against Moosehead, when all is said and done, the most that might happen is a private letter to Dr. Boux advising her to instruct her staff to be more guarded in what they say to applicants during the Endgame. Bambi Gazelle may feel some satisfaction, but she is still left without a position.

In short, adherence to the Guidelines cannot be adequately enforced with sanctions. Because the process is so difficult and the rewards so slight, few aggrieved individuals file complaints, even if they have no reason to worry about possible retaliation for being a whistle blower. From a legal standpoint, the new Rule makes things worse because it criminalizes behavior that is even vaguer and more difficult to define than "soliciting" information. Conceivably, a case coordinator could determine whether an ITD "accepted" ranking information, but how can he or she decide whether the ITD "used" it? How can APPIC enforce prohibitions against ADCTs and students who "offer" ranking information when they are not subject to APPIC's jurisdiction or sanctions? Obviously, APPIC and ASARC can only hope that all parties voluntarily comply with these regulations for the good of the system as well as for their own benefit.

The problem is that as much as everyone would like to behave honorably, the present rules give an advantage to those ITDs who can predict which applicants are least likely to "hold" their offers on UND. And, whether or not it is true, many applicants will no doubt continue to believe that voluntarily "first choicing" an internship gives them an edge on the competition, a powerful incentive in the era of shortfalls. This makes it difficult for those who play by the rules. As Pogo, cartoonist Walt Kelly's ubiquitous 'possum said, "We has met the enemy, and it is us."

Computer Matching: Back to the Future

How do we deal with the 'possum's observation on human nature? If we are the problem, how do we change our behavior? APPIC has tried sanctions and has tried appealing to people's sense of fairness. If this does not work, then perhaps we should change the rules or, as a good behaviorist would say, alter the contingencies. If the present system benefits those who violate the Guidelines, we should devise a system in which crime does not pay. Such a plan is already in the works. Some time on or about the beginning of the next millennium, APPIC will switch from Uniform Notification to computer matching. This change should eliminate the differences in power and control that now exist. In this section, I will explain how computer matching works and why it should help solve the problems associated with UND.

Why computer matching?

All three selection strategies used thus far have had the same basic flaw: sequential decision-making that gives one party or the other an unfair advantage. In "*laissez faire,*" the strategy used prior to APPIC, ITDs had the leverage because they could make an offer and rescind it whenever they chose. With Uniform Notification, the training center makes a binding unilateral commitment to an applicant and must then wait until the candidate decides whether or not to accept. The short-lived Early Acceptance policy forced applicants to make a unilateral binding commitment to a training center to accept a position if it was offered. In terms of the poker analogy I have been using throughout this book, some players had to reveal their hands before the others did. Since the beginning, this disparity has created the differences in power and control that led some players to try to equalize the differences by "cheating."

"Computer matching" is an attempt to resolve this problem by allowing the players to make their selections independently and reveal them simultaneously to a neutral third party, in this case a computer, which will examine their selections, seek the best fits, and advise all the players of the results. In other words, all the players expose their cards at the same time, and the computer figures out who wins and who loses, just like the "house" does in a casino poker game. Proponents of the system swear that there will be no advantage in knowing the cards in the other players' hands or how they plan to play them. The best chance for the various players to achieve the results they want is to "call them as they see them," that is, to rank their choices solely on the basis of their desirability. No other strategy will accomplish their goals better. Once the players realize this, there will be no incentive for the ITDs to know the students' choices, and there will be no advantage to the students in "first choicing" one or more internships.

Matching schemes have been employed in other disciplines such as medicine, dentistry, accountancy, and law for many years. They have been discussed for psychology intern matching since the 1970s, but in the early days of APPIC, the cost was prohibitive. Growing dissatisfaction with Uniform Notification on the part of the universities and the students as well as the internship training centers led to a reexamination of computer matching and a pilot test during the 1989-1990 intern selection season. That study failed because many sites and applicants did not participate. A five-year moratorium on making major changes in the selection system was declared. That time has passed. Unless there are drastic changes in the composition of the APPIC Board, it seems evident that computer matching will soon become a reality.

How computer matching will work

Plans for a new computer matching system are now being developed. A "Request for Proposals" (RFP) will be issued, bids will be collected, and at some point in 1997 or 1998, a contract will be awarded to a software company to develop and manage a system for conducting computerized matching. Although the specific details have yet to be worked out, the broad outlines of the proposed system are in place.

Who will participate? When computer matching is adopted, anyone and everyone who plans to apply to an APPIC-member internship will have to participate to be accepted. You will obtain the necessary materials from APPIC, and you will be assigned a unique individual PIN (Personal Identification Number). Each APPIC internship will also have its own unique number.

How applicants select their internships. In the pilot study, applicants and training centers recorded their internship selections on a special optically scannable form that they then mailed to APPIC; this proved disastrous. In addition to relying on the vagaries of the U.S. Postal Service, the forms proved to be optically unscannable, so all the data had to be entered by hand (Pederson, 1997).

The plan is for the new computer matching system to be done on line, with applicants and training centers entering their choices electronically. As an applicant, you will access the system, which will probably be through the APPIC web site, enter your personal PIN (and probably some other identifiers), and then list the numbers of your choices in rank order. The present plan allows you to list as many as 17 choices. No ties will be permitted; you must assign each internship its own unique rank from 1 to 17. Depending on how the matchings work out, you could be assigned to any of the internships on the list, so you obviously should not list any that you would not be willing to attend. Entering an internship's number signifies that you are willing to attend that placement and you will accept a position there if the Computer Gods say you are matched to that setting.

The selection algorithm will be designed in such a way that your best chance to get the internship of your choice is to rank your selections in your preferred order. If there is some dream internship that you would love to attend but fear you have no realistic chance of obtaining, put it first. You have absolutely nothing to lose. If they listed you sufficiently high, you will get your dream match. If your "dream internship," or even several dream internships, did not rank you high enough for you to get a match there, the program will proceed on to your next choices. The planners assure us that you and the training centers have nothing to lose and everything to gain by calling it exactly as you see it.

The web site will remain open for a specified period of time. During that period, if you have second thoughts, you can change your rank order. The fact that you can change the order of your selections at any time "up to one nanosecond" before the system closes is viewed as a safeguard against pressure to disclose your first choices to any internship (Pederson, 1997). At the specified time, the system will be closed, and the applicants' choices will be compared with those submitted by the internships. Subsequently, the training centers will be informed of the trainees assigned to them, and you will be notified of the internship to which you were matched. That is where you must go if you are to go on any APPIC internship that year. If you did not get matched with any site, you will be informed of all those places that still have openings, and you can then negotiate with them directly. Thus, under computer matching, access to the Clearinghouse is automatic and begins immediately. Under what circumstances might an applicant not get matched to a site? Basically, the same as at present, namely not having enough viable selections, limiting choices to a circumscribed geographical area, getting low ranks because of inadequate preparation, and so on.

<u>How internships select their applicants.</u> For the internships, the task will be more complex. They will have to decide between "global" and "single slot" rankings or some combination thereof. What does this mean?

In *global ranking*, an internship simply lists all their applicants in their preferred order, just as you did with the internships. If Halibut Hospital has 36 acceptable applicants, they rank them from 1 to 36 and submit the entire list. They should not list anyone that they are unwilling to have as an intern. If they have six slots, the first six candidates will constitute the first "tier." Unlike the medical matching program, the APPIC program will begin with applicants rather than institutions. The results make no difference except in the rare example of a gridlock such as the one I described in Chapter Two. The APPIC model will decide such stalemates in favor of the student, whereas the medical model resolves them in favor of the internship setting. In the past, this disgruntled some APPIC members, but this situation is so rare that it makes little difference.

Let us suppose that your first four choices are as follows:

1. Halibut Hospital
2. Codliver Consortium
3. Septicemia School of Medicine
4. Moosehead Medical Center

When the program comes to your entry, it will note that Halibut Hospital is your first choice. It will check Halibut's list to see how you stand; if you are in the first tier, you are automatically matched. You have a position at Halibut and you are dropped from further consideration by the computer program. Meanwhile, one of Halibut's slots is marked as filled.

Suppose, however, you miss the first tier at Halibut. Instead of being in the top six, you are ranked seventh. Your first-choice bid will be put on hold for a time until the computer has examined all the other applicants' rankings. If all six of the people in Halibut's first tier also rated Halibut as their first choice, they would be matched, and Halibut would be filled. When the computer gets back to you, it would then note that your first choice, Halibut Hospital, is filled and would move all your other choices up a notch. The Codliver Consortium is now your #1 pick. If you are listed in the first tier at Codliver, that is where you will be matched. If Codliver is also filled, then Septicemia becomes your first choice and so on. If you think about it, you can see why, under computer matching, putting a long shot in first place does not hurt your chances at your lower-ranked settings. If your first choice is filled or you are not listed, your second choice becomes your first choice. In the pilot study, 90% of the applicants who were matched obtained their first or second choices.

Consider another scenario. Again, suppose you ranked Halibut first and they ranked you seventh. Let us suppose that in the first round Halibut filled only three slots with their first-tier selections. With applicants applying to an average of 12 or 13 places each, it would be remarkable if all six listed Halibut first, especially if Halibut took the opportunity to try for some superstars that they had little chance of attracting. (Under computer matching, unlike Uniform Notification, Halibut can afford to give ranks to very desirable but unlikely candidates without hurting its chances of filling.) Halibut now has three slots filled and three still vacant. Their seventh, eighth, and ninth selections are now promoted to their first tier. This time, when the computer gets back to you, it notes that Halibut is your first choice. Since they ranked you seventh, you are now in their first tier and you are matched with Halibut. You are dropped from the program, and Halibut now has only two slots left to fill. Halibut stays in the program until all their six slots are filled or until their list is exhausted.

Global ranking considers nothing except the overall ranks made by the internships and applicants. Halibut's fourth, fifth, and sixth slots are matched with candidates with no consideration of the nature of their first three matches. This can pose problems for internships that have track-specific selection or that prefer a class stratified according to gender, ethnicity, theoretical orientation, or some other variable. To deal with these problems, the APPIC program will allow them to adopt "single slot selection." If, for example, Halibut has a child track, they could set aside one of their six slots exclusively for that track. Only students who had applied for the child track would be ranked for that position. They would not be considered for any of the other five Halibut positions.

Let us suppose that seven applicants are applying for Halibut's child slot and that three ranked Halibut first. If one of those three was ranked first for that slot by the Halibut child staff, then a match would be declared and that slot would be filled. The remaining six applicants could be matched with other internship centers, but they would not be considered for any of the other five Halibut slots. (Under Uniform Notification, Halibut could have called their second-ranked child person and said, "I'm sorry, our child slot is filled, but we have a general opening; will you accept a general opening with a major child rotation?" Computer matching does not permit this flexibility.)

Each internship will have the option of setting aside as many specific slots as it wants and using global ranking for the remaining ones. The advantage of slot-specific ranking is it allows an internship to specify to some extent the composition of its entering class. If Halibut wants equal numbers of male and female applicants, for example, they can reserve three slots for women and three for men. However, an internship adopting the single-slot strategy will run a greater risk of leaving a vacancy unfilled. Suppose that 26 of Halibut's applicants are female and ten are male. By the time the program comes to Halibut's third "male" slot, it might find that all ten men have already been assigned. Since that slot is reserved for men, none of Halibut's female applicants would be considered for it, and the slot would go unfilled.

Pros and cons of computer matching

Because of sequential decision-making, internship selection has always suffered from differences in the relative power of the applicants and the ITDs. By forcing both applicants and internships to make their rankings independently and disclose them simultaneously, computer matching seems to ensure equality better than any system used thus far.

The major benefit of computer matching in my opinion is that it eliminates the "stalemates" and "gridlocks" that occur under Uniform Notification when candidates hold offers from lower-ranked internships while they await offers from those higher on their lists. It is this waiting while candidates hold offers that appears to cause the internships the most difficulty, because their alternates can disappear before the position is freed up. With computer matching, everyone enters their decisions, and the ranks are then frozen in place while the matching proceeds. Once the choices are entered, candidates and ITDs cannot change their minds, so "alternates" cannot "decide to go elsewhere" while there is still a chance they may be matched. The approach-avoidance conflict that presently occurs as the selection period draws to a close will disappear. The cards are all face up on the table, and the Computer Gods will decide who goes where.

There are, of course, some drawbacks as there are with any method. The major casualty is sequential or contingent decision-making. Instead of starting the day with a locked-in list, such as the computer match calls for, some ITDs like to wing it, basing their later calls on who accepts their initial offers (i.e., "First I'll first call the analytically-oriented black male student from the Midwest; if he accepts, I'll go after the cognitive-behavioral white female from New York, but, if he turns me down, I'll next call the research-oriented black lesbian from Missouri, and then go after the Jungian white male from San Francisco"). Single-slot selection will enable them to exercise some control over class composition, but after one has controlled for a couple of variables, the lists start getting very short.

Like the ITDs, the students who will suffer most under computer matching are those who wish to make contingent decisions, especially couples who wish to accept internships in geographic proximity. "If my spouse gets an internship at the Southwest Schizophrenia Center, I would want to go to Arizona

Anorexia, but if my partner is going to New England Neuropathology, I would prefer to attend Boston Bulimia." When computer matching was being debated prior to the pilot test, some argued that there ought to be a special provision whereby married couples were linked so that they could be sure of staying together. However, Blom and Pederson (1988) noted that, "...giving preference to married couples negatively affects the matching outcomes of unmarried candidates applying to those same sites...." Concerned about possible lawsuits, they asked, "...what about [special] provisions for engaged couples, cohabiting couples, siblings, other relatives, lifelong friends, future business partners or couples where the non-applicant spouse has a job in a specific locality?" The best strategy for partners who wish to remain in proximity under computer matching will continue to be to submit all their applications to a reasonably contiguous geographic area with a high density of internship training centers.

Under computer matching, ITDs will no longer gain any benefits from knowing how applicants rank them. Ideally, this should put a halt to ITDs pressuring students to reveal their rankings or make "first choice" pledges, the violations that appear to bother applicants the most. This does not mean that the ITDs will necessarily be persuaded. Old habits die hard, and even if it does not gain them a real advantage, some players may continue to bend or break the rules if only because it gives them a feeling of being in control. I have heard it said that there are pressure tactics used in medical internship selection even though it has been computerized for many years.

For example, I can see where settings that choose single-slot selection might think they could benefit from pressure tactics during the Endgame. Think back to the Halibut Hospital example in which they put all seven applicants for the child rotation on the list for a single slot. If our old friend, Dr. Almondine Dover-Sole of Halibut had an advance commitment from Tom Cod, her first-choice child candidate, to rank Halibut at the top of his list, *and* if Dover-Sole was convinced of Tom's veracity, she could list only Tom Cod's name under that slot. This would give her an opportunity to call the other six applicants to see if they would be willing to be considered for other slots. Of course, if Tom decided not to list Halibut first, he could be assigned elsewhere and Halibut would not fill that slot. A couple of experiences such as this might convince the more cynical players that "honesty is the best policy."

Nor would computer matching solve the problem posed by the APPIC member who used to call me every fall when I was ADCT.

He did not care for Uniform Notification, interviewing applicants, or any other aspect of the organized internship-selection process. Every year he would tell me that if I had a good candidate, he would give her or him a position based solely on my recommendation. The candidate would then apply only to his internship, and he would call and award that student the slot on UND. I used to mention that possibility to my students, but none was ever interested; they preferred to go through the process, see the internships for themselves, make their choices, and take their chances on the outcome. I felt they were wise.

The Bottom Line

Applying for internships is stressful no matter what the ground rules are. Whether it is the Uniform Notification poker game or the Computer Match roulette wheel, don't let the selection strategy bother you. No matter what matching procedure is employed, it is in your best interest to be ranked as high as possible by the internship of your choice.

Although applying for internships is challenging, you should be able to cope with it successfully now that you understand what it is all about. Remember that everybody concerned is seeking the optimal match between interns and programs in order to achieve the best possible educational experience for all involved. Many applicants experience needless anxiety because of unrealistic expectancies. Put aside any irrational concerns, and you will be able to cope with the real issues effectively.

No matter what sort of internship you decide is best for you, you want to make the best possible impression. First, make sure you are ready for internship. Develop your skills and credentials to the utmost. Take the right courses, work hard, get good grades, and earn outstanding recommendations. Read on your own, and develop your knowledge of all things clinical. Do well in a variety of practicum settings; be the person who is responsive to supervision, who can be relied on to keep cool in a crisis, and who cheerfully handles his or her share of the tough tasks. Produce quality research and get it published. Have a dissertation project approved and in progress. Above all, be honest, responsible, and ethical. In short, do everything you can to be the kind of student you will want to supervise in the years to come.

Once you have established your qualifications, review your priorities and preferences, investigate the various internships, and select those that best meet your needs. Then go for it. Make the best possible presentation via your CV, letters, and interviews. In your site visits, obtain the information you need to make your decision, follow the rules, and be honest and forthright with the internship faculties. Work with your ADCT, discuss your options with the internship ITDs, and convince the programs that you have what it takes to succeed. I hope you get what you are looking for and that this book has helped.

NOTES

APPENDIX 1

APPIC POLICY

INTERNSHIP OFFERS AND ACCEPTANCES

Revised June, 1996

Adherence to these policies is a condition of membership in APPIC

"Selection day" currently begins at 9:00 a.m. Central Standard Time on the second Monday in February and ends at 1:00 p.m. that same day. This definition is subject to change.

1. **These policies must be made known to all students applying to APPIC member internship programs and to all others affected by these policies.**
   a. APPIC member programs must include a copy of these policies in internship materials sent to applicants.
   b. Directors of APPIC internship programs must ensure that all people involved in recruiting or selecting interns are familiar with the policies, the need to communicate policies to applicants, and the importance of adhering to the policies.
   c. Directors of academic training programs (universities and professional schools) whose students intend to apply to APPIC member internship programs are requested to ensure that these policies are understood and adhered to by their students.

2. **Internship program directors must make every effort to inform, prior to selection day, those applicants who are no longer under consideration.**
   a. Students who remain under consideration may be notified that they remain under consideration after others have been excluded.
   b. No other information (such as agency's ranking of the applicant, status as alternate/first choice, etc.) may be communicated to applicants prior to selection day.

3. **No internship offers in any form may be extended by agencies before the beginning of selection day.**
   a. The *only* information that agencies may communicate to applicants prior to this time is whether or not the applicant remains under consideration for admission (see item 2). The spirit of this item precludes any communication of an applicant's status prior to the time above, however "veiled" or indirect such communication might be.
   b. "Alternates" may be fully informed of their status any time after the start of selection day. Applicants may not be told whether they are considered alternates or first choices prior to that time.
   c. Internship programs may not solicit information regarding an applicant's ranking of programs or his/her intention to accept or decline an offer of admission until after that offer is officially tendered.

4. **Applicants must reply to all offers no later than the closing time on selection day.**
   a. This deadline applies to all offers including those to applicants who are initially considered alternates and are subsequently extended an offer any time prior to the end of selection day.

b. Agencies may inquire as to the applicant's progress towards making a decision at any time after an offer is formally extended. Under no circumstances, however, may an agency implicitly or explicitly threaten to or actually rescind an offer if a decision is not made prior to the end of selection day (except as noted in item 6).
c. It is in everyone's best Interest that applicants make and communicate decisions to accept or reject each offer as quickly as possible.
d. Any offer that has not been accepted is void as of the ending hour of selection day.

5. An applicant must respond immediately to each offer tendered in one of three ways. The offer may be accepted, rejected, or "held."
a. *Accepting* the offer constitutes a binding agreement between applicant and internship program;
b. *Rejecting* the offer terminates all obligations on either side and frees the internship program to offer the position to another applicant;
c. *Holding* the offer means that the offer remains valid until the applicant notifies the program of rejection or acceptance, or until the end of selection day.

6. Applicants may "HOLD" no more than one active offer at a time.
a. If an applicant is holding an offer from one program and receives an offer from a more-preferred program, s/he may accept or "hold" the second offer provided the less-preferred program is notified *immediately* that the applicant is rejecting the previously held offer.
b. If a program confirms that an applicant is holding more than one offer, the program is free to withdraw their previously tendered offer of acceptance, and to offer that position to another applicant *after* the offending applicant is notified of that decision.

7. An offer of acceptance to an applicant is valid only if the applicant has not already accepted an offer of admission to another program.
a. An applicant's verbal acceptance of an offer constitutes a binding agreement between the applicant and the program that may not be reversed unilaterally by either party.
b. Before programs extend an offer, they must first explicitly inquire whether the applicant has already accepted an offer elsewhere. If so, no offer may be tendered.
c. A program may in no way suggest that an applicant renege on previously accepted offers.
d. If an applicant who has accepted an offer receives a second offer, s/he is obligated to refuse the second offer and inform the agency that s/he is already committed elsewhere.
e. Any offer accepted subsequent to a prior commitment is automatically null and void, even if the offering agency is unaware of the prior acceptance and commitment.

8. When an applicant accepts an offer of admission, s/he is urged to immediately inform all other internship programs at which s/he is still under consideration that s/he is no longer available.

9. Applicants who have not accepted a position prior to the end of selection day may receive offers of admission after that deadline.
a. Applicants should be prepared to accept or reject such late offers quickly, since most other deliberations should have already taken place.
b. Programs may legitimately place short but reasonable deadlines for responses to such late offers.

10. **Once a program has filled all available positions, all candidates remaining in their applicant pool must be notified that they are no longer under consideration.**
    a. Applicants who have not notified the agency that they have accepted a position elsewhere and who have not been selected by the agency should be notified by phone as soon as all positions are filled.
    b. If an applicant cannot be reached by phone, s/he should be so notified by letter postmarked no later than 72 hours after the end of selection day.

11. **Internship training directors should document their verbal agreement with each applicant in a letter postmarked no later than 72 hours following the end of selection day.**
    a. The letter should be addressed to the applicant and should include confirmation of conditions of the appointment, such as stipend, fringe benefits, and the date on which the internship begins.
    b. A copy of that letter should be sent simultaneously to the applicant's academic program director.

12. **Applicants who receive offers which do not comply with these policies or who in other ways detect violations of these policies by an APPIC member program are urged to request compliance with APPIC policies from the program representative.**
    a. Applicants should immediately report any problems unresolved after such request to his/her academic program director.
    b. Academic program directors are urged to contact internship training directors immediately regarding such unresolved problems.
    c. Such compliance problems should be resolved through consultation among applicant, internship program, and academic training director whenever possible.
    d. Problems not amenable to resolution through such consultation should be reported as soon as possible to the APPIC Standards and Review Committee at the address listed at the end of this document.

13. **Internship directors who become aware of violations of policies on the part of students, academic training directors, or other internship directors are urged to immediately request compliance to the policies.**
    a. Internship directors are urged to contact academic training program directors immediately regarding problems that remain unresolved after such a request for compliance.
    b. Internship program directors who become aware of violations of these policies by other internship programs should urge the applicant and academic training directors involved to follow the procedures outlined in 12 a-d above, and/or to directly contact the other internship director.
    c. Such compliance problems should be resolved through consultation among applicant, internship programs, and academic training director whenever possible.
    d. Failure to resolve compliance problems through consultation should be reported to the APPIC Standards and Review Committee.

14. **All reported violations of these policies will be considered by the APPIC Standards and Review Committee (ASARC). ASARC policies are described in the *APPIC Directory*. Violations of these policies should be reported to:**

Chair, APPIC Standards and Review Committee
733 Fifteenth Street, N.W.
Suite 719
Washington, DC 20005-2112
(202) 347-0022

Reprinted by permission of the Association of Psychology Postdoctoral and Internship Centers.

NOTES

APPENDIX 2

AVAILABILITY OF 1996-1997 INTERNSHIP POSITIONS BY REGION AND STATE

Region 1: East Coast: Northern section

State	Number of Agencies APA Accredited	Number of Agencies Not Accredited	Funded Positions Full-Time	Funded Positions Part-Time	Mean Full Stipend	Number of Applications	Mean No. of Applications per Position
Connecticut	8	0	49	0	$16,919	779	15.9
Delaware	2	0	7	0	$16,550	129	18.4
Massachusetts	19	4	117	4	$13,801	2,213	18.9
Maine	2	0	6	0	$16,660	111	18.5
New Hampshire	4	0	18	0	$13,775	245	13.6
New Jersery	9	5	48	1	$14,121	820	17.1
New York	52	8	294	15	$15,967	5,812	19.8
Pennsylvania	18	4	97	0	$15,472	1,655	17.1
Rhode Island	0	1	17	0	$16,224	265	15.6
Vermont	0	1	2	1	$14,000	7	3.5
Total	114	23	655	21	$15,349	12,036	15.8

Region 2: East Coast: Southern section

State	Number of Agencies APA Accredited	Number of Agencies Not Accredited	Funded Positions Full-Time	Funded Positions Part-Time	Mean Full Stipend	Number of Applications	Mean No. of Applications per Position
District of Columbia	8	0	33	0	$19,225	671	20.3
Georgia	8	2	37	1	$18,280	584	15.8
Maryland	13	0	64	0	$21,002	993	15.5
North Carolina	6	1	37	0	$17,330	727	19.6
South Carolina	3	0	20	0	$15,333	325	16.3
Virgina	13	0	55	0	$18,665	1,089	19.8
Total	54	3	246	1	$18,306	4,389	17.9

Region 3: Eastern Central

State	Number of Agencies APA Accredited	Number of Agencies Not Accredited	Funded Positions Full-Time	Funded Positions Part-Time	Mean Full Stipend	Number of Applications	Mean No. of Applications per Position
Alabama	2	1	13	0	$15,133	130	10.0
Florida	14	14	127	0	$12,837	1,730	13.6
Michigan	14	5	66	7	$14,496	819	12.4
Mississippi	2	0	18	0	$17,000	140	7.8
Ohio	14	3	81	3	$15,957	909	11.2
Tennessee	7	5	51	1	$15,302	670	13.1
West Virginia	4	0	12	0	$16,460	137	11.4
Total	57	28	368	11	$15,312	4,535	11.4

Region 4: North Central

State	Number of Agencies: APA Accredited	Number of Agencies: Not Accredited	Funded Positions: Full-Time	Funded Positions: Part-Time	Mean Full Stipend	Number of Applications	Mean No. of Applications per Position
Illinois	24	13	141	6	$15,009	2,635	18.7
Indiana	11	3	47	0	$14,711	758	16.1
Kentucky	4	1	19	0	$18,696	312	16.4
Minnesota	9	1	40	0	$15,090	759	19.0
Wisconsin	6	3	35	2	$14,759	562	16.1
Total	54	21	282	8	$15,653	5,026	17.3

Region 5: Western Central

State	Number of Agencies: APA Accredited	Number of Agencies: Not Accredited	Funded Positions: Full-Time	Funded Positions: Part-Time	Mean Full Stipend	Number of Applications	Mean No. of Applications per Position
Arkansas	3	0	12	0	$17,342	137	11.4
Iowa	4	0	13	0	$15,762	176	13.5
Kansas	4	0	21	1	$16,527	228	10.9
Louisiana	4	1	18	0	$15,331	235	13.1
Missouri	10	1	47	4	$16,139	549	11.7
Nebraska	2	0	27	0	$21,300	136	5.0
Oklahoma	3	1	21	0	$14,075	248	11.8
South Dakota	2	0	6	0	$17,250	73	12.2
Texas	20	6	124	0	$17,596	1,645	13.3
Total	52	9	289	5	$16,813	3,427	11.4

Region 6: West Coast and Mountain

State	Number of Agencies: APA Accredited	Number of Agencies: Not Accredited	Funded Positions: Full-Time	Funded Positions: Part-Time	Mean Full Stipend	Number of Applications	Mean No. of Applications per Position
Arizona	4	2	24	0	$15,129	397	16.5
California	33	18	199	17	$13,799	3,702	18.6
Colorado	7	1	34	1	$14,619	779	22.9
Hawaii	4	3	22	0	$16,523	252	11.5
Montana	1	0	3	0	$15,338	47	15.7
New Mexico	2	0	11	0	$16,065	207	18.8
Nevada	1	0	3	0	$17,000	58	19.3
Oregon	6	2	35	0	$14,282	578	16.5
Utah	5	3	30	1	$15,161	361	12.0
Washington	6	1	41	0	$14,632	655	16.0
Wyoming	1	1	6	0	$15,174	96	16.0
Total	70	31	408	19	$15,247	7,132	17

APPENDIX 3

A SAMPLE CURRICULUM VITAE

Curriculum Vitae
Rosa Thorne
(Formerly Rosa Cholla)

Addresses

Home:	2702 Elm Street University City West Idabama 82046 (111) 222-3333 (Leave message)	Work:	Psychology Clinic 102, West Idabama State University University City, WI 82032 (111) 888-7777, Ext 240

Personal Data

Birthplace:	Santo Loco, Costa Rojo
Citizenship:	U.S. (naturalized 10/1/95)
Birthdate:	2/27/72
Marital Status:	Married
Ethnicity:	Hispanic
Social Security:	222-33-4444

Education

1996 to Present

Doctoral Candidate, Psychology Department
West Idabama State University
Major: Clinical Psychology
Minor: Nutrition
Dissertation Topic: The influence of grain price fluctuations on posttraumatic stress disorders among Midwestern farmers.
(Prospectus Defended: July 4, 1997)
Major Professor: B. J. Mentor, Ph.D.
Comprehensive Examination: Passed, December 25,1996
Areas of Concentration: Psychopathology, Food psychology

1993 to 1996	Master of Science, Psychology Department West Idabama State University Major: Clinical Psychology Major Professor: Mary Grayhead, Ph.D. Thesis Title: Personality changes resulting from pesticide exposure in rural children.
1988 to 1992	Bachelor of Science, *magna cum laude* Horatio Alger College Collegetown, West Idabama Major: Psychology Minor: Home Economics Honors: Phi Beta Kappa, Sigma Xi

Other Educational Experience

February 12, 1996: Advanced 8 PF Test workshop (6 hrs.)
Presented by Raymond Stenscore, Ph.D.
Sponsored by American Personality Association, Central City, West Idabama

April 18, 1995: Eating Disorders Workshop (8 hrs.)
Presented by Duncan Donut, Ph.D.
Sponsored by West Idabama Psychology Association, University City, WI

Special Skills

Native fluency in Spanish.

Professional Affiliations

West Idabama Psychology Association
Student Member
Vice President, 1995

American Association of Food Psychologists
Associate Member

Professional Credentials

Licensed Food Psychologist, West Idabama (License #000248)

Supervised Clinical Experience

June, 1997 to Present — Psychology Trainee
University City Community Mental Health Center
University City, West Idabama

Duties: Outpatient based assessment and therapy with adult, adolescent, and child populations. Client population includes a variety of developmental, anxiety, mood, personality, and organic disorders. Complete assessments performed for learning disabilities, neuropsychological, attention deficit hyperactivity, and personality disorders. Therapy experience includes group, family, conjoint, and individual using an eclectic approach. (20 hrs/wk - estimate 1,000 hrs. by August, 1998)

Supervisor: Alice Sage, Ph.D., ABPP

June, 1995 to May, 1997 — Psychology Trainee
West Idabama State Hospital
Central City, West Idabama

Duties: Inpatient-based assessment and therapy with an adult population. Responsibilities include screening admissions using objective and projective devices; intellectual and personality testing as requested by resident psychiatrists; and leading assertiveness training groups. (10 hrs/wk, 1,000 hrs. total)

Supervisors: George Thyme, Ph.D.,
& Mary Marjoram, Ph.D., ABPP

June, 1996 to Present — Crisis Management Unit Team Member
West Idabama State University
University City, West Idabama

Duties: On-site intervention and evaluation of psychotic, suicidal, and homicidal crises; assess dangerousness and need for hospitalization; transport clients to psychiatric receiving facilities with a member of the West Idabama State University Police Department. (On call for 24 hours, roughly 6 days a month.)

Supervisor: Rosemary Mace, Ph.D.

June, 1994 to May, 1995	Psychology Trainee West Idabama State University Campus Psychology Clinic

Duties: Individual, family, and marital therapy involving clients with wide variety of presenting problems (including: child management, marital issues, social skill deficits, low self-esteem, substance abuse, depression, stress management, impulse and anger control, and learning disabilities). Assessments for learning disabilities, attention deficit hyperactivity disorder, behavior problems, and emotional problems. (10 hrs/wk for 80 weeks = 800 hrs)

Supervisor: Sara Nutmeg, Ph.D.

Total hours of supervised clinical experience = 2,800

Instrument Competence

Type of Test	Number Administered and Interpreted
Intellectual Abilities	
WISC-R	75
WAIS-R	120
Stanford Binet (4th ed.)	20
Woodcock-Johnson Tests of Cognitive Ability	25
Achievement Tests	
Wide-Range Achievement Test	50
Woodcock-Johnson Test of Achievement Revised	25
Personality	
Rorschach (Exner System)	30
Thematic Apperception Test	20
California Psychological Inventory, Revised	25
MMPI-2; MMPI-A	75
Neuropsychological	
Luria Nebraska Neuropsychological Test Battery	20

(In addition, I have been exposed to and administered five or less Columbia Mental Maturity Examinations, Rosenzweig Picture Frustration Studies, and Cattell 16-PF Inventories.)

Teaching Experience

June, 1996 to Present	General Psychology for Honors Students Freshman/Sophomore Level Course Department of Psychology West Idabama State University

Duties: Responsible for all phases of teaching including the preparation and administration of lectures, selection of reading materials and assignments, construction of examinations, and the assignment of course grades.

May, 1995 to August, 1995	Sensation and Perception Junior/Senior Level Course Department of Psychology West Idabama State University

Duties: Responsible for all phases of teaching including the preparation and administration of lectures, the selection of reading materials and assignments, the development of experiments to demonstrate sensory and perceptual principles, the construction of examinations, and the assignment of course grades.

August, 1994 to May, 1995	General Psychology Freshman/Sophomore Level Course, Department of Psychology, West Idabama State University

Duties: Responsible for all phases of teaching including the preparation and administration of lectures, the selection of reading materials and assignments, the construction of examinations, and the assignment of course grades.

Research

June, 1996 to Present — Dissertation in progress.

This study is using a time series analysis to investigate the association of fluctuations in grain prices on the incidence of posttraumatic stress disorders among Midwestern farmers, covarying for interest rates, in comparison with the incidence of PTSD among service workers in the same area.

My prospectus was defended July 4, 1997, and data collection is almost complete. I anticipate defending the dissertation before leaving for internship.

June, 1994 to May, 1996 — Research Assistant
B. J. Mentor, Ph.D.

Worked 10 hrs/wk on Dr. Mentor's NAA-funded epidemiological study of nutrition and stress in rural Americans. In the course of this research, I administered 350 Structured Clinical Interviews and was responsible for coding Demographic Data.

June, 1995 to May, 1996 — Master's Thesis Research

In this study, I compared the Eight-Personality Factor (8PF) profiles of 25 male and 25 female adolescent farm children who had been exposed to significant levels of malathion and DDT as children with matched samples of suburban children from the same school. As predicted by Bovine's Dissipation theory, the exposed male children were higher on scales assessing Threshia and Harvestia and the suburban boys were lower in Reaping. No differences were noted for the girls.

Publications and Presentations

Thorne, R. C., & Grayhead, M. (1996). Effects of herbicide exposure on personality factors in rural adolescents: A test of Bovine's hypotheses. *Journal of Food Psychology, 12,* 432-441.

Thorne, R. C. (1996, May). Environmental influences on personality development. Paper presented at the meeting of the West Idabama Psychological Association, Central City, West Idabama.

Under Submission

Mentor, B. J., Grayhead, M., & Thorne, R. C. Nutritional stresses in adolescence. Chapter to appear in C. Bovine and B. Allspice (Eds.), *Comprehensive handbook of food psychology,* to be published by the West Idabama State University Press.

References

B. J. Mentor, Ph.D.
Professor of Psychology
Psychology Department
West Idabama State University
University City, West Idabama 82032
(111) 555-1234

Alice Sage, Ph.D.
Chief Psychologist
University City Community Mental Health Center
2102 River Road
University City, West Idabama 82066
(111) 555-5678

Basil Oregano, Ph.D.
Director of Clinical Training
Psychology Department
West Idabama State University
University City, West Idabama 82032
(111) 555-9101

NOTES

APPENDIX 4

A SAMPLE TRAVEL PLANNER

TRAVEL PLANNER
Traveler(s):____________________
Destination:____________________
Purpose:____________________
Duration:____________________

==

Day # Day: Dates:
Plan:

==

Air: Place Time Carrier Flt No.

Leave____________________
Arrive____________________

Leave____________________
Arrive____________________

Leave____________________
Arrive____________________

Ground:
Carrier:__________ Confirm #__________

Hotel:__________ Confirm #__________

Address:__________ Phone No:__________

Rate:__________ How Paid:__________

Contacts:
1)Name:__________ Phone No.:__________
Where:__________ When:__________

2)Name:__________ Phone No.:__________
Where:__________ When:__________

==

==
Day # Day: Dates:
Plan:
==

Schedule:

____
____
____
____
____
____

Contacts:
1)Name:__________________ Phone No.:__________________
Where:__________________ When:__________________

2)Name:__________________ Phone No.:__________________
Where:__________________ When:__________________

3)Name:__________________ Phone No.:__________________
Where:__________________ When:__________________

==

Air: Place Time Carrier Flt No.

Leave____
Arrive____

Leave____
Arrive____

Leave____
Arrive____

APPENDIX 5

QUESTIONS INTERVIEWERS ASK INTERN APPLICANTS

These last two appendices are placed at the end so you can find them easily. If you have a few minutes while you are waiting for an interview, you may want to review these questions.

Hersh and Poey (1985) provided an outline of questions that may be asked by internship directors. Their list of topics to be covered is rather formal and represents a systematic exploration of your experience in various areas such as individual adult therapy, group therapy, inpatient, outpatient, assessment, supervision, and so on. In each area, you are asked about your past experience, orientation, work style, and areas that need improvement. Some ITDs use this outline, so you should familiarize yourself with it and be prepared to respond to the questions posed.

The interviews my students have experienced have often been less structured and more personal. In standard employment interviews, personal topics are off limits, but many ITDs do not feel that this prohibition extends to internship applicants and inquire about personal matters. The big question, which is off limits but may be asked covertly, is, "Are you really interested in this internship? If we make you an offer, will you accept?"

Remember that most interviewers are as interested in <u>how</u> you respond as they are in the actual content of your answers. Humor, flexibility, good eye contact, and a firm handshake are important.

Personal/Professional Questions

--How did you become interested in psychology?

--How did you become interested in (specific professional/research interest areas)?

--What would you be doing if you were not in psychology?

--What do you see as your personal strengths and weaknesses? How do they influence your work? What have you done to deal with your shortcomings?

--Have you ever been in therapy? How did this affect how you conducted therapy?

--What are your goals after internship? In five years?

--What is your favorite supervision style. Why?

--Why are you here?

Purely Personal Questions

--Tell me about yourself.

--What do you see as your personal strengths and weaknesses? Who are you, personally?

--Tell me about your family. Are you married? Do you have any children? Tell me about them. What arrangements will you be making for them while you are interning?

--Tell me about your family problems.

--What was the worst thing about your father? Your mother?

--What do you do in your spare time?

--How is your health?

Questions About Your Credentials

--What were your GRE scores? GPA?

--How many graduate programs accepted you?

--Why did you choose your training program?

--Why should we accept *you* over the other equally qualified candidates?

--What do you have to contribute to us?

Questions About Research

--What is your dissertation topic? How is your research progressing? Where do you see it going?

--How did you get interested in that topic?

--What is the clinical relevance of your research?

Questions About Assessment

--Tell us about an instrument with which you feel competent.

--What is your opinion of projective techniques?

-- Read this case and conceptualize it.

Or, conceptualize a recent case.

--What Rorschach scoring system do you use? Why?

--What do you think of this Rorschach response?

--What is you opinion of MMPI-2?

--Comment on this MMPI profile.

--What further assessment training or experiences do you need?

--What role should managed care implications have in arriving at a diagnosis?

Questions About Treatment

--What is your greatest strength as a therapist?

--What type of client is most difficult for you to work with? What type of feelings do you have toward such cases? How do these feelings interfere with your treatment?

--What is your orientation in therapy? What do you think of [dynamic, behavioral, etc.] approaches?

--What experience have you had with [family, group, inpatient, etc.] treatment?

--Talk about a therapy case you had. How did you conceptualize the case? What was most effective?

--Describe a difficult case.

--Describe a case that was unsuccessful. Why?

--What sorts of supervisors have you had? What type of supervision is best for you?

--What further therapy training or experiences do you need?

--What empirically validated treatments are you familiar with?

--What is you opinion of psychologists having prescription privileges?

--In your opinion, how has managed care impacted treatment? What can be done about it?

Questions About Clients

--What sorts of clients have you worked with? Which were you most comfortable with? Most effective? Least comfortable? Least effective?

--Have you worked with clients such as we have here?

--What is your opinion of the most recent diagnostic nomenclature? How could it be improved?

--Questions about the assessment, dynamics, or treatment of specific disorders, especially those in which you have claimed some expertise.

Questions About Ethics

--Tell me about an ethical problem you have been faced with and how you handled it.

--Describes a situation and asks ethical implications.

--Under what conditions can/should a psychologist break confidentiality?

--When is a psychologist legally obligated to notify authorities about a client's behavior?

Questions Dealing with Recruiting

--What can we do to make you want to come here?

--How do you see us as fitting with your goals?

--What is your favorite rotation?

--Which of your interest areas are (are not) addressed by our program?

--Where else have you applied and what attracted you to these places? How do they compare with us?

--Why would someone from an ("X-oriented") department want to come to a ("Y-oriented") program?

--What attracts you most to our internship?

--Where did you apply? At what (geographic) locations are you interviewing?

--What settings are you actively considering?

--What is your top choice?

--If we make you an offer, will you accept it?

Others

--What else would you like me to know about you that is not apparent from your CV?

--What is the one question you would *not* like me to ask you?

--What do you hope we will not find out about you?

--I notice you did not take any coffee. Have you been reading Megargee's book? Are you the kind of person who always "does things by the book"? (New question that followed publication of the first edition in 1990.)

NOTES

APPENDIX 6

QUESTIONS INTERN APPLICANTS CAN ASK INTERVIEWERS

Questions Regarding the Setting/Professional

--What are you looking for in an intern?

--What does an intern do during a typical work week?

--Do you anticipate any staff or program changes within the next year?

--What is the relation between psychology and other disciplines?

--Are interns here regarded as employees or students?

--What is the balance between service and training? Does funding for the program depend on fees generated by the interns and staff?

--How does the program here compare with where you interned?

--Does this program encourage specialization or diversification in training?

--What are the possibilities of doing research during the internship? Would you say there is a research focus here?

--(To a present intern): What do you like most about this internship? What do you like least?

--Is this a congenial setting? How do trainees and staff get along?

Questions Regarding the Setting/Personal

--What is the cost of living here? Does the program provide health care?

--Are any changes in stipends or benefits expected?

--Is day care for children difficult to find? How are the schools in this area?

--How available are jobs in my spouse's field?

--What is the availability of affordable housing here?

--Do many interns take outside jobs during the intern year?

Questions Regarding Rotations

--Do you anticipate any changes in the rotations being offered next year?

--How are rotations determined? Are they fixed or flexible?

--Do interns negotiate for rotations?

--What are the common presenting problems on the [insert] rotation? What is the typical duration of treatment? What is the ratio of therapy to assessment?

--(To an intern): What rotations do you regard as being truly outstanding? Which ones should you avoid?

Questions Regarding Assessment

--Is there a standard assessment battery? Are projectives used much?

--What are the opportunities for neuropsych assessment?

Questions Regarding Therapy

--What opportunities are there for [family, group, etc.] therapy?

--Are there opportunities to conduct groups on the inpatient unit? What kinds of groups are done? Supportive, problem-centered, insight-oriented?

--How many long-term clients does an intern carry?

--Are interns expected or encouraged to have personal therapy? If so, who provides it and what are the goals?

Questions Regarding Supervision

--How many supervisors does an intern have? How are they assigned?

--Is all supervision provided on site? Is supervision on an individual or group basis?

--How much and what type (audio, video, live) supervision is provided?

--What are the theoretical orientations of the supervisors? Which is predominant?

Questions Regarding Didactics

--What types of seminars are offered? What are some typical topics?

Questions Regarding Future Opportunities

--Where do your interns go after finishing their internship? Where are some of your former interns now? What kinds of job opportunities are there for psychologists in this area?

--Does the internship play an active role in trying to place its graduates?

REFERENCES

American Psychological Association. (1986). *Accreditation handbook.* Washington, DC: Author.

American Psychological Association. (1993). *Directory of the American Psychological Association, 1993 Edition.* (Vols. 1-2). Washington, DC: Author.

American Psychological Association Committee on Accreditation. (1991). APA accredited predoctoral internships for doctoral training in psychology: 1991. *American Psychologist*, *46,* 1308-1331.

ASARC (1994, August 13). ASARC statistics: 1990-1994. Report presented at the annual APPIC Business Meeting at the 102nd annual meeting of the American Psychological Association, Los Angeles, CA.

Association of Psychology Postdoctoral and Internship Centers. (1991). Preliminary pre-doctoral summaries. *APPIC Newsletter*, *16*(2), 47.

Association of Psychology Postdoctoral and Internship Centers. (1994). Selection day: Internship offers and acceptances--Summary of results. Report presented at the annual APPIC Business Meeting at the 102nd annual meeting of the American Psychological Association, Los Angeles, CA.

Belar, C. D., Bieliauskas, L. A., Larsen, K. G., Mensh, I. N., Poey, K., & Roehlke, A. J. (Eds.). (1987). *Proceedings of the National Conference on Internship Training in Psychology.* Washington, DC: Association of Psychology Internship Centers.

Belar, C. D., Bieliauskas, L. A., Larsen, K. G., Mensh, I. N., Poey, K., & Roehlke, A. J. (1989). The national conference on internship training in psychology. *American Psychologist, 44,* 60-65.

Belar, C., & Orgel, S. (1980). Survival guide for intern applicants. *Professional Psychology*, *11*, 672-675.

Blanchard, J. J. (1994). *Directory of research opportunities for clinical psychology interns.* Albany, NY: Graywind Publications.

Blom, B. E. (1990). Remarks from the editor. *APIC Newsletter, 15* (2), 5-7.

Blom, B. E. (1991). Remarks from the editor. *APPIC Newsletter, 16* (2), 2-3.

Blom, B. E., & Pederson, S. L. (1988). Results of the APIC survey. *APIC Newsletter, 13*(1), 43 - 49.

Blom, B. E., Pederson, S. L., & Klepac, R. K. (1990). The computerized internship matching pilot study. Further results, cautions and excuses. *APIC Newsletter, 15* (1), 20-22.

Brems, C., Thevenin, D. M., & Routh, D. K. (1991). The history of clinical psychology. In C. E. Walker (Ed.), *Clinical psychology: Historical and research foundations* (pp. 3-35). New York: Plenum.

Burt, C. E. (1985). Reflections on interviewing for internship. *Clinical Psychologist, 38*, 91-93.

Cantrell, P., & Garfield, N. (1997, April). Universal application forms. Paper presented at the First APPIC Membership Meeting and Conference, Orlando, FL.

Carifio, M. S., & Grace, W. C. (1992). Ignored data on the development of psychology internships. *American Psychologist, 47,* 428.

Carifio, M. S., Buckner, K. E., & Grace, W. C. (1987). APIC guidelines: Are they really that helpful? *Professional Psychology: Research and Practice, 18*, 407-409.

Carlin, A. S. (1982, August). Is there a free lunch? Experiences with unfunded interns. Paper presented at the annual meeting of the Association of Psychology Internship Centers. Washington, DC. Reprinted in R. H. Dana & W. T. May (Eds.). (1987). *Internship training in professional psychology* (pp. 497-500). Washington, DC: Hemisphere.

Clay, R. (1997, April). Concerns about internships lead APA to conduct survey. *APA Monitor*, p. 51.

Constantine, M., & Gloria, A. (1996). Managed health care and predoctoral internship sites: Preliminary findings and implications for training programs and internship candidates. *APPIC Newsletter, 21*(1), 4, 18.

Constantine, M., & Keilin, W. G. (1996). Association of Psychology Postdoctoral and Internship Centers' guidelines and the internship selection process: A survey of applicants and academic and internship training directors. *Professional Psychology: Research and Practice, 27*, 308-314.

Daehnert, C., & Carter, J. D. (1987). The prediction of success in a clinical psychology graduate program. *Educational and Psychological Measurement, 47,* 1113-1125.

Dana, R. H., & May, W. T. (Eds.). (1987). *Internship training in professional psychology*. Washington, DC: Hemisphere.

Davies, R. (1987). Demise of the 3rd year internship: The changing role of the internship in graduate training. *Professional Psychology: Research and Practice, 18*, 481-484.

Douce, L. A. (1990). Intern selection advisory. *APIC Newsletter, 15*(1), 59-60.

Eggert, M. A., Laughlin, P. R., Hutzell, R. R., Stedman, J. M., Solway, K. S., & Carrington, C. H. (1987). The psychology internship marketplace today. *Professional Psychology: Research and Practice, 18*, 165-171.

Fox, R. E. (1990). The history of the APIC selection process: A personal prequel. *APIC Newsletter, 15*(1), 27-28.

Fox, R. E. (1991). Improvements still needed in selection process. *APIC Newsletter, 16*(2), 33-36.

Gavzer, B. (1992, June 14). Fly smart. *Parade Magazine*, pp. 4-6.

Gill, D. (1997, March 12). Internship. Personal communication.

Gollaher, K. K., & Craig, N. W. (1994). *Securing a pre-doctoral internship: A student's perspective on how to succeed in the internship application process*. Torrance, CA: NWC Enterprises.

Grace, W. C. (1985). Evaluating a prospective clinical internship: Tips for the applicant. *Professional Psychology: Research and Practice, 15*, 475-480.

Hall, R. G., & Cantrell, P. J. (Eds.). (1996). *Directory of internship and postdoctoral programs in professional psychology, 25th ed.: 1996-1997.* Washington, DC.: Association of Psychology Postdoctoral and Internship Centers.

Hardin, G. (1968). The tragedy of the commons. *Science, 162*, 1243-1248.

Hersh, J. B., & Poey, K. (1985). A proposed interviewing guide for intern applicants. *Professional Psychology: Research and Practice, 15*, 3-5.

Hollander, P. A. (1990). Internships and the law: Questions and answers. *APIC Newsletter, 15*(1), 56-57.

Jacob, M. C. (1987). Managing the internship application: Advice from an exhausted but content survivor. *The Counseling Psychologist, 15*, 146-155.

Johnson, M. C. (1986). The pre-doctoral internship selection process. *Professional Psychology: Research and Practice, 17*, 291-293.

Kingsley, K. (1985). Reflections on internship year. *Clinical Psychologist, 38*, 93-94.

Krause, A. A. & Lawlor, R. (1990). Internship selection and early acceptance procedures: Students' evaluations. *Professional Psychology: Research and Practice, 21*, 144-146.

LaGana, C. (1997, April). Panel discussion on funding and managed care. First APPIC Membership Meeting and Conference, Orlando, FL.

Larsen, K. G. (1991). Chair's column. *APPIC Newsletter, 16*(2), 1-2.

Larsen, K. G., & Klepac, R. K. (1991). How to survive intern calling day: A guide for training directors. *APPIC Newsletter, 16*(2), 32-33.

Laughlin, P. R., & Worley, J. L. (1991). Role of the American Psychological Association and the Veterans Administration in the development of internships in psychology. *American Psychologist, 46*, 430-436.

Lonigan, C. J. (1994, August). How to be right for the place that you want: Results from a survey of internship directors. In K. Foster (Chair). Obtaining internships in clinical psychology. Symposium presented at the 102nd annual meeting of the American Psychological Association, Los Angeles, CA.

Lopez, S. J., Oehlert, M. E., & Moberly, R. I. (1996). Selection criteria for American Psychological Association-accredited internship programs: A survey of training directors. *Professional Psychology: Research and Practice, 27*, 518-520.

May, T. M., & Dana, R. H. (1990). Issues concerning the internship selection process. *APIC Newsletter, 15*(1), 29-32.

May, T. M., Rice, K., & Birckhead, L. (1990). A current perspective on intern selection: The state of the art. *APIC Newsletter, 15*(2), 37-42.

Megargee, E. I. (1992). *A guide to obtaining a psychology internship* (2nd ed.). Muncie, IN: Accelerated Development.

Miller, R. K., & Van Rybroek, G. J. (1988). Internship letters of recommendation: Where are the other 90%? *Professional Psychology: Research and Practice, 19*, 115-117.

Mitchell, S. (1996). Getting a foot in the door: The written internship application. *Professional Psychology: Research and Practice, 27*, 90-92.

Monti, P. M. (1985). Interviewing for internships. *The Behavior Therapist, 10*, 205-206.

Ochroch, R. (1990). The need for half-time internships: Affirmative action on behalf of parents of young children. *APIC Newsletter, 15*(2), 35-37.

Pederson, S. (1994). The history of computerized internship matching in APPIC. APPIC *Newsletter, 19*(1), 56-61.

Pederson, S. (1996, August). Chair's report. APPIC business meeting conducted at the annual meeting of the American Psychological Association, Toronto, ONT.

Pederson, S. (1997, April). Computer matching. Paper presented at the First APPIC Membership Meeting and Conference, Orlando, FL.

Peterson, D. R. (1985). Twenty years of practitioner training in psychology. *American Psychologist, 40*, 441-451.

Peterson, D. R. (1991). Connection and disconnection of research and practice in the education of professional psychologists. *American Psychologist, 46*, 422-429.

Petzel, T. P., & Berndt, D. (1980). APA internship selection criteria: Relative importance of academic and clinical preparation. *Professional Psychology, 11*, 792-796.

Plante, T. G. (1987). Comments on the internship application process. *Professional Psychology: Research and Practice, 18*, 7-8.

Resnick, R. J. (1997). A brief history of practice--Expanded. *American Psychologist, 52*, 463-468.

Rickard, H. C., & Clements, C. (1986). An evaluation of interviewed versus noninterviewed clinical psychology students. *Professional Psychology: Research and Practice, 17*, 78-79.

Shemberg, K. M., & Leventhal, D. B. (1981). Attitudes of internship directors toward pre-internship training and clinical models. *Professional Psychology, 12,* 639-646.

Spruill, J. (1997). The business side of psychology. In C. Zimet (Chair), Funding and managed care. Panel discussion at the First APPIC Membership Meeting and Conference, Orlando, FL.

Stanford University Career Planning and Placement Center. (1988). *How to write your resume*. Stanford, CA: Author.

Stedman, J. M. (1983). Fear and loathing on intern selection day. American Psychological Association *Monitor*.

Stedman, J. M. (1989). The history of the APIC selection process. *APIC Newsletter, 14*(2), 35-43.

Stedman, J. M. (in press). What we know about pre-doctoral internship training: A review. *Professional Psychology: Research and Practice.*

Stedman, J. M., Costello, R. M., Gaines, T., Jr., Schoenfeld, L. S., Loucks, S., & Burstein, A. G. (1981). How clinical interns are selected: A study of decision-making processes. *Professional Psychology, 12,* 415-419.

Stedman, J. M., Costello, R. M., Gaines, T., Jr., Solway, K., Zimet, C., & Carrington, C. (1990) Intern supply and demand: The rest of the story. *APIC Newsletter, 15*(1), 33-43.

Stedman, J. M., Neff, J. A., Donahoe, C. P., Kopel, K., & Hays, J. R. (1995). Applicant characterization of the most desirable internship training programs. *Professional Psychology: Research and Practice, 26,* 396-400.

Stewart, A. E., & Stewart, E. A. (1996a). A decision-making technique for choosing a psychology internship. *Professional Psychology: Research and Practice, 27,* 521-526.

Stewart, A. E., & Stewart, E. A. (1996b). Personal and practical considerations in selecting a psychology internship. *Professional Psychology: Research and Practice, 27,* 293-303.

Stricker, G. (1997, April). *Slouching toward the millennium.* Keynote address delivered at the First APPIC Membership Meeting and Conference, Orlando, FL.

Thorne, B. (1997, March 17). Results of the CUDCP Internship Survey. Personal communication.

Weiner, E. (1990, January 21). Why plane travel isn't always fast. *New York Sunday Times, National News,* pp. 1, 15.

Williams, G. (1997, May 26). APPIC clearinghouse summary. Personal communication.

Winiarski, M. (1986). *Applying for internship.* Unpublished manuscript, Psychology Department, Florida State University, Tallahassee.

Zimet, C. N. (1988). Further comments on the internship application process. *Professional Psychology: Research and Practice*, *19*, 5.

Zimet, C. N. (1990). Chair's column. *APIC Newsletter*, *15*(2), 4-5.

Zimet, C. N. (1991). Chair's column. *APPIC Newsletter*, *16*(1), 1-3.

Zimet, C. N. (1996). Report of the APPIC Standards and Review Committee. *APPIC Newsletter*, *21*(1), 16.

Zimet, C. N. (1997, April). ASARC report. Report presented at the APPIC Business Meeting at the First APPIC Membership Meeting and Conference, Orlando, FL.

Zimet, C. N., & Lamb, D. H. (1992). Addressing alleged internship selection violations: A response to Carifio and Grace. *APPIC Newsletter*, *17*(1), 27-29.

BIOGRAPHIES

Photo by Bob Celander

Edwin I. Megargee received his Ph.D. in Clinical Psychology from the University of California at Berkeley in 1964. He has been Professor of Psychology at the Florida State University since 1970, where he served as Director of Clinical Training for seven years. The author of over 100 journal articles, review chapters, and books, he has received three life-time achievement awards for his research on personality assessment, criminal behavior, and the psychology of aggression.

Sanford L. Pederson received his Ph.D. in Clinical Psychology from the University of Maine in 1984. He has been involved in internship training in a variety of settings since that time. He has served in a variety of capacities with the Association of Psychology Postdoctoral and Internship Centers (APPIC), serving as Chair of the Board of Directors from 1995 to 1997. He is currently an Associate Professor in the School of Professional Psychology at Wright State University.